Excavation of later prehistoric and Roman sites along the route of the Newquay Strategic Road Corridor, Cornwall

Andy M Jones

with contributions from

Ryan P Smith, Dana Challinor, Julie Jones, Graeme Kirkham, Anna Lawson-Jones, Henrietta Quinnell and Roger Taylor

ARCHAEOPRESS ARCHAEOLOGY

Archaeopress Publishing Ltd
Summertown Pavilion
18-24 Middle Way
Summertown
Oxford OX2 7LG

www.archaeopress.com

ISBN 978-1-78969-152-8
ISBN 978-1-78969-153-5 (e-Pdf)

© the individual authors and Archaeopress 2019

All rights reserved. No part of this book may be reproduced, or transmitted, in any form or by any means, electronic, mechanical, photocopying or otherwise, without the prior written permission of the copyright owners.

Printed in England by Holywell Press, Oxford

This book is available direct from Archaeopress or from our website www.archaeopress.com

Contents

List of Figures iii
List of Tables vi
Acknowledgements vii

SECTION 1 BACKGROUND TO THE PROJECT

Chapter 1 Introduction to the project 3
Andy M Jones

    Background 3
    Report structure 3
    Terminology used in this report 3
    Location and background 6
    Methodology 9

SECTION 2 INVESTIGATIONS

Chapter 2 The results from the fieldwork 13
Andy M Jones and Ryan P Smith

    The Neolithic 13
    The Bronze Age: *circa* 2500 to 1300 cal BC 13
    The Middle Iron Age: *circa* fifth to third century cal BC 17
    The Late Iron Age: last century cal BC to first century AD 20
    The Roman period: first to fourth centuries AD 28
    Undated features 40

SECTION 3 THE ANALYSES

Chapter 3 The ceramics 43
Henrietta Quinnell

    Beaker 43
    Middle Bronze Age 43
    The Middle Iron Age to early Roman period sequence 45

Chapter 4 The stonework 52
Henrietta Quinnell with petrological comment by Roger Taylor

    Bronze Age 52
    Later Iron Age and Roman period 52

Chapter 5 The flint 57
Anna Lawson-Jones

    The assemblage 57

Chapter 6 The plant macrofossils 65
Julie Jones

    Crop plants and weed assemblages 65
    Results 66
    Discussion 67

Chapter 7 The charcoal 75
Dana Challinor

    Methodology 75
    Results 75
    Discussion 81

Chapter 8 The radiocarbon dating 83
Andy M Jones

    Results 83

SECTION 4 INTERPRETATION AND CONCLUSIONS

Chapter 9 Introduction: Themes for discussion 89
Andy M Jones

Chapter 10 Structures and boundaries: The wider later prehistoric and Roman period context 92
Andy M Jones

Chapter 11 Inscribing the landscape and hiding in plain view 115
Andy M Jones and Graeme Kirkham

Chapter 12 Review and overview 146
Andy M Jones

Bibliography 150

List of Figures

Figure 1.1 Location map showing archaeological features located by geophysical survey and the National Mapping Programme in the area around the Newquay Strategic Road corridor. The urban core of Newquay town centre is to the north west; shading represents modern suburban and leisure development on the resort's western fringe. 4

Figure 1.2 Results from the geophysical survey of the Newquay Strategic Road corridor and Field numbers. 5

Figure 1.3 The truncated Structure 2, located at the southern end of the road corridor. 6

Figure 1.4 Overview showing excavated archaeological features in relation to the results from the geophysical survey. 7

Figure 1.5 Archaeological sites in the area surrounding the Newquay Strategic Road corridor, including, barrows, large enclosures, cliff castles and rounds. 8

Figure 2.1 Overview of the results from the excavations shown by Field and phase (Bronze Age, Middle Iron Age Late Iron Age and Roman). 14

Figure 2.2 Features of Bronze Age date. Middle Bronze Age Structure 1 and Beaker pit [163] (inset). 15

Figure 2.3 Features of Middle Iron Age date. Structure 2 and Structure A1. 17

Figure 2.4 Plan of Middle Iron Age Structure 2 and ditch [274]. 18

Figure 2.5 Plan of Middle Iron Age Structure A1. 20

Figure 2.6 Features of Late Iron Age date, including Hollow 1, Hollow 2, ditch [120] and Area A2. 21

Figure 2.7 Plan of Late Iron Age Hollow 1. 22

Figure 2.8 Plan of pits within Late Iron Age Hollow 2. 24

Figure 2.9 Plan of Late Iron Age Hollow 2. 25

Figure 2.10 Plan of Late Iron Age features and the north end of Field 2, ditch [120] and Area A2. 27

Figure 2.11 Features of Roman period date, including Structure A3, Structure 3, Structure A6 and ditch [230]. 29

Figure 2.12 Plan of Roman period Structure A3 and adjacent features. 30

Figure 2.13 Plan of Roman period features in Enclosure Area, including ditches [125] and [129] and [20] and [204]. 32

Figure 2.14 Plan of Roman period features to the north and west of Hollow 1. 34

Figure 2.15 Plan of Roman period Structure A6 and adjacent features. 36

Figure 2.16 Plan of Roman period Structure 3. 37

Figure 2.17 Plan showing the location of the Romano-British enclosure, associated features and geophysical features outside the stripped area. 38

Figure 3.1 Middle Bronze Age pottery P1–P4, Middle Iron Age pottery P5–P7. (Drawing Jane Read.) 45

Figure 3.2 Pottery of Late Iron Age and Roman date P8–P13. (Drawing Jane Read.) 48

Figure 4.1 Worked stone S1 saddle quern fragment, S2 rotary quern fragment, S4 spindle whorl fragment, S5 Cornish mortar, S6–S7 large Cornish mortars or small Trethurgy bowls. (Drawing Jane Read.) 53

Figure 4.2 Worked stone S8 whetstone. (Drawing Jane Read.) 54

Figure 4.3 Worked stone S12 Beach cobble with slight peck marks from anvil or hammerstone use. (Photograph: Gary Young.) 55

Figure 4.4 Worked stone S13 Slate discs, S13 top right, S14 bottom right, S15 left. (Photograph Gary Young.) 55

Figure 4.5 Worked stone S16 split tuffaceous slate beach cobble trimmed as chopper. (Photograph Gary Young.) .56

Figure 5.1 Four worked flints. The first two are of a broadly Late Neolithic to Early Bronze Age date, the second two came from Bronze Age Structure 1. L1 is a cutting flake or simple knife flake from pit fill (162); L2 is a cortical flake scraper from curvilinear gully fill (219), L3 is a slightly denticulated blade from Structure 1 stone lined pit fill (257) and L4 is a short, utilized blade from central pit fill (299). 58

Figure 7.1. Taxonomic composition of charcoal by phase (based upon fragment count, excluding indeterminates; N=841). 82

Figure 8.1 Radiocarbon date ranges from the Newquay Strategic Road corridor. 83

Figure 9.1 Photograph of ring-gully [332] which is probably part of a structure of Roman period date which lies outside the road corridor. The size and form of the structure are unknown.. 89
Figure 9.2 Photograph showing the quartz filled gully encircling Richard Lander Iron Age house 9, looking east. 90

Figure 10.1 Photograph of Pit [300] within Middle Bronze Age Structure 1. Note the lighter colour of the upper part of the pit which may represent a floor layer or infilling deposit.. 94
Figure 10.2 Photograph of Middle Bronze Age Structure 1 taken from the east. Note the lighter colour of the lower part of the section, which is likely to be a Bronze Age infilling deposit. 95
Figure 10.3 Middle Iron Age structures in Cornwall and Devon: (1) Twinyeo structure 3, (2) Twinyeo structure 1, (3) Penryn College structure 2, (4) Twinyeo structure 2, (5) Nansledan and (6) Newquay Structure 2. 96
Figure 10.4 Iron Age roundhouses in Cornwall: Camelford School structure 4, Trevelgue Head house 1, Belowda, Threemilestone houses 8 and 12, and Penmayne structure 2. 98
Figure 10.5 Aerial photograph of the Manuels enclosure, showing an inner roughly circular cropmark approximately 50m diameter; the site as a whole may have an overall diameter of around 250m. Part of the south-eastern side is preserved in the hedge bank (© Cornwall Council). 100
Figure 10.6 The plotting of the cropmark enclosure at Manuels by the National Mapping Programme revealed that there are up to five concentric ditch circuits and that the space between the two inner enclosures and the next concentric ditch appears to have been divided radially into a number of cells. 101
Figure 10.7 Photograph of half excavated pit [309], which may have been associated with the preparation of food. ... 101
Figure 10.8 Plan showing the open 'working hollows' at Little Quoit Farm. These hollows were associated with small-scale smithing. (After Lawson-Jones and Kirkham 2009–10.) 102
Figure 10.9 Photograph of Roman period Structure 3 during excavation. Note standing section and material filling the hollow which includes quartz blocks.. 104
Figure 10.10 Selection of Roman period oval-shaped structures found across Cornwall: (1) Newquay Structure 3, (2) Tremough structure 338, (3) Trebarveth structure 3, (4) Grambla structure 1, (5) Chysauster structure 5, (6) Castle Gotha and (7) Porth Godrevy... 106
Figure 10.11 Selection of Roman period oval-shaped structures found across Cornwall: (1) Trethurgy A1, (2) Trethurgy T4, (3) Trethurgy T2 and (4) Trethurgy Z2.. 107
Figure 10.12 Plan showing Tremough structure 338. This oval shaped structure associated with small-scale metalworking and occupation. (After Gossip and Jones 2007.) 108
Figure 10.13 Photograph of stone-capped 'grave' [108] prior to excavation. Note the in situ stone capping covering the feature.. 111
Figure 10.14 Photograph of 'grave' feature [109] after excavation. 111
Figure 10.15 Map showing the distribution of Iron Age cist graves and pit graves in the south west peninsula.... 112
Figure 10.16 Photograph of Forrabury stone-capped feature 13, which is of Iron Age date and similar to feature [108]... 113
Figure 10.17 Photograph of Forrabury cist 4, with in situ water rolled quartz pebble. 114

Figure 11.1 Distribution of key Iron Age and Roman wetland sites associated with metalwork and coin deposition in Cornwall referred to in Chapter 11. 117
Figure 11.2 Photograph showing the Roman patera and jug recovered from the shaft / well at Bosence. (AN1836 p.126.146 and AN1836 p.127.179. Image © Ashmolean Museum, University of Oxford.)........................... 118
Figure 11.3 Photograph of Camelford enclosure 1, showing the pit cut into the southern ditch terminal............. 119
Figure 11.4 Post excavation photograph of pit [367]. 122
Figure 11.5 Photograph of worked stone objects found within Higher Besore pit [5027]. 123
Figure 11.6 Photograph of the cache of worked stone artefacts found within Tremowah pit [345]. 123
Figure 11.7 Photograph of the pottery deposit placed the bottom of pit [337] at Tremough............................. 124
Figure 11.8 Photograph showing charred grain deposit in section within pit [2-05], Middle Amble. (Photograph Mark Borlase.) 124
Figure 11.9 Photograph of the quartz filled gully encircling Richard Lander Iron Age house 9, looking north west. 126
Figure 11.10 Distribution of 'special deposits' within Structure 3 and in adjacent ditches... 128
Figure 11.11 Photograph showing the deposit of iron ore in section within [210] / [212]................................... 129
Figure 11.12 Distribution of artefacts within the Roman period enclosure at Tremough... 130
Figure 11.13 Photograph of the pottery deposit placed within the Roman period enclosure at Tremough........... 131
Figure 11.14 Photograph of the Roman period burial (note body stain in the bottom of grave) located at the upper margin of the field system at Scarcewater. 132
Figure 11.15 Photograph of the decorated stone spindle whorl found within pit [491].. 132
Figure 11.16 Photograph of Camelford enclosure 2, showing infill deposits within the northern ditch terminal. 133
Figure 11.17 Photograph of the quern fragment found in Camelford enclosure 2 ditch... 134

Figure 11.18 Distribution of key Iron Age and Roman sites with possible evidence for ritualized abandonment / special deposits in Cornwall referred to in Chapter 11 (star = Newquay Strategic Road corridor). 135

Figure 11.19 Photograph of in situ rotary quern found within a posthole inside structure 2 at Penryn College..... 137

Figure 11.20 Photograph of a copper-alloy toiletry set found within a gully associated within structure 2 at Penryn College. 137

Figure 11.21 Plan of Trevelgue Head, house 1 showing the distribution of Roman coins within and outside the structure (after Nowakowski and Quinnell 2011)...138

Figure 11.22 Photograph of the stone mensuration weight within a posthole close the entrance into structure 338 at Tremough. 139

Figure 11.23 Key sites beyond Cornwall referred to in Chapter 11..141

Figure 11.24 From roundhouse (top) to round mound (bottom). Abandoning the Middle Bronze Age roundhouse at Callestick. (Drawing Nigel Thomas.) 144

Figure 12.1 Photograph of the iron carding comb from Atlantic Road, Newquay. In a region lacking in good organic preservation this artefact acts as a proxy for the importance of wool in the local economy.................146

Figure 12.2 Photograph showing Roman period plough marks (foreground) at Atlantic Road, Newquay. Despite being in a marginal location ploughing had taken place, before being covered by windblown sand.................147

Figure 12.3 Reconstruction of the Manuels enclosure. (Painting Freya Lawson-Jones.) 147

Figure 12.4 Photograph of late fourth century AD Roman coins buried in a pit outside the entrance to Trevelgue Head, house 1. (Photograph Anna Tyacke.)..148

Figure 12.5 Photograph of the Roman period bell found within the midden deposit covering Penhale Round structure 2045/5054. 148

Figure 12.6 Photograph of the Roman period tin dish which had been placed within a pit at Killigrew Round......149

List of Tables

Table 3.1 Details of Bronze Age pottery fabrics by sherd numbers and weight in grams. All material comes from Structure 1 except that from the old land surface (OLS) (218). 44
Table 3.2 Details of ceramic fabrics from Structure 2 by sherd numbers and weight in grams. 47
Table 3.3 Details of ceramic fabrics from Structure A1 by sherd numbers and weight in grams. 47
Table 3.4 Details of ceramic fabrics from Hollow 1 by sherd number and weight in grams. 47
Table 3.5 Details of ceramic fabrics from Hollow 2 by sherd numbers and weight in grams. 49
Table 3.6 Details of ceramic fabrics from Area A2 by sherd numbers and weight in grams. 49
Table 3.7 Details of ceramic fabrics from Structure A3 by sherd numbers and weight in grams. 49
Table 3.8 Details of ceramic fabrics from Enclosure Area (north) by sherd numbers and weight in grams. 49
Table 3.9 Details of ceramic fabrics from Enclosure Area (south) ditches by sherd numbers and weight in grams..50
Table 3.10 Details of ceramic fabrics from features north west of Hollow 1 by sherd numbers and weight in grams.......50
Table 3.11 Details of ceramic fabrics from Structure A6 by sherd numbers and weight in grams. 50
Table 3.12 Details of ceramic fabrics from Structure 3 by sherd numbers and weight in grams. 51
Table 3.13 Totals of sherds by fabric, sherd numbers, weight and period. 51
Table 3.14 Suggested chronology for the ceramics of different structures and areas, presented in broad sequence. ...51

Table 5.1 Late Neolithic and Early Bronze Age flint. NOTE: the bags of unstratified material have been individually distinguished by letters A to G. Bag D came from Field 1, bag C from Field 2 and bag F from Field 3. Bags A, B, E and G include material from all fields. 60
Table 5.2 Bronze Age flint from Structure 1. 63
Table 5.3 Other probable Bronze Age material. NOTE: the bags of unstratified material have been individually distinguished by letters A to G. Bag D came from Field 1, bag C from Field 2 and bag F from Field 3. Bags A, B, E and G include material from all fields. 63

Table 6.1 Bulk samples from the Newquay Strategic Road corridor. 68
Table 6.2 Charred plant remains from the Newquay Strategic Road corridor. 71

Table 7.1 Charcoal from Early and Middle Bronze Age features. 76
Table 7.2 Charcoal from Middle Iron Age features. 77
Table 7.3 Charcoal from Late Iron Age features. 78
Table 7.4 Charcoal from Area A2, Structure A3 and Enclosure Area (north). 79
Table 7.5 Charcoal from Enclosure Area (south) features. 80
Table 7.6 Charcoal from Roman period features. 80

Table 8.1 Radiocarbon determinations from Newquay Strategic Road corridor. 85

Acknowledgements

The author would like to thank Ryan Smith for supervising the fieldwork and the excavation team: Megan Val Baker, Graham Britton, Anna Lawson-Jones, Richard Mikulski and Ian Rose. I would also like to thank Graeme Kirkham for reading the manuscript and for discussions about other Roman period sites in the west of Britain where ritualized abandonment may also have occurred. Thanks are also due to Dave Field, Henrietta Quinnell, Paul Rainbird and Andrew Young for reading the draft, to Francis Shepherd for assisting with the production of the publication drawings and to Jane Read and Gary Young for the artefact illustrations. I am also grateful to Freya Lawson-Jones for her painting of the Manuels enclosure.

I am grateful to Paul Rainbird of AC Archaeology for forwarding a draft copy of the Nansledan report, Mark Borlase for supplying Figure 11.7, Middle Amble pit [2-05] and Anna Tyacke for Figure 12.4. I would also like to thank the Ashmolean Museum for giving permission to reproduce Figure 11.2, the photograph of the pewter *patera* and jug from Bosence.

Henrietta Quinnell would like to thank Paul Bidwell and Alex Croom for providing comment on the amphorae sherds.

The project was funded by Cormac Solutions, Cornwall Council.

SECTION 1
BACKGROUND TO THE PROJECT

Chapter 1

Introduction to the project

Andy M Jones

Background

In 2014 Cornwall Archaeological Unit was commissioned by Cormac Solutions, Cornwall Council, to undertake a programme of archaeological excavations in advance of the construction of the first stage of the Newquay Strategic Road (SW 832 604) (Figs 1.1 and 1.2). This report covers the archaeological recording carried out along the road corridor during the winter of 2014.

This project led to the uncovering of a large number of archaeological features, spanning later prehistory to the Roman period. They included a Middle Bronze Age roundhouse, structures and field boundaries of Middle and Late Iron Age date, and settlement features belonging to the Roman period. The excavated features provided evidence for increasing enclosure and occupation in the Late Iron Age and early Roman periods. The chronological range and density of features was greater than anticipated and the outcome has resulted in a far more significant set of results than were envisaged at the outset.

In the light of the very significant results relating to the later prehistoric and Roman periods (Smith 2015), the decision was made to draw the results together into a single publication, which could allow for the consideration and synthesis of the results at a local, regional and, where appropriate, national level.

Report structure

This resulting monograph is divided into four sections. The first (this section) provides the background to the project and gives a brief overview of related sites and the programme of archaeological recording undertaken. It also describes the setting of the project area and the geological background.

The second section outlines the stratigraphical results from the major excavated sites, by chronological periods: Neolithic, Bronze Age, Middle Iron Age, Late Iron Age and Roman. As will be seen, although these are treated as discrete entities in this chapter and in Chapter 2, the following sections break down these rigid distinctions somewhat, especially between the Late Iron Age and Roman periods, where there is little to differentiate the two archaeologically.

The third section contains detailed specialist reports on the artefacts, including the ceramics, flint and worked stone (Chapters 3, 4 and 5). Analyses of the plant macrofossils and the charcoal (Chapters 6 and 7) are also reported in this section, as well as the results from radiocarbon dating (Chapter 8).

The concluding section draws together the results from the analyses of the excavated sites and places them within a wider context with other excavated sites in Cornwall and beyond (Chapters 9, 10, 11 and 12). This section is in three principal parts. After an introduction (Chapter 9), the first synthesises the results from the excavation and post-excavation analyses and uses this material to examine comparanda for the excavation results (Chapter 10). Structure, form and function and comparanda for the excavated structures are considered, as well as the evidence for the development of the surrounding landscape. In particular, the possible importance of the large multi-circuited enclosure at Manuels, which lies 700m to the south east, is highlighted in relation to the excavated sites. Chapter 11 can almost be read as a stand-alone essay, as it reviews the evidence for placed deposits in structures, pits and ditches and other contexts. It also considers the evidence for deliberate abandonment of structures, which it is suggested was not only a feature of the Middle Bronze Age but was also associated with Late Iron Age and Roman period buildings. The similarities and contrasts in practice are discussed and the opportunity is taken to review these practices in Cornwall and other parts of Britain. The final chapter provides a brief overview of the results and suggests avenues for further research (Chapter 12).

Terminology used in this report

Throughout this report structures are denoted by numbers without brackets; for example, Structure 2. Context numbers for cuts – ditches, pits, postholes and similar features – are shown in square brackets [127] and their fills, layers and other deposits are shown with round brackets: (126).

The term ring-gully is used throughout the report to denote ditching around the perimeter of both structures and hollows of circular or oval shape.

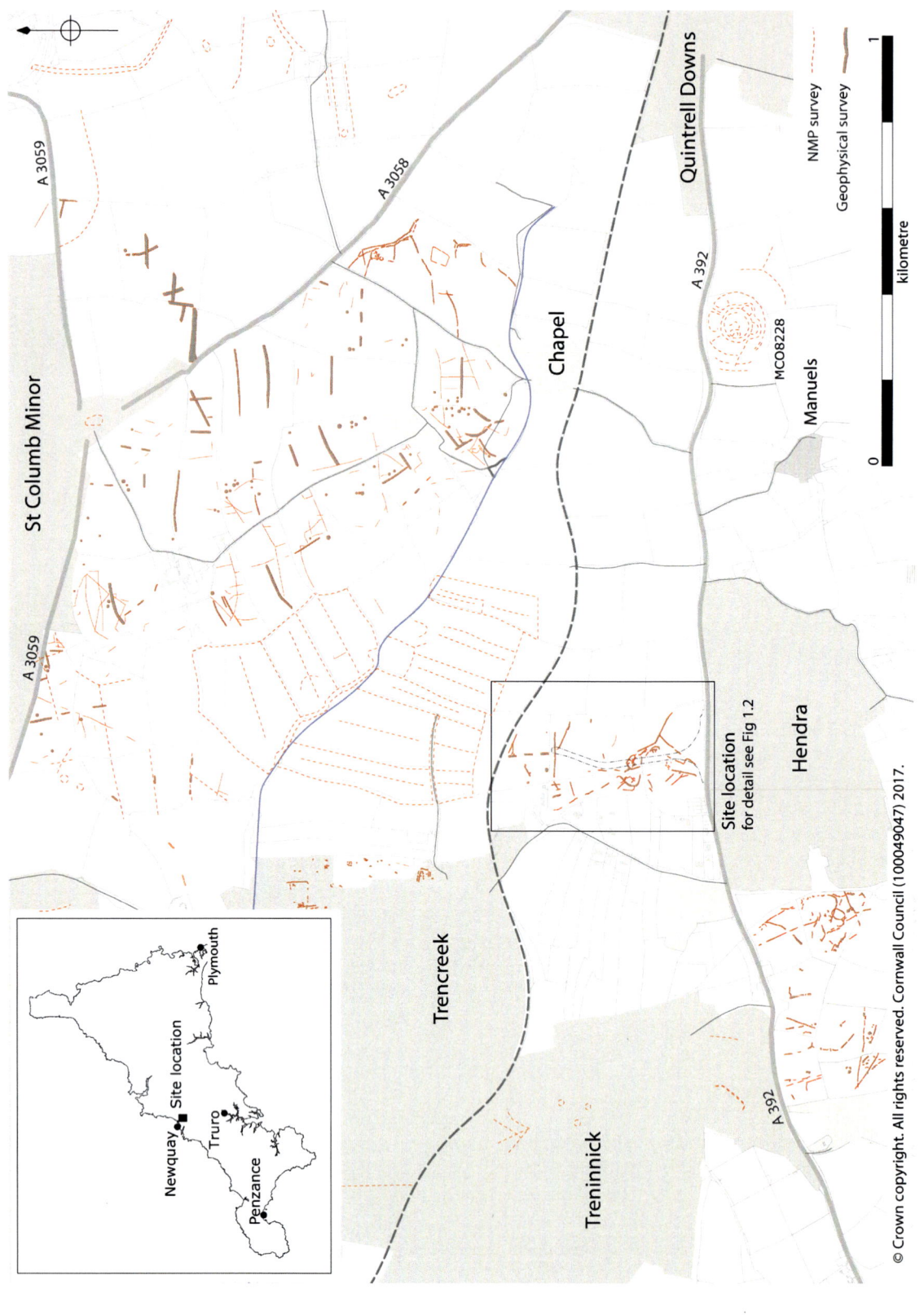

Figure 1.1 Location map showing archaeological features located by geophysical survey and the National Mapping Programme in the area around the Newquay Strategic Road corridor. The urban core of Newquay town centre is to the north west; shading represents modern suburban and leisure development on the resort's western fringe.

INTRODUCTION TO THE PROJECT

Figure 1.2 Results from the geophysical survey of the Newquay Strategic Road corridor and Field numbers.

The radiocarbon dating probability distributions (Chapter 8, Fig 8.1 and Table 8.1) were calculated using OxCal v4.2, including those from earlier excavations; calibrated determinations cited in the text may therefore differ from older published sources. Unless stated otherwise, the 95 per cent level of probability has been used throughout this volume.

Location and background

The investigated road corridor lies on the eastern edge of Newquay, on the north side of the Trevemper Bridge to Quintrell Downs road, directly opposite Hendra Tourist Park, Newquay (Fig 1.1). The scheme comprised a road corridor which measured approximately 375m in length and 15m wide, except for the southern end which was widened to 100m to accommodate a new roundabout.

The underlying bedrock geology has been identified as part of the Meadfoot Group Mudstone, Siltstone and Sandstone of the Devonian period (Geological Survey of Great Britain 1974), overlain by well-drained fine loamy soils. Prior to the excavations the land had been used for pasture, although aerial photographs reveal that the fields had been ploughed in the recent past.

The road corridor cut across the western edge of an east–west orientated ridge. The southern end of the corridor was located on the south side of the summit of the ridge. The overlying topsoil in this area was quite thin and the exposed archaeological features quite shallow; ploughing is likely to have truncated archaeological deposits including the poorly preserved Structure 2 (Fig 1.3). The stripped area became more level, reaching a height of approximately 75m OD, and the covering soil was deeper across this area. The northern half of the corridor sloped increasingly steeply down towards the valley which lay beyond.

As the ridge is elevated above the surrounding landscape, there are extensive views from the excavated sites across the surrounding area. The north Cornish coast and at least two Early Bronze Age barrows are clearly visible three kilometres to the north, and the Gannel estuary, a historically important waterway with many prehistoric and Roman period sites and find-spots adjacent to it, lies a similar distance to the west (Nowakowski et al 2009). Castle-an-Dinas hillfort, approximately 11.5 kilometres to the east, is a prominent landscape feature (Wailes 1963; Jones, forthcoming a) (Fig 1.5). In addition to large monuments, the Newquay hinterland also contains a large number of later prehistoric to Roman period settlement sites (see Nowakowski and Quinnell 2011, fig 17.1). These include a crop mark round 1 kilometre to the north of the site (Cornwall HER MCO33168) and archaeological investigations at Tregunnel and Trevithick Manor have revealed evidence for prehistoric settlement (Cotswold Archaeology 2012; Cornwall HER MCO55974).

A complex cropmark enclosure at Manuels (Cornwall HER MCO8228) lies 700m to the south east. This,

Figure 1.3 The truncated Structure 2, located at the southern end of the road corridor.

INTRODUCTION TO THE PROJECT

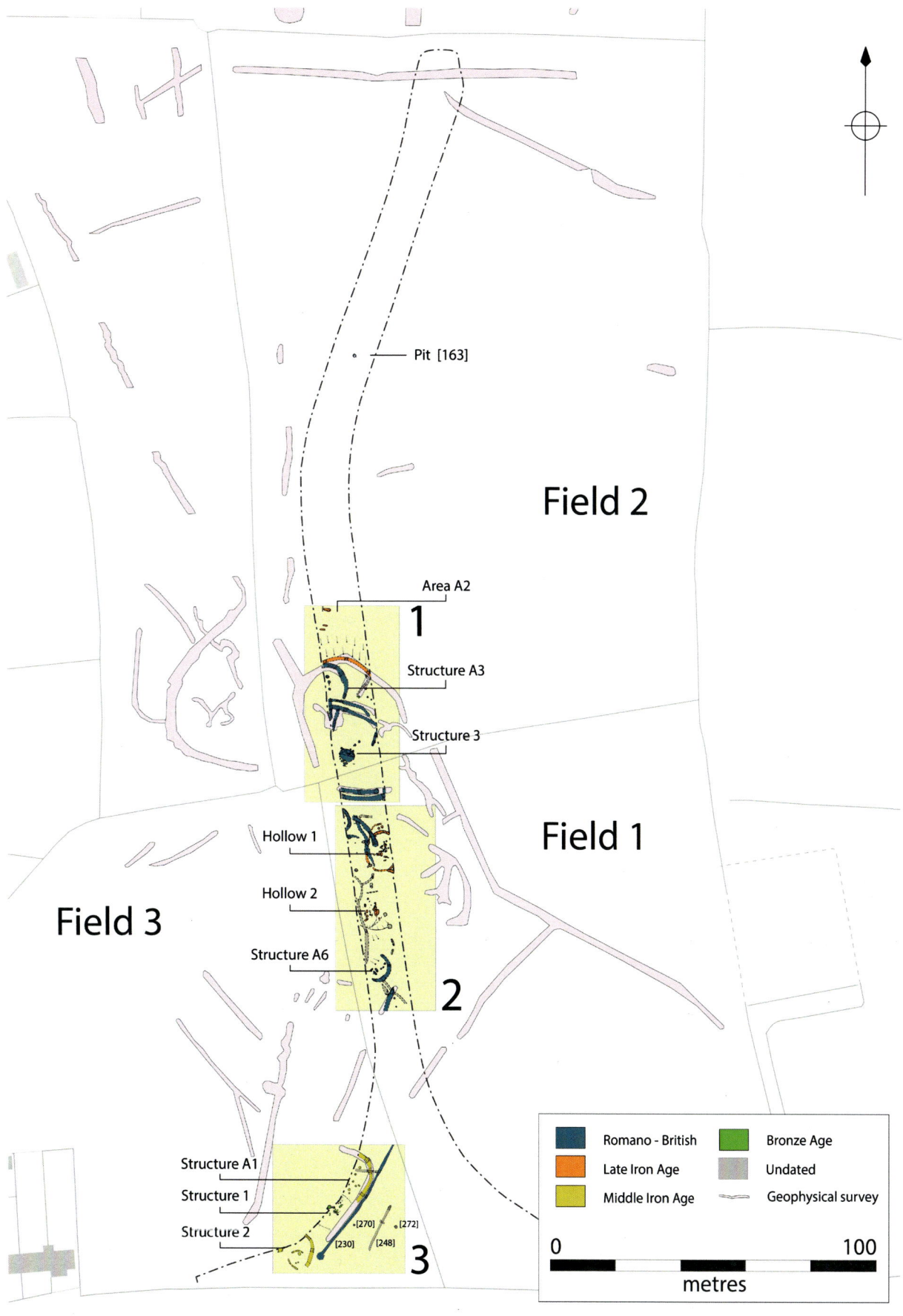

Figure 1.4 Overview showing excavated archaeological features in relation to the results from the geophysical survey.

Later prehistoric and Roman sites along the route of the Newquay Strategic Road Corridor

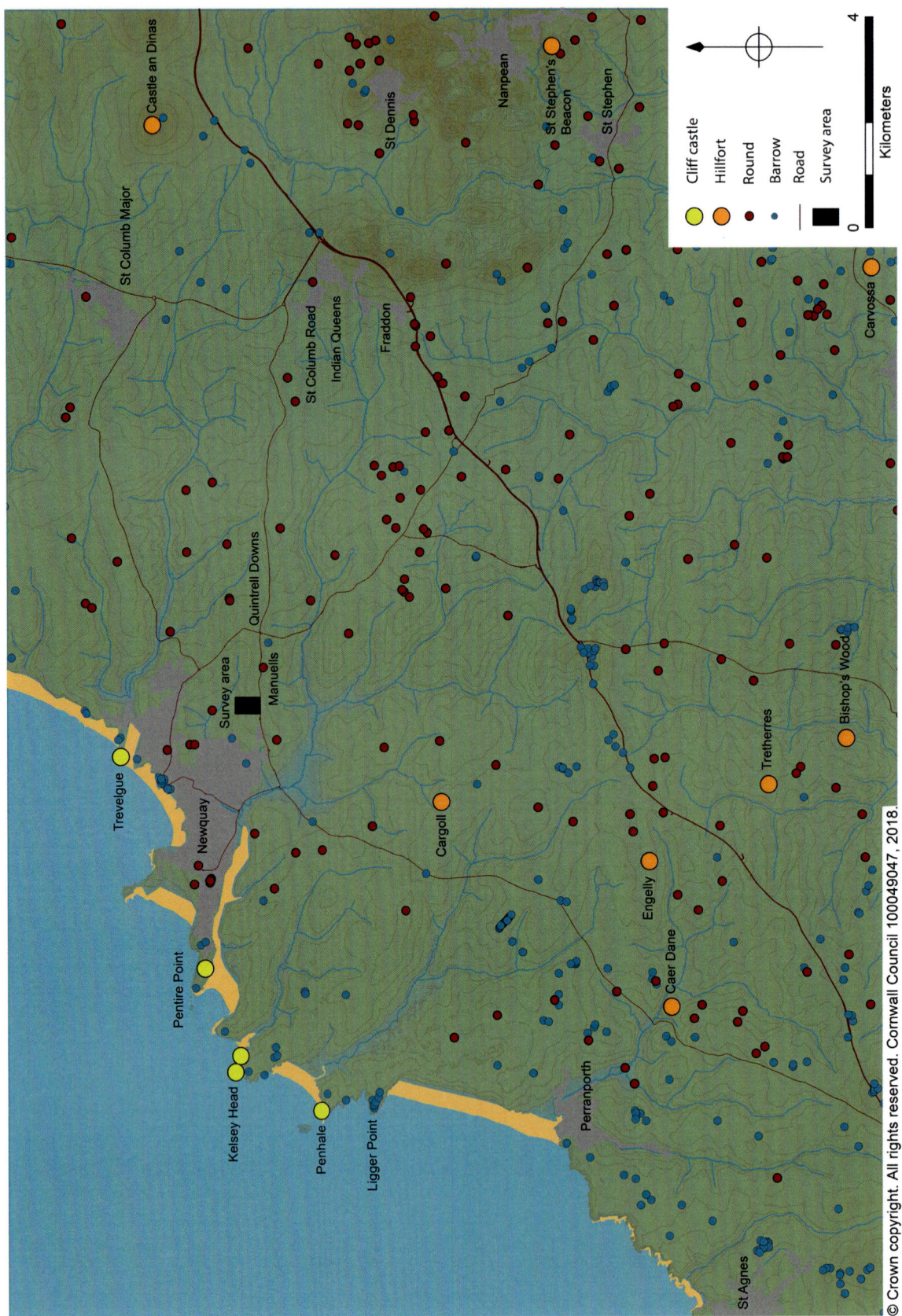

Figure 1.5 Archaeological sites in the area surrounding the Newquay Strategic Road corridor, including, barrows, large enclosures, cliff castles and rounds.

although now substantially levelled, is likely to have been the most significant site in the immediate area during the later prehistoric and Roman period (chapter 10). This site is located on the north-eastern slope of the end of the ridge and is a very large, multiple ditched enclosure, the eastern side of which is partially fossilized in an upstanding field boundary. Although the enclosure has not been investigated archaeologically it is probably of first millennium cal BC and / or Roman period date and is likely to have been an important place in the landscape (Jones and Smith 2015; Chapter 10, below).

Prior to the excavations little was known of the archaeology of the immediate area of the development. The potential for the road corridor to contain buried archaeological remains had, however, been shown by a geophysical survey (Figs 1.2 and 1.4) and archaeological evaluation trenching. Subsequent archaeological excavation of fields approximately 1.5 kilometres to the north east at the development site known as Nansledan has revealed substantial evidence for later prehistoric and Roman period settlement activity (Rainbird and Pears, forthcoming).

The geophysical survey was carried out in evaluative strips across the fields through which the road would be cut. Despite the gaps between the surveyed areas, it identified a large number of features of potential archaeological interest (Bunn 2011). The anomalies included an enclosure of probable prehistoric or Roman period date at the centre of the surveyed area, which appeared to be surrounded by ditches associated with a field system (Fig 1.1). A large number of pit-type anomalies were also detected, indicative of an intense occupation. The route of the road corridor was set to pass through this area of high activity, although many of the features identified by the survey lay beyond the east and west boundaries of the road scheme and were therefore outside the scope of the subsequent mitigation work.

In 2011 Cotswold Archaeology (Joyce 2011) excavated a series of evaluation trenches along the route of the proposed road corridor and in the fields to the east and west of the projected line of the road. The results from the trenching confirmed the presence of buried archaeological features, including pits and ditches, together with artefacts of Bronze Age, Iron Age and Roman date. The evaluation confirmed the results of the geophysical survey, established the character of the archaeology within the road corridor and demonstrated the need for detailed archaeological recording to take place in advance of construction of the road.

Methodology

The soil stripping along the length of the road corridor was carried out under archaeological supervision using a machine fitted with a toothless bucket. Where significant features were encountered, their location was recorded and highlighted as an area requiring further investigation (Smith 2015).

The stripped road corridor was divided into three zones deriving from the fields through which it passed: the northern part of the site fell within Field 2; Fields 1 and 3 were located at the southern end and demarcated the eastern and western parts of the corridor respectively (Figs 1.2 and 2.1). Archaeological features within these areas were then grouped. Potential buildings were given structure numbers (for example, Structure 1). Hollows with associated features were also given unique identifying numbers (for example, Hollow 1).

SECTION 2
INVESTIGATIONS

Chapter 2

The results from the fieldwork

Andy M Jones and Ryan P Smith

The results from the excavations are described below by chronological period and are subdivided by type (for example, Structure 1) and by area (for example, Field 3). Where appropriate the features are described from north to south (Fields 2, 1 and 3) (Fig 2.1).

The Neolithic

Flints and radiocarbon dating

No archaeological features were identified which can be assigned to the Neolithic period. There were, however, two strands of evidence which suggest a phase of Neolithic activity in the immediate area of the road corridor. The clearest indication of this took the form of 48 flints, which were recovered both within later period features and as unstratified finds (Lawson-Jones, Chapter 5). Although not closely diagnostic, many of the pieces appear to be of later Neolithic type. These include an unmodified knife **L1** and a cortical scraper **L2**.

The broad dating from the flints matches one of the radiocarbon determinations from the site. The lower fill (208) within ditch [204] produced a Middle to Late Neolithic radiocarbon determination of 4420 ± 28 BP, 3316–2992 cal BC (SUERC-63278), obtained on a hazelnut shell from a cluster of 472 shells. The radiocarbon date is, like the flint assemblage, problematic in that it was obtained from a feature which also contained iron ore and is clearly of much later date than the deposit of hazelnut shells (Chapters 8 and 11, below).

Nonetheless, despite the residuality of the flint and of the material sampled for radiocarbon dating, the results are significant because they hint at an occupation site of Middle to Late Neolithic date in the vicinity of the road corridor and highlight the potential for undisturbed features of this date such as pits or land surfaces to survive beyond the edges of the project area. The location of the hazelnut shell concentration in the bottom of a much later ditch is of interest, and this is discussed below in Chapter 11.

The Bronze Age: *circa* 2500 to 1300 cal BC

Early Bronze Age Beaker pits and flint

The earliest securely stratified evidence from the road corridor took the form of a small assemblage of Beaker pottery which was recovered from pits [163] and [398].

Pit [163] was an isolated feature in Field 2 cut by one of the evaluation trenches (Fig 2.2). It was sub-oval in plan, measuring 1m long by 0.7m wide, and was 0.45m deep. It contained four fills, (170), (171), (172) and (162). The upper fills (162) and (172) contained seven abraded sherds of Beaker pottery decorated with traces of probable comb-stamped horizontal lines and a row of fingernail impressions (Quinnell, below). The topmost deposit (162) was found to contain four flints, including a possible knife of later Neolithic to Early Bronze Age type, **L1** (Lawson-Jones, Chapter 5). The pit also included charred cereal grains and fragments of hazelnut shell (J Jones, Chapter 6). A radiocarbon determination on a charred hazelnut shell fragment from fill (162) produced a date of 3635 ± 29 BP, 2131–1912 cal BC (SUERC-64607).

Pit [398] was located in Hollow 1. It was a shallow, circular feature, measuring 0.26m in diameter by 0.24m deep. It was filled by (397), which produced an abraded sherd of Beaker pottery with a fabric similar to the sherds in pit [163]. Pit [398] was, however, located in an area with a large number of pits of Iron Age to early Roman period date. Consequently, there is a possibility that the sherd had been redeposited.

In addition to the Beaker pottery, some of the flint assemblage is also of Bronze Age date (Lawson-Jones, Chapter 5); however, with the exception of the pieces in pit [163], it was all recovered from residual contexts.

Middle Bronze Age

Old land surface

Only one feature of Middle Bronze Age date, Structure 1, was uncovered within the road corridor. However, an old land surface, layer (218), was identified in Field 3. This silty clay layer survived across the field in natural hollows and depressions. Several artefacts were recovered from it, including 16 sherds of Middle Bronze Age Trevisker Ware pottery and three pieces of fresh flint (Quinnell and Lawson-Jones, Chapters 3 and 5). The condition of the flint and the survival of the pottery suggest that the layer was formed in prehistory, although it is not possible to closely date it.

Structure 1

Structure 1 was a Middle Bronze Age roundhouse of hollow-set type (Fig 2.2), comparable with a significant

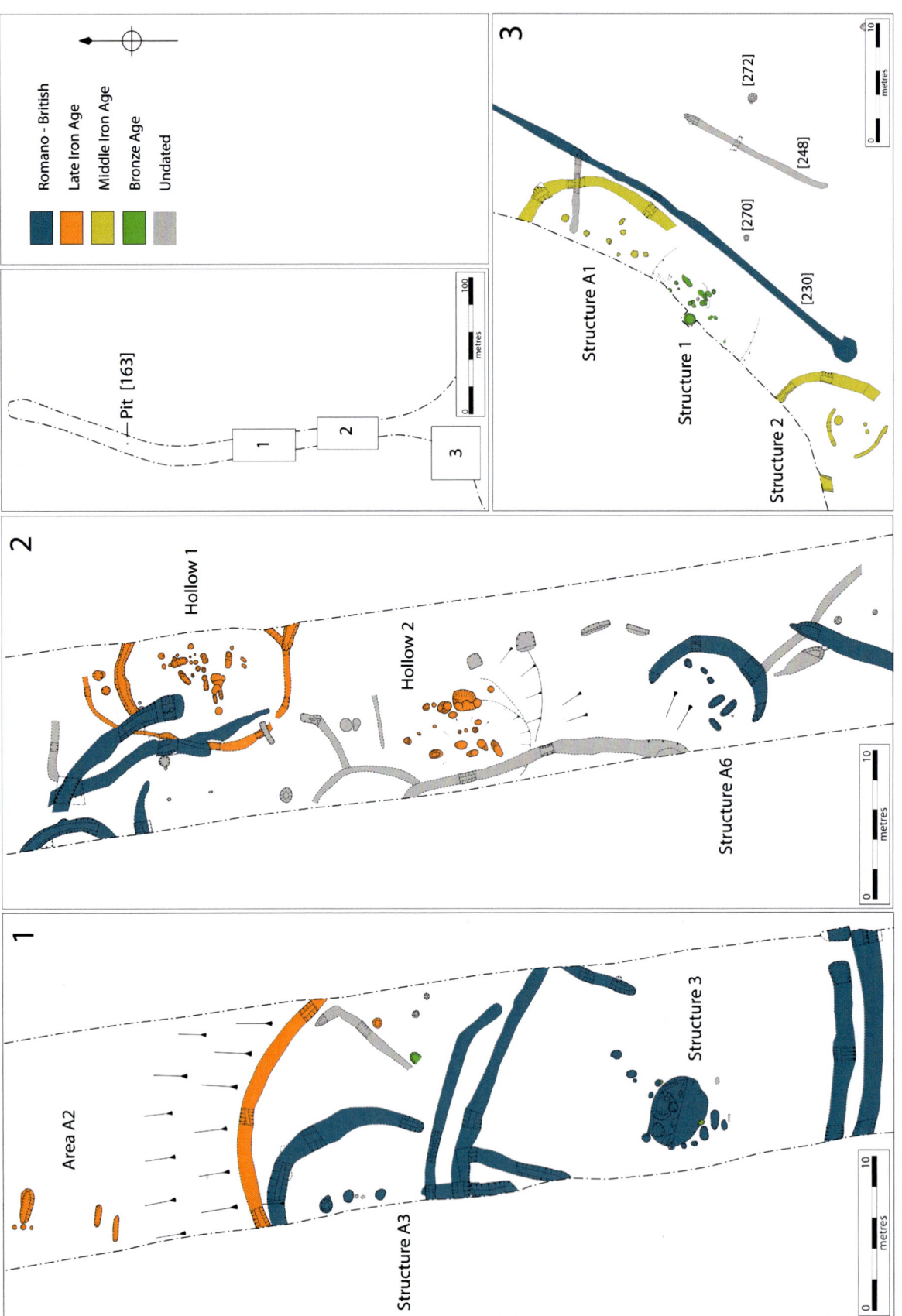

Figure 2.1 Overview of the results from the excavations shown by Field and phase (Bronze Age, Middle Iron Age Late Iron Age and Roman).

THE RESULTS FROM THE FIELDWORK

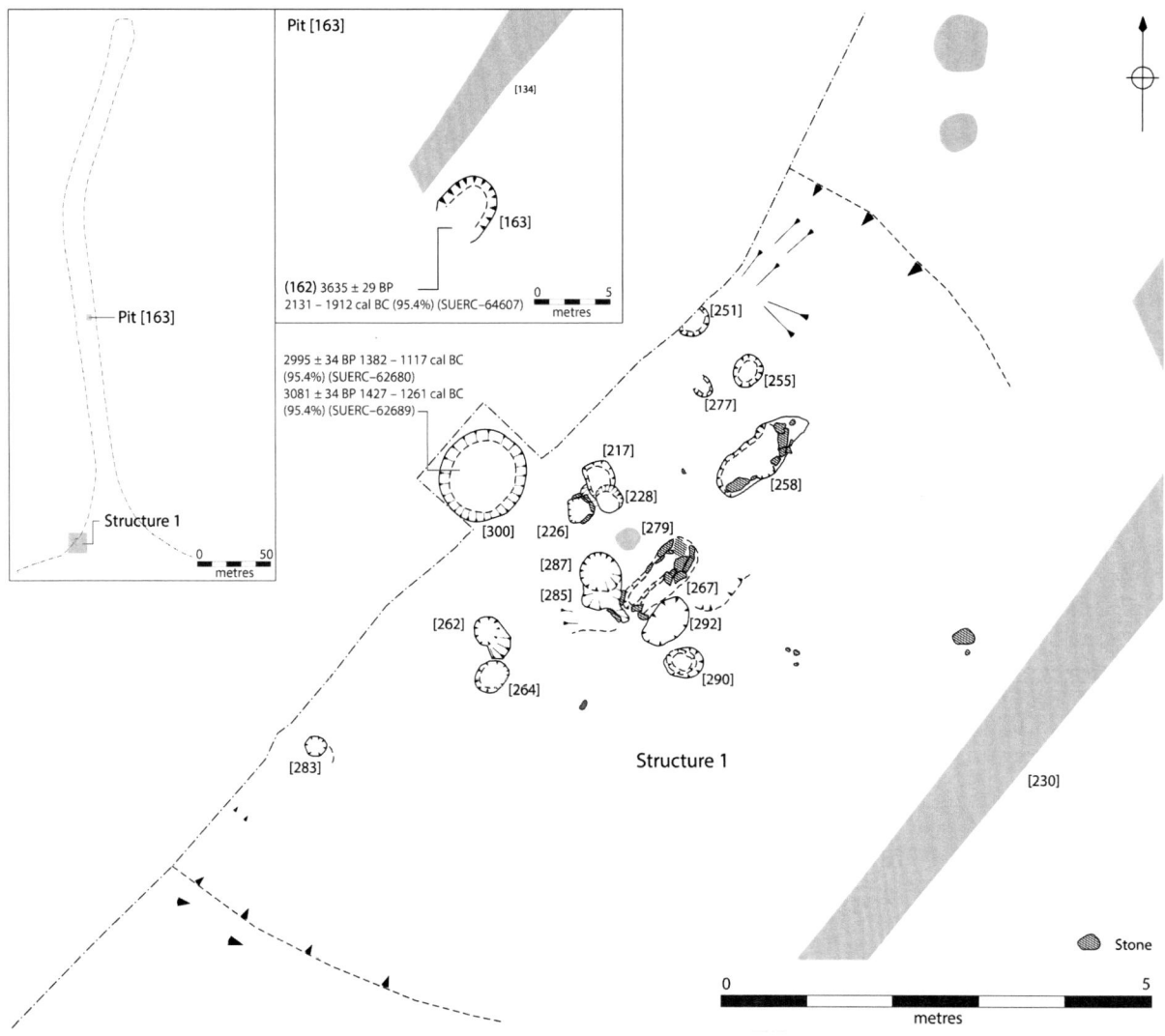

Figure 2.2 Features of Bronze Age date. Middle Bronze Age Structure 1 and Beaker pit [163] (inset).

number of others excavated in lowland Cornwall (Gossip and Jones 2008).

Most of the structure lay outside the western edge of the cutting for the road corridor, and less than half of its probable extent was investigated. The investigated portion did, however, include the entrance, which was located on the south east side of the building. In total, the area of the roundhouse excavated measured 10.5m by 4.5m.

The edges of the roundhouse were defined by a shallow cut into the natural. This was most clearly evident on the north east and south west sides but less apparent on the east. This is, however, likely to be due to the entrance having been on this side of the house rather than a result of plough-truncation. Although the full dimensions of the building cannot be precisely determined, it is likely to have had a diameter of approximately 10m.

The roundhouse was sealed beneath a deposit of dark brown loamy ploughsoil (101), up to 0.7m deep. The ploughsoil was especially thick in this part of the site and it is likely that the lower portion of the layer was in fact an infill deposit over the house floor. This is indicated by the fact that the lower portion of (101) was of a slightly lighter colour than the deposit above (see Fig 10.2). Weather conditions, however, were not good when the site was stripped and the layer was devoid of artefacts, which meant that this subtle division was not noted until the post-excavation stage of the project.

The overlying infill layer sealed a number of internal features, including a deeply cut pit, four deep postholes, a potential floor surface and a number of small pits and postholes.

Close to and partially under the baulk was a deeply cut circular pit [300]. This measured 1m in diameter and was up to 0.45m deep. The baulk was cut back in order to fully excavate the feature. Within the pit was fill (299), which held a structured deposit that included selected sherds of Trevisker Ware pottery (including **P1–P4**), two flints (including **L4**) and part of a saddle quern, **S1** (Quinnell, Chapters 3 and 4; Lawson-Jones, Chapter 5) (Figs 3.1 and 5.1). The pot appeared to have been placed on its side within the fill and a large piece of slate covered it. The upper part of the pit cut was covered by a lighter deposit which could either be a floor layer or an infilling deposit sealing the pit (Fig 10.1). Two radiocarbon determinations were obtained: *ilex* charcoal from the pit fill produced a date of 2995 ± 34 BP, 1382–1117 cal BC (SUERC-62680), and residue from ceramics a date of 3081 ± 34 BP, 1427–1261 cal BC (SUERC-62689). The determinations fall in the Middle Bronze Age and are discussed below (Chapter 8).

Four deep postholes, [228], [251], [262] and [283], were initially interpreted as part of an internal post-ring (Smith 2015) which would have supported the covering roof. The posts were spaced between 2.1m and 2.4m apart. They measured from 0.3m to 0.5m in diameter and were 0.5m to 0.6m deep. However, the arc formed by these posts is quite shallow and the ring may actually have included postholes [290] and [255]. Posthole [283] was close to the edge of the hollow and may not have been part of the ring. There were very few finds from these features, although (282), the fill of posthole [283], did contain a broken flint blade (Lawson-Jones, Chapter 5).

On the south eastern side of the roundhouse were two elongated oval pits or sockets, [258] and [267]. Pit [258] measured 1.2m long by 0.5m wide and 0.2m deep. Cut [267] was of very similar size, 1m long by 0.4m wide and 0.3m deep. Both pits were stone-lined and they were set on a similar alignment with their adjacent ends just under 1m apart. It is probable that they formed part of the entrance to the roundhouse and were situated on either side of the doorway. Pit [258] produced two flints, including **L3**, a distinctive black cortical flake which had been burnt (Lawson-Jones, Chapter 5), and a single sherd of Trevisker Ware pottery. Two sherds of Trevisker Ware pottery were recovered from pit [267].

Pit [258] appeared to have been cut through a floor layer (256). This comprised a mixture of broken shillet and clay silt which had been laid up to 0.2m thick across the interior of the house hollow. The floor surface covered an area of 4m by 3m on the eastern side of the roundhouse. It was above layer (105), which was a very smooth, possibly worn area of natural clay shillet.

Several postholes, including [255] and [277], unless the floor was laid around them, had also been cut through the floor surface (256), and may indicate the presence of internal features within the building. Posthole [228] cut posthole [217] and may represent a renewal of the post-ring. The same may be true of [264], which could have replaced [262]. Eighteen sherds of Trevisker Ware pottery were recovered from posthole [217] and a further four were found in posthole [226]. However, the majority of these postholes and pits, which include [292], [285], [277], [287] and [279], did not form a regular pattern and their function remains uncertain. Only one of these, posthole [277], produced an artefact, in the form of a single sherd of Trevisker pottery.

Although small amounts of charcoal were recovered from several postholes, the only large quantity was found in pit [300] (Challinor, Chapter 7), and must have been deposited after it had cooled as there was no sign of burning and the feature was not a hearth. Much of the charcoal, which is of oak, was derived from small diameter roundwood. By contrast, the lack of charred plant materials, especially from within pit [300], is of interest.

Discussion

The two pits with Beaker pottery are comparable with other known sites in the county. Sherds from Cornwall with similar decoration have associated radiocarbon dates in the twenty-second to twentieth centuries cal BC (Jones and Quinnell 2006a; Jones *et al* 2012) and the radiocarbon determination from pit [163] falls within this period. The second pit [398] found to contain Beaker pottery is also likely to date to the earlier part of the Bronze Age (*circa* 2500–1900 cal BC).

Middle Bronze Age activity (*circa* 1500–1000 cal BC) was represented by Structure 1, a hollow-set roundhouse, less than half of which was investigated. Nonetheless, despite the limitations of the evidence, it is possible to make some general points about the site stratigraphy (see also the discussion in Chapter 11, below).

Despite the limited investigation, the roundhouse in many ways conforms with other lowland roundhouses in Cornwall which have been more fully excavated. The entrance was located on the south east side of the house and a post-ring was set within an artificial cut or hollow. The survival of a clay floor layer is more rarely encountered but a small number of roundhouses – for example, one at Trevalga, near Tintagel, and roundhouse 1 at Tremough (Jones and Quinnell 2014, 33; Jones *et al* 2015, 36) – have been found to have patches of remnant clay flooring surviving within them, and more complete floors were found within roundhouses 2001 and 2222 at Trethellan Farm (Nowakowski 1991).

Pit [300] with its 'structured deposit' is also paralleled at other lowland roundhouse sites, as at Scarcewater house 1500 and at Trethellan, the latter lying just 3.5 kilometres away to the west (Jones and Taylor 2010; Nowakowski 1991), and pits flanking the entrance may also have formed an aggrandized entrance which is found at other lowland roundhouses (Chapter 10). However, by contrast with the majority of other investigated hollow-set roundhouses, most of the other excavated features were almost devoid of artefacts; unusually, the infill layer covering Structure 1 also lacked finds, and was not readily distinguished from the ploughsoil above during the soil stripping.

The Middle Iron Age: *circa* fifth to third century cal BC

Two discrete features of Middle Iron Age date were uncovered and investigated in Field 3. They comprised a ring-gullied feature, Structure 2, and a group of postholes and a gully which formed a possible building, Structure A1 (Fig 2.3). Three ditches were also located in the vicinity, and although not securely dated, these may have been associated with a field system or compound of broadly the same period.

Structure 2

Structure 2 comprised a segmented curvilinear gully [303], which encircled a pit and two postholes (Fig 2.4). The two segments of the gully did not link up and there were wide gaps between the ends of the gullies to east and the west. The overall space enclosed was roughly oval and measured approximately 4.5m by 4m.

The excavated sections through the gully were 0.35m wide and up to 0.2m deep. The eastern ends of both

Figure 2.3 Features of Middle Iron Age date. Structure 2 and Structure A1.

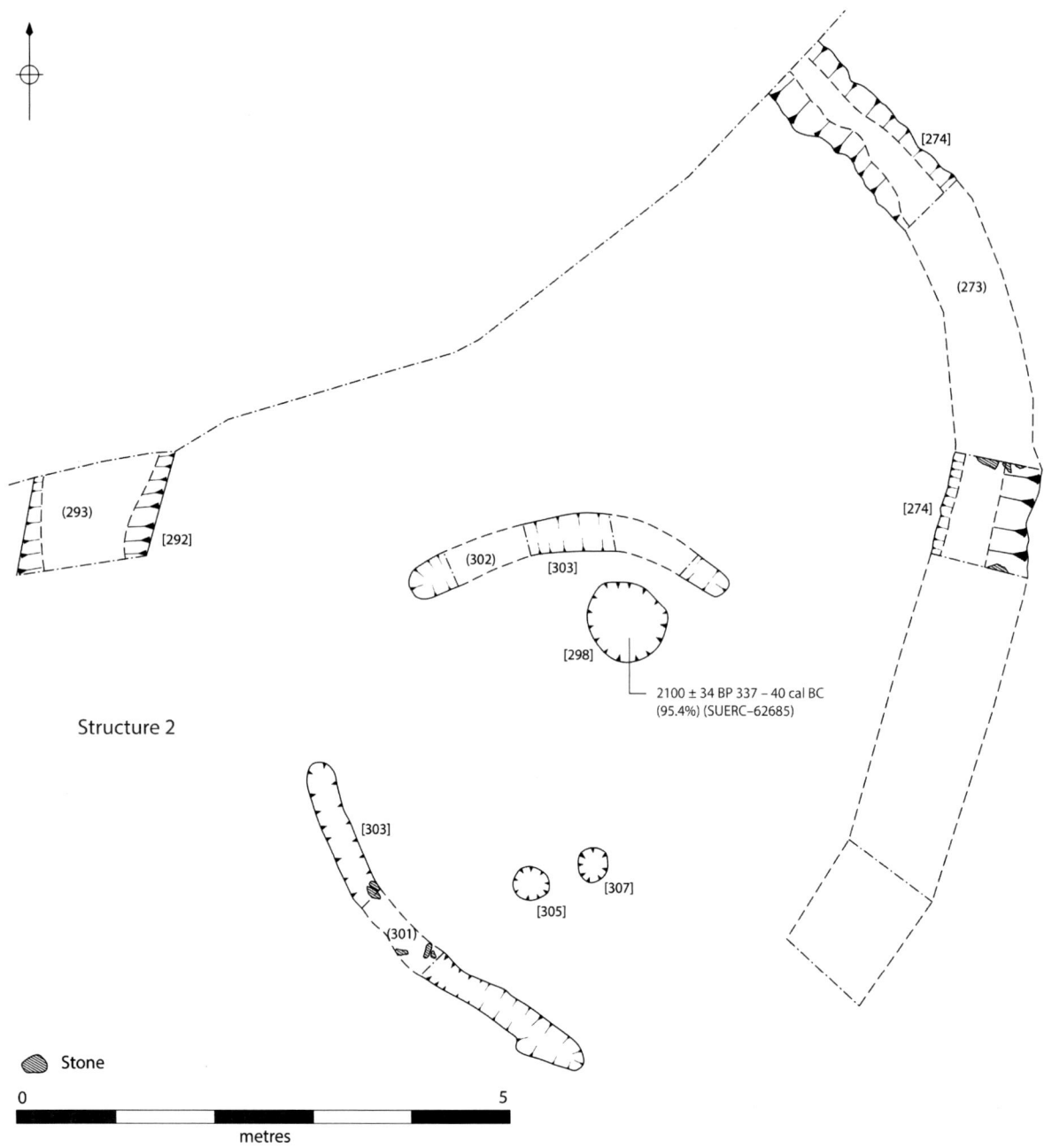

Figure 2.4 Plan of Middle Iron Age Structure 2 and ditch [274].

segments, north and south, may have been cut by a modern water main (not shown) and a larger curvilinear ditch [274]. The overlying ploughsoil was quite shallow in this area and it is likely that ploughing has truncated the feature. The gully could not be radiocarbon dated, although a few sherds of Middle Iron Age pottery were recovered from it, which would be consistent with the radiocarbon dating from pit [298] (Quinnell; Chapter 3; Chapter 9).

Within the interior of Structure 2, close to the north eastern side of the ring-gully, was a large pit [298]. The cut was roughly circular in shape and measured 0.82 in diameter by 0.29m deep. The fill (297) contained some sherds of Middle Iron Age pottery, a single polished stone and a large amount of charcoal consistent with a domestic fuel assemblage (Challinor, Chapter 7). There was, however, no indication of burning on either the sides or base of the pit. The charcoal from the pit produced a radiocarbon determination of 2100 ± 34 BP, 337–40 cal BC (SUERC-62685), which suggests that Structure 1 is of Middle to Late Iron Age date.

Only two other features were found inside the ring-gully. On the southern side of the enclosed area was a pair of postholes, [305] and [307]. Both were circular and similar in size, with [305] measuring 0.4m in diameter by 0.2m deep and [307] 0.3m in diameter by 0.15m deep.

Neither of the postholes produced any artefacts and their function remains uncertain, although it is likely that they were structural.

A short length of a well-defined ditch [293], measuring 1.3m wide and 0.64m deep, was found to the north west of Structure 2. Two sherds of Middle Iron Age pottery and a burnt flint tool were recovered from the ditch fill (296) (Quinnell, Chapter 3; Lawson-Jones, Chapter 5). The full extent of the ditch could not be determined, but it may have continued to the south east and connected with ditch [274].

To the north east of Structure 2 was ditch [274] (Fig 2.4). This was 0.7m wide and between 0.12m and 0.37m deep. The northern end of the ditch continued under the baulk, but the section in the stripped area curved toward the south west, where it was truncated by later disturbance; its full extent could not be determined. The only dating evidence from the ditch was a few sherds of Middle Iron Age pottery (Quinnell, Chapter 3). It is possible that it was a field boundary ditch and that it was associated with Structure 2, but this is uncertain and the finds may have been residual.

Structure A1

Structure A1 was located immediately north of Structure 1, the Middle Bronze Age roundhouse, and Middle Iron Age Structure 2 (Fig 2.3 and 2.5). It is intriguing that it did not cut and appears to respect the Middle Bronze Age roundhouse site, which implies the infill mounding over Structure 1 may still have existed as an above ground feature. It comprised what appeared to be a shallow curvilinear ditch or ring-gully [220], the area enclosed by which was possibly open to the south (Fig 2.5). It measured 0.77m wide and 0.2m deep and was exposed over a distance of 15m (Fig 2.5). However, its full extent is unknown as the western side of the feature lay beyond the stripped area. The gully was found to contain a few sherds of Middle Iron Age pottery (Quinnell, Chapter 3); a radiocarbon determination, 2179 ± 34 BP, 365–119 cal BC (SUERC-62695), was obtained from the ring-gully on ceramic residue. A beach cobble with whetstone use on one side was also recovered from it (Quinnell, Chapter 4).

The gully encircled a number of pits and postholes, including [215], [233], [237]/[239], [235], [241], [243], [245] and [253]; most of these were laid out in what appeared to be a roughly linear fashion (with two others offset to the east).

Several of the postholes contained artefacts. Posthole [237] produced sherds from two vessels (Quinnell, Chapter 3) and another sherd was found with a residual flint tool in posthole [239], which probably recut [237]. Pit [215] contained a whetstone **S8** and posthole [233] produced a sandstone beach cobble with some hammerstone use on one corner (Quinnell, Chapter 4).

A radiocarbon determination was obtained from (232), the fill of posthole [233]: 2114 ± 34 BP, 346–45 cal BC (SUERC-62687). This falls in broadly the same period as the date from the gully, which suggests that they are likely to be contemporary.

The ring-gully [220] was cut by short length of ditch [223] (Fig 2.5), which unfortunately could not be closely dated (below).

Structure A1 may represent either an open working area bounded by the curvilinear ring-gully [220], or another roofed structure, much of which lay beyond the stripped area. The line of spaced postholes would lend weight to the latter interpretation, suggesting a broadly rectilinear structure. In either case, it appears to be broadly contemporary with Structure 1 and part of an episode of Middle Iron Age activity.

Discussion

The Middle Iron Age phase was confined to Field 3, at the southern end of the road scheme. Two structures and possibly two or three boundary ditches have been assigned to this phase.

The structures were different in form from one another and neither of the buildings were classic roundhouses. Structure 2 was roughly sub-oval in shape and would have enclosed a space of around 4m by 5m. The ring-gully could have held a wall or enclosed a space in which a building stood (Chapter 10). Too little is available of the complete plan of Structure A1 to make any firm comments on its overall form, beyond suggesting that ring-gully [220] may have encircled a line of postholes forming one side of a rectilinear timber building. Again, the gully could have held a wall-line, although it is possible that the structure represented by the postholes actually sat in its own ditched enclosure. Structures encircled by non-structural gullies are known from elsewhere in Cornwall, as, for example, at the Late Iron Age settlement at Higher Besore, Truro, and at Camelford (Gossip, forthcoming; Jones and Taylor 2015; and see discussion in Chapter 10).

The radiocarbon and artefactual dating is too broad to identify which of the structures was the older and given their proximity to one another it is possible that they were contemporary. They may have been situated within a larger open settlement as there was no evidence for enclosure. Neither of the possible buildings produced any charred remains of cereals or crop processing (J Jones, Chapter 6, below), neither was there any sign of industrial activity or occupation

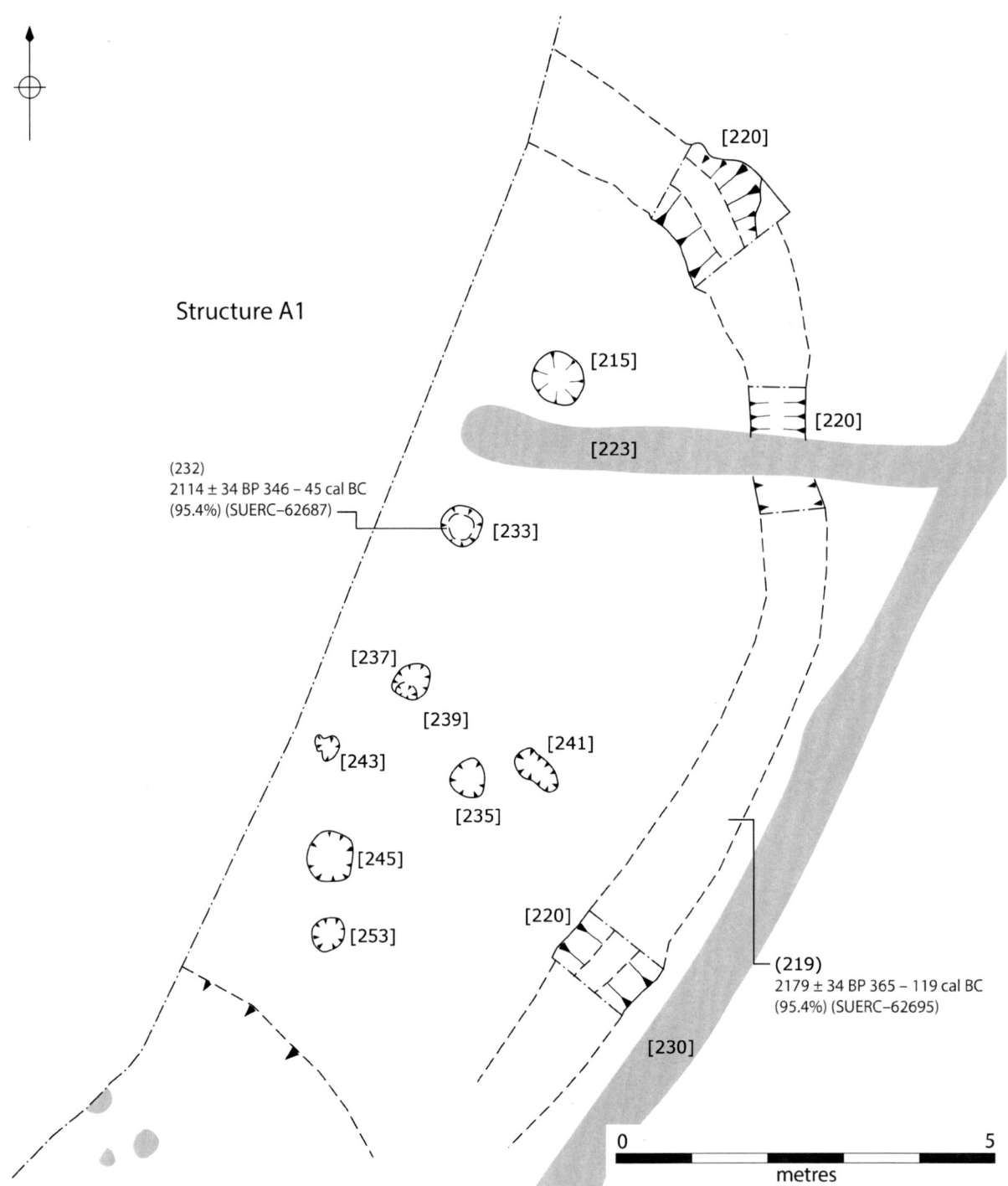

Figure 2.5 Plan of Middle Iron Age Structure A1.

deposits within them. This makes interpretation difficult, although both may be interpreted as roofed buildings.

The linear ditches [223], [274] and [292] may have been part of a field system or part of a compound around Structure 2. Unfortunately, they had few direct relationships with the identified structures and secure dating is quite limited, reliant upon the small ceramic assemblage found within them not having been redeposited or residual. However, ditch [223] certainly cut ring-gully [220] forming Structure A1 and it is also possible that ditches [274] and [293] were later than Structure 2. It is therefore conceivable that the field ditches post-dated the use of the structures and belong to a later phase.

The Late Iron Age: last century cal BC to first century AD

The Late Iron Age phase of activity on the site centred on two hollowed areas in Field 1, Hollow 1 and Hollow

2, which were associated with pits and ring-ditches and gullies (Fig 2.6). Other features of this period included a substantial boundary ditch and a group of isolated rectangular cut features towards the southern end of Field 2 (Area A2).

Hollow 1

Hollow 1 was located towards the northern end of Field 1 in a slightly depressed area although there was no sign of a cut. It was oval and measured approximately 12–14m by 7.5m (Fig 2.7). The eastern side of the hollow lay outside the stripped area. The edge of the hollow was defined and enclosed by three ditches, interpreted as ring-gullies, including [360], [336] and [408]. None of the gullies were associated with banks.

Ring-gully [360] was 0.35m wide and was 0.25m deep and defined the outer western and northern parts of the hollow. The upper fill (446) contained six sherds of Late Iron Age pottery. The ring-ditch was cut by two features of Roman date, ring-gully [322] and ditch [317] (see below). It was also cut by a shallow east-west aligned sub-rectangular pit [414], 1.6m long by 0.43m wide and up to 0.15m deep.

Ring-gully [336] was located on the northern side of the hollow, approximately 1.6m south of ring-gully [360]. It was 1m wide and 0.6m deep and was also cut by ditch [322]. The fill (335) produced 28 sherds of Late Iron Age pottery, including parts of vessel **P11** (Quinnell, Chapter 3), a slate 'pot lid' **S13** (Quinnell, Chapter 4) and a residual flint pebble. The artefacts may have been associated with a deliberate 'structured' deposit (Chapter 11), as the ditch fill material (335) had been spread beyond the confines of the ditch cut and over pit [346] immediately to the north. A Late Iron Age radiocarbon determination from fill (335) was obtained from ceramic residue: 1981 ± 34 BP, 52 cal BC – cal AD 85 (SUERC-62690).

Between gullies [360] and [336] were pits [346] and [309]. Pit [346] was circular, 0.5m in diameter and 0.4m deep. The natural subsoil around the pit had become reddened, suggesting that it had been used as a hearth. The fill contained several sherds of Late Iron Age pottery, including **P10,** a well-made storage vessel (Quinnell, Chapter 3). Two radiocarbon determinations were obtained from pit [346]: charcoal from fill (345) produced a date of 2028 ± 34 BP, 159 cal BC – cal AD 55 (SUERC-62679), and a second date on ceramic residue fell in the period 2077 ± 34 BP, 189–1 cal BC (SUERC-62694). Both fall in the Late Iron Age and are consistent with the pottery (Chapters 3 and 8).

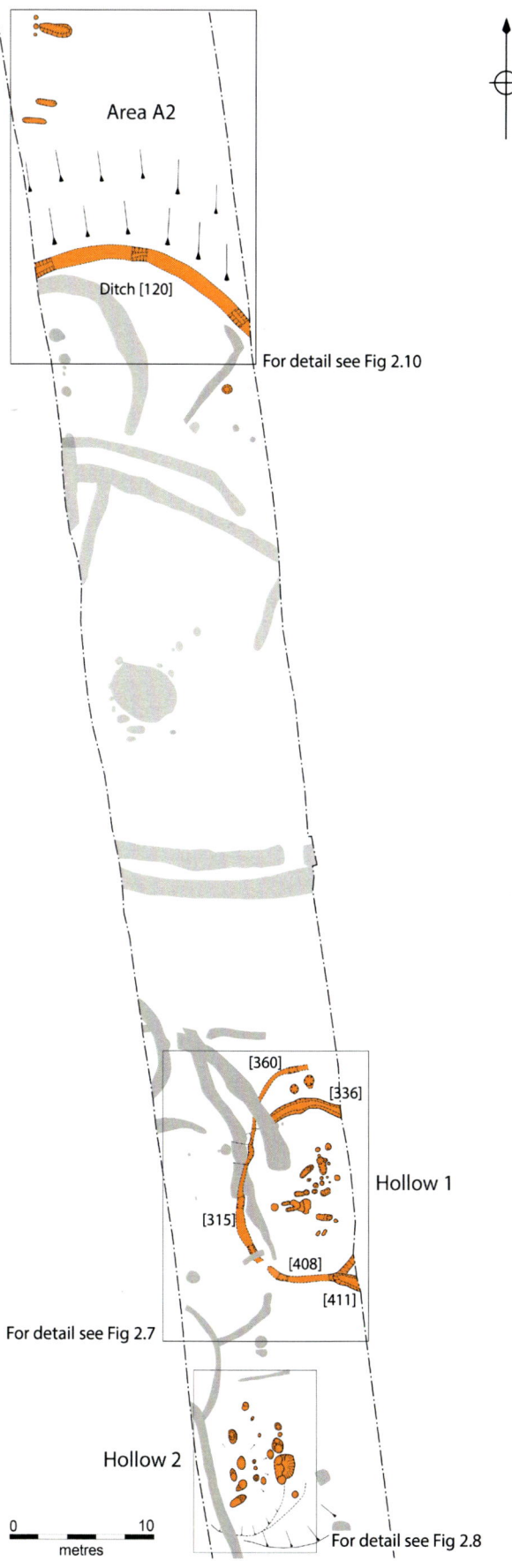

Figure 2.6 Features of Late Iron Age date, including Hollow 1, Hollow 2, ditch [120] and Area A2.

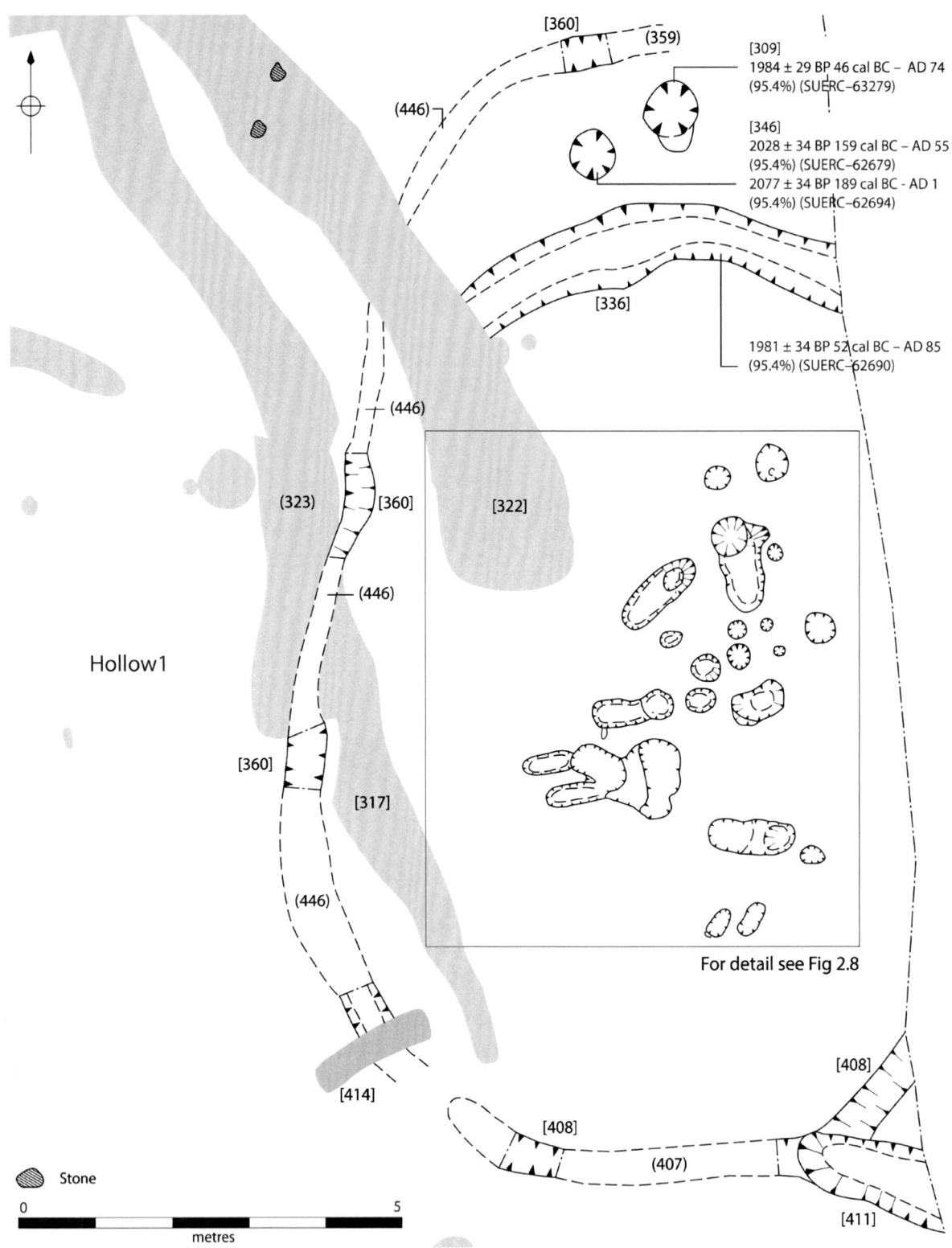

Figure 2.7 Plan of Late Iron Age Hollow 1.

Pit [309] was sub-circular, 0.9m by 0.6m and 0.4m deep. It was filled by (308), which contained 13 sherds from a Late Iron Age Cordoned Ware vessel **P9** (Quinnell, Chapter 3). A number of burnt granite stones were recorded in the fill, from which a small amount of cereal grain was also recovered (J Jones, Chapter 6). A radiocarbon determination was obtained on charred hulled wheat from fill (308): 1984 ± 29 BP, 46 cal BC – cal AD 74 (SUERC-62694). This is broadly similar to the Late Iron Age dating from pit [346], although it could indicate that pit [309] was a little later.

The southern side of the hollow was demarcated by ring-gully [408]. It was 0.6m wide by 0.24m deep and was filled by (407). The fill did not produce any artefacts; ring-gully [408] was, nevertheless, certainly later than ditch or gully [411], which it cut. Ditch [411] was excavated over a length of 1.2m and was 0.9m wide and 0.6m deep. The date of [411], however, is unknown and, as most of the ditch circuit lay outside the stripped area, it is not possible to say if it was associated with the hollow.

Indeed, it is possible that not all of these elements were contemporary with one another: ring-gullies [336] and [360] both appeared to define the northern side of the hollow and there was no direct relationship between gullies [360] and [408] to the west and south. It may be that the perimeter of the hollow was redefined on more than one occasion but it is not possible to determine a sequence for the gullies. The radiocarbon date from ring-gully [336] could be a little later than those from two of the pits but this cannot be demonstrated for certain.

Hollow 1 contained a large number of internal features, at least 23 pits and postholes, some of which were intercutting or had been recut. They clustered in the central part of the hollow but, unlike the pits and postholes found within the other excavated hollows and ring-gullies, there seemed to be no patterning or other indication of a post-built structure.

The internal features included nine probable postholes, [330], [340], [344], [350], [351], [352], [355], [390], [394] and [398]. All but one, posthole [355], were located in the north east part of the central cluster of features. It is not, in fact, certain that all of these features held posts and they have been described as postholes because of their circular form and size. They ranged in diameter from 0.2m to 0.37m and in depth from 0.1m to 0.3m. The majority were, however, around 0.15m deep.

Only one of the postholes, [330], produced any finds, in the form of sherds of Late Iron Age pottery (Quinnell, Chapter 3), and none contained any material suitable for radiocarbon dating, which makes their phasing within the hollow difficult. It is, however, apparent from the stratigraphic relationships that they did not all belong to one phase. Posthole [340], for example, was cut into the fill of pit [334] and posthole [330] was located at the west end of pit [334].

Activity around pit [348] was particularly complicated. Posthole [351], which appeared to have been deliberately capped with slates, was cut through pit [348]. By contrast, posthole [352] was earlier and had been cut by posthole [351]. A small assemblage of charred cereals was recovered from postholes [340] and [351] (J Jones, Chapter 6).

Fourteen pits were found inside the hollow: [334], [348], [364], [373], [375], [377], [380], [382], [384], [386], [388], [400], [402] and [404] (Fig 2.8). Of these, pits [334], [348], [373], [375], [377], [380] and [388] were of particular interest. All were sub-rectangular in shape, between 0.7m and 1.2m long and 0.1m to 0.25m deep, with signs of heating evident around the sides and containing charcoal and burnt stone. Pit [334] also contained large stones in its west end, subdividing the pit into two parts. At the east end of the pit fill (333) was a fragment from a stone bowl of Trethurgy type, S5, and trimmed slates (Quinnell, Chapter 4). This artefact suggests that the hollow continued to be used into the earlier part of the Roman period.

There are no radiocarbon determinations from any of the elongated pits; however, pit [380] produced a few small sherds of pottery of Late Iron Age date (Quinnell, Chapter 3).

Pits [364], [373], [375] and [377] were arranged in a tight, intercutting group, concentrated within an area no more than two metres square. Pit [364] was oval, measuring 1m by 0.8m and 0.2m deep. Pieces of slate were concentrated on the northern edge of the pit, one of which appeared to have been held in position by a deposit of clay. A smooth pebble and the rim from a Late Iron Age Type O jar were found within the fill. A second oval pit [373] measured 0.9m by 0.4m and 0.25m deep; no artefacts were recovered but evidence for burning was found within it and a small quantity of cereal grains (J Jones, Chapter 6). Pit [375], on the south west side of the group, was one of the elongated pits noted above and appears to have been cut by [373]. On the north west side of the group, pit [377] also appeared to have been cut by pit [373]. It was oval, 0.7m long by 0.34m wide and 0.14m deep.

There are no radiocarbon determinations from any of the central pits; however, in addition to the finds described above, pit [382] produced 40 small sherds of pottery of Late Iron Age date (Quinnell, Chapter 3), together with a vein quartz cobble which had been used as a rubber, a beach cobble trimmed into a rough chopper S16 and a beach cobble S12 which had been used as a hammerstone. Pit [404] also contained a hammerstone (Quinnell, Chapter 4).

In addition to these cut features, an amorphous layer (412) was situated just beyond the western end of pit [377]. This produced two sherds of Late Iron Age pottery, indicating that it was broadly contemporary with activity within the hollow.

To the south west of Hollow 1 (and north west of Hollow 2) were a number of miscellaneous features (Fig 2.11). These included a shallow curvilinear gully [442], which measured 0.6m to 0.85m wide and 0.12m deep. The

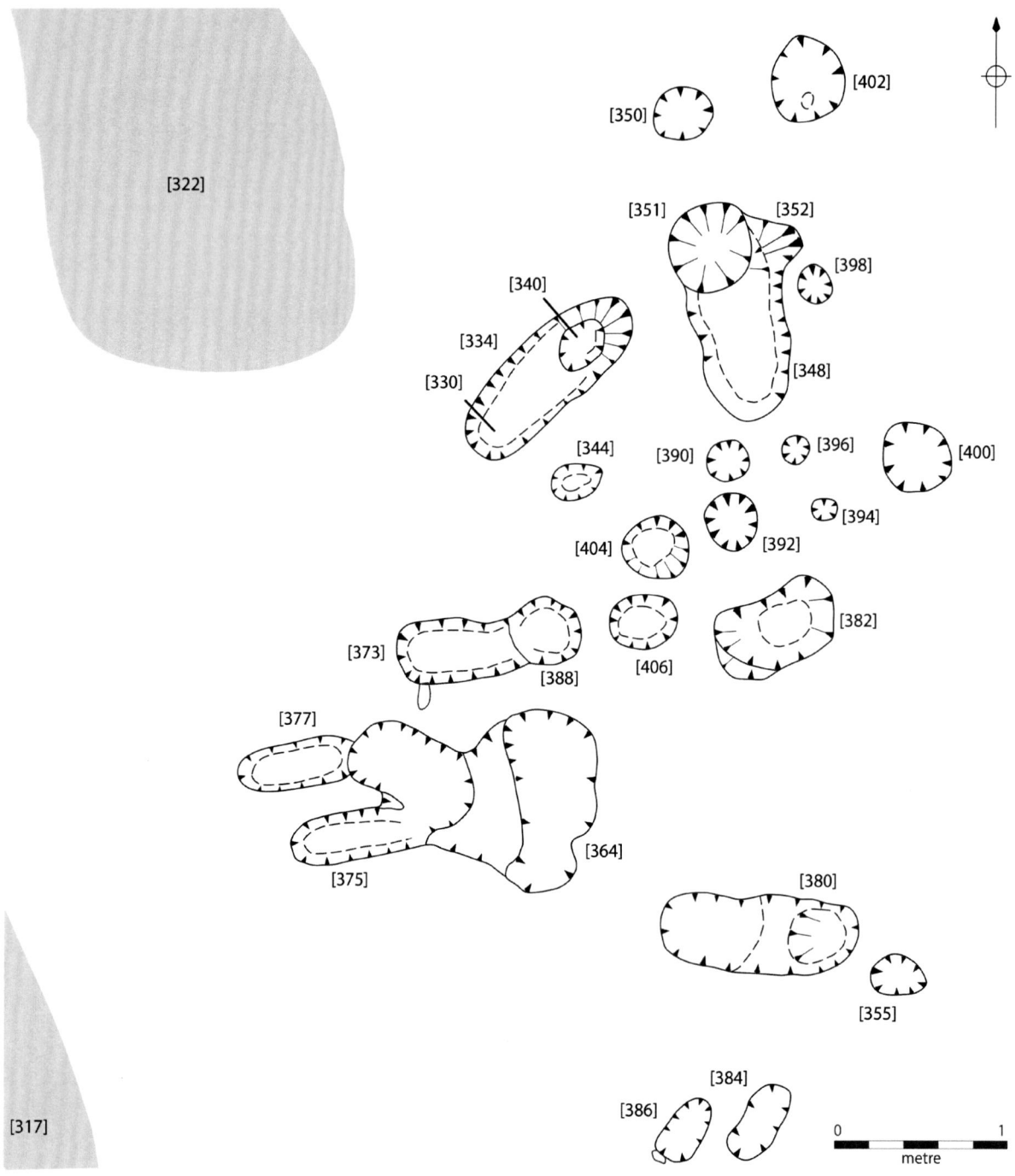

Figure 2.8 Plan of pits within Late Iron Age Hollow 2.

western end ran into gully [495] but their relationship was not established as the latter was unexcavated. The feature is not well-dated. The fill (441) contained a flint and three sherds of Late Iron Age pottery, which could mean that it is contemporary with Hollow 1. However, the finds may be residual and gully [442] could be associated with the nearby pit [367].

Hollow 2

Hollow 2 was situated towards the western side of the stripped area. It was roughly oval, approximately 8m long by 7m wide and 0.1m to 0.15m deep at the southern end (Fig 2.9). Its western side lay outside the road corridor. Hollow 2 petered out to the north and was most clearly defined on its southern side where it had been heightened by (486), a layer of redeposited natural clays and loamy soil. This deposit had been dumped against the edge of the hollow, where it may originally have formed a low bank or bund around it. Layer (486) may have been derived from within the area of the hollow and represent upcast removed in order to create a level area to hold a structure and other features. Within the hollow itself there was a

THE RESULTS FROM THE FIELDWORK

Hollow 2

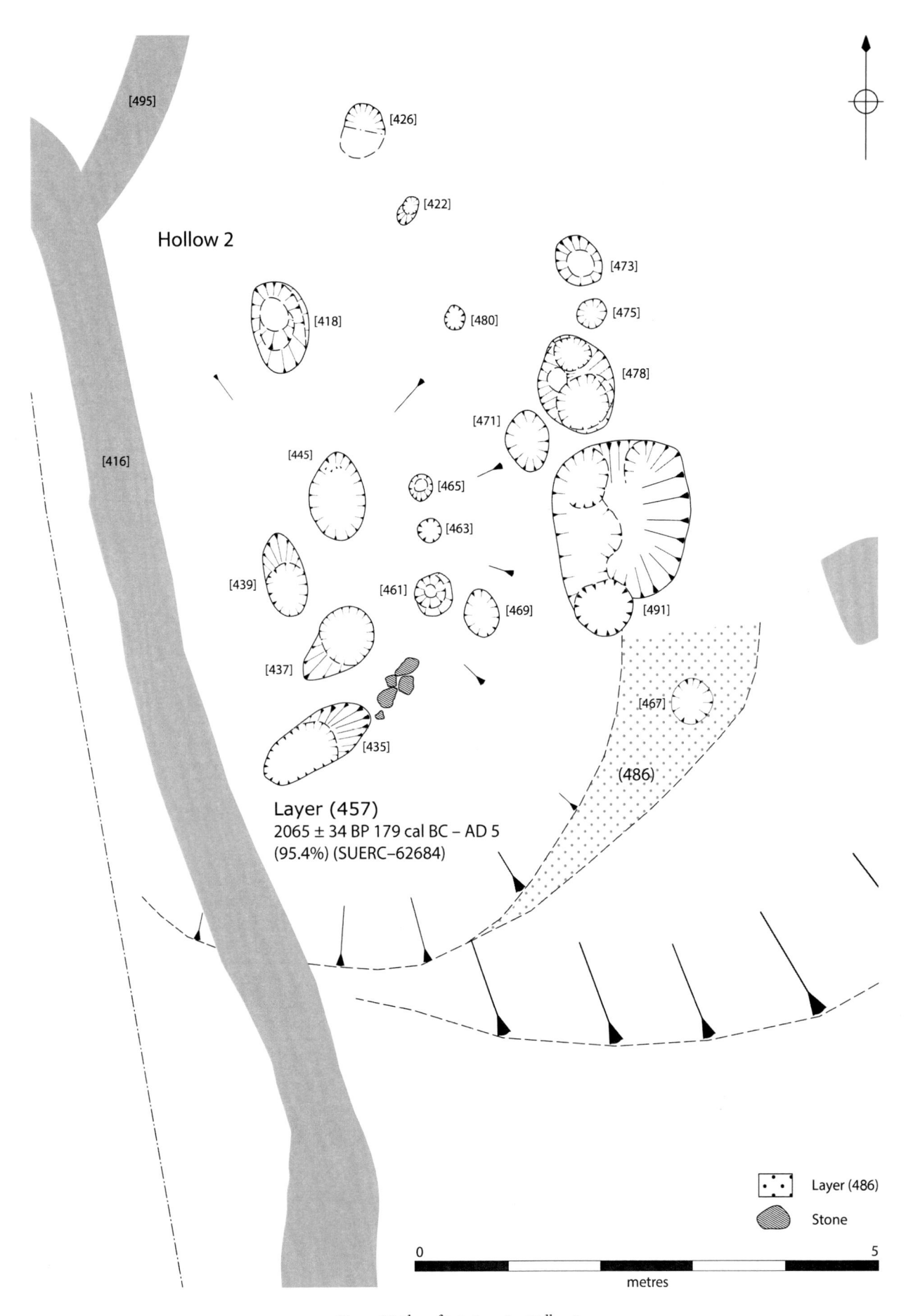

Layer (457)
2065 ± 34 BP 179 cal BC – AD 5
(95.4%) (SUERC–62684)

Figure 2.9 Plan of Late Iron Age Hollow 2.

patchy, thin 60mm to 90mm layer (457) of compact clay and charcoal. It produced a few sherds of Late Iron Age pottery and the deposit may represent a remnant occupation layer inside the hollow. A Late Iron Age radiocarbon determination, 2065 ± 34 BP, 179 cal BC – cal AD 5 (SUERC-62684), was obtained on charcoal from (457). This date is consistent with the date of the pottery recovered from the layer, as well as from other features within the hollow (Chapters 8 and 10).

Within the area defined by the hollow were a number of pits and postholes forming a roughly rectangular arrangement measuring approximately 4m by 4.5m, which are interpreted as representing a building. The features defining this were [418], [437], [439], [445], [469], [471], [473], [475], [478], [480], and two more postholes which were identified in the bottom of pit [491]. Some of these features, such as [473], were clearly postholes; others, for example [471], may have been pits.

Feature [418] was also recorded as a pit, although it seems more likely that it was in fact a posthole that had become distorted by a post that had been removed at an angle. The amorphous shapes of other features, such as [437] and [439], may also have been produced by the removal of posts from their sockets. Two other features seem to have been a combination of posthole and pit. Pit [478] had two postholes, [477] and [476], in the bottom of the cut, and is likely to have post-dated them. Pit [491] appeared to have been cut through two earlier postholes. It was large: 2m long, over 1m wide and 0.47m deep. A posthole was located at both ends of the pit. A single deposit (490) filled both the pit cut and the postholes and this strongly implies that pit [491] post-dated the post-built structure. The fill contained frequent large quartz inclusions and occasional flecks of charcoal, as well as a decorated stone spindle whorl **S4** from one end of the pit and a sherd of pottery from the other. Both artefacts were of Late Iron Age date (Quinnell, Chapters 3 and 4). The homogenous nature of the deposit makes it probable that it had entered the pit after the posts had been removed and the decorated spindle whorl may be regarded as having been deliberately selected for deposition (Chapter 11, below).

Small quantities of Late Iron Age pottery were also recovered from [418], [437], [445], [447], [471], [478] and [480]. The largest quantity was from pit [437], which contained 10 sherds (Quinnell, Chapter 3).

Three small postholes, [461], [463], and [465], formed a north-south alignment within the southern part of this structure. These features can probably be best interpreted as an internal division of space within a small, roughly rectangular post-built structure; they did not contain any artefacts.

Several features were located just outside the probable structure. To the north of the hollow were two pits or postholes, [426] and [428]. Both were shallow and neither produced any artefacts. A small pit or posthole [467] was located beyond the south east corner of the building and a large pit [435] was located just beyond the south west corner of the structure. Pit [435] was oval, measuring 0.8m by 0.45m and 0.4m deep. A lining of vertically set pieces of slate was found along the inside edge of the pit and the clay natural had been scorched red. Immediately to the north east was an area of stones and burnt clay (497) (not illustrated). Taken together, these suggest that the pit may have been used as a hearth. Deposit (424), the fill within the pit, contained 20 sherds of Late Iron Age pottery, the largest quantity of pottery from Hollow 2, together with a trimmed slate (Quinnell, Chapters 3 and 4).

The western side of the hollow was cut by a north–south aligned ditch [416]. This feature was not dated and remains unphased (see below).

Area A2

Area A2 was located at the southern end of Field 2, beyond ditch [120], and away from the concentration of hollows and structures to the south (Fig 2.10).

Within this area were three rectangular pits with rounded corners orientated east-west, and three postholes on a north-south alignment situated at the western end of one of the rectangular pits.

The southernmost pit [110] was 0.9m long by 0.4m wide but only 0.1m deep. North of this pit [118] was 1.5m long by 0.37m wide and 0.24m deep. Both of the pits were steep-sided and had flat bases. Each was filled by a single deposit of yellowish-brown silty clay. Neither feature, however, produced any artefacts with which to date them.

The third rectangular pit [108] was of a similar size, 2m long, 0.48m wide and 0.32m deep. By contrast with pits [110] and [118] it had been capped by large slates placed transversely along its length. One sherd of undiagnostic pottery of Late Iron Age or Roman date (Chapter 3) and a small, dark grey water-rolled pebble were recovered from its fill, (106).

At the west end of pit [108] were the three small postholes [112], [114] and [116]. These formed a short alignment and as they did not cut, but respected the end of pit [108] they may have been contemporary with it. The postholes did not contain any artefacts.

The features in Area A2 are of interest as they are completely different from those found elsewhere along the corridor and are spatially separated from the intense areas of activity to the south. It is possible

The results from the fieldwork

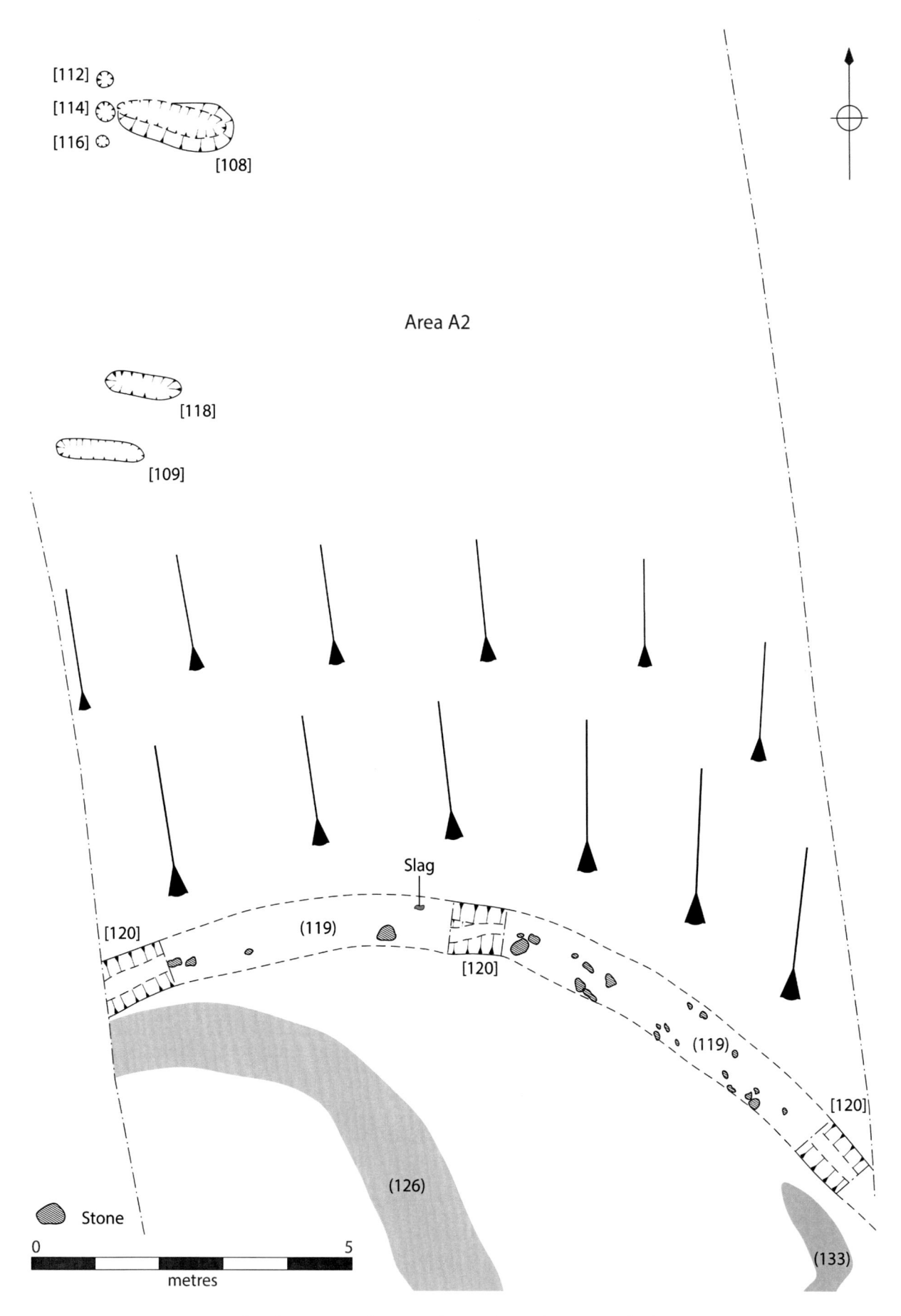

Figure 2.10 Plan of Late Iron Age features and the north end of Field 2, ditch [120] and Area A2.

that these features were inhumation graves and this interpretation will be discussed below (Chapter 10).

Ditch [120]

Ditch [120] was located towards the southern end of Field 2, a few metres to the south of the rectangular pits described above (Fig 2.10). The ditch measured 0.9m wide and was approximately 0.5m deep. It was curvilinear, following the upper edge of a natural break in slope. It ran right across the stripped area but its full extent is unknown. It was filled by (119), from which a sherd of Late Iron Age pottery (Quinnell, Chapter 3) and a piece of iron slag were recovered. A small assemblage of charred cereal grain was also recovered (J Jones, Chapter 6).

Ditch [120] was quite a substantial feature and would have appeared more so because of its location along the break of slope. Although ditch [120] may have been part of a field system, it could instead have been part of a curvilinear enclosure, which can be made out on the geophysical survey (Figs 1.2, 1.4 and 2.17). This possibility is discussed below (Chapter 10).

Discussion

Evidence of the Late Iron Age phase was confined to Fields 1 and 2. Two hollows and a major boundary ditch and a group of rectangular pits have been assigned to this phase.

The two hollows were rather different from one another. Hollow 2 was an poorly defined sunken area measuring 8m by 7m which was not demarcated by any kind of bounding feature (for example a gully or ditch). Numerous pits and postholes were found inside the hollow and there were indications that there was a rectangular central structure. Just outside this building were further pits and postholes. Radiocarbon dating and the artefactual assemblage placed this activity at the end of the Iron Age. Hollow 1 was much larger, up to 14.5m long by 7.5m wide, and was defined by several ring-gullies. It contained a large number of pits and a smaller number of postholes which did not form an identifiable structure. Instead, several of the pits showed signs of burning and there was evidence for recutting. A charred grain assemblage was recovered from Hollow 1 and from ditch [120], which, although small, provides the first evidence for the cultivation and consumption of cereals on the site. Activity within Hollow 1 also seemed to have continued for longer than Hollow 2, with radiocarbon dating and the ceramics suggesting Late Iron Age activity and the fragment from a stone bowl demonstrating continuing occupation into the Roman period. Both hollows provided evidence for abandonment activities and these are discussed in Chapter 11.

The three rectangular pits in Area A2 were isolated from the other features of this period and were located to the north of Late Iron Age ditch [120]. There was limited direct evidence with regard to their function. They were, however, all of a similar shape and laid out on an east-west orientation, and spaced so that they did not intercut one another, implying that they had been marked above ground in some way. All three features were filled with a homogenous single fill. One was covered by a capping of slate slabs and this feature may also have been marked above ground by a short line of timber posts. One plausible interpretation is that these rectangular features were graves, in which the bones have not been preserved: unless cremated, human bone would not survive in the acidic soil conditions on the site, which would explain why they appeared to contain nothing but soil. East-west graves can be Christian or pagan, and broadly comparable Iron Age graves, of similar mixed form, size and orientation, have been found elsewhere in Cornwall. At Forrabury, near Boscastle, for example, cists, simple cut graves, and stone-capped graves of Iron Age date were found together in one cemetery, and at Scarcewater, simple cut graves and a cist of Roman date were found in close proximity to one another away from a settlement area (Jones and Quinnell, 214, 38–50; Jones and Taylor 2010, 55–59) (Chapter 11).

The Roman period: first to fourth centuries AD

Several discrete features of Roman date were investigated along the road corridor. They were located along the length of Field 1 and the southern part of Field 2 and included ditches and gullies in the Enclosure Area, ditches and pits to the north west of the earlier Hollow 1 and Structure A3, Structure A6 and Structure 3. Ditch [230] in Field 3 may also have belonged to this phase although it was not well-dated (Fig 2.11).

Structure A3

Structure A3 was located on the western side of the excavation area in Field 2 and was made up of a partial ring-gully [127] enclosing a linear arrangement of large pits or, more probably, postholes (Fig 2.12). The gully took the form of a shallow curvilinear ditch, 1m wide and 0.25-0.5m deep. It may have enclosed a circular or oval space of around 10m in diameter. Unfortunately, as it mostly lay beyond the western side of the stripped area, its original shape and overall size are unknown. The ditch was filled by (126), a dark greyish brown silty clay containing large pieces of quartz and granitic stone. The amount of stone in the ditch could indicate that it had held a wall which was subsequently robbed out or that the stone had been pushed into the cut from an adjacent bank. Several sherds of Middle Iron Age pottery from vessel **P7** (Quinnell, Chapter 3) were recovered from fill (126); however, a radiocarbon

THE RESULTS FROM THE FIELDWORK

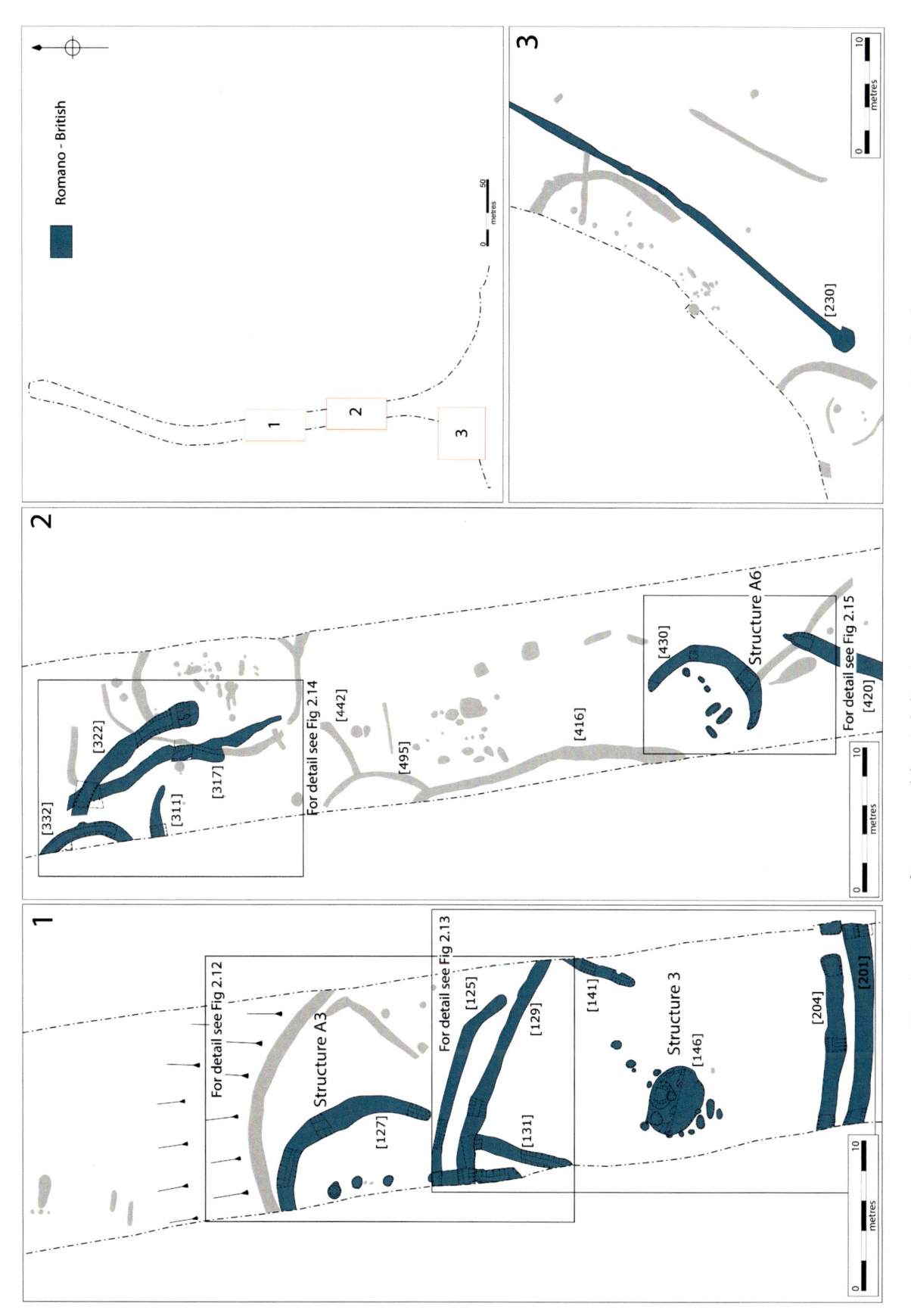

Figure 2.11 Features of Roman period date, including Structure A3, Structure 3, Structure A6 and ditch [230].

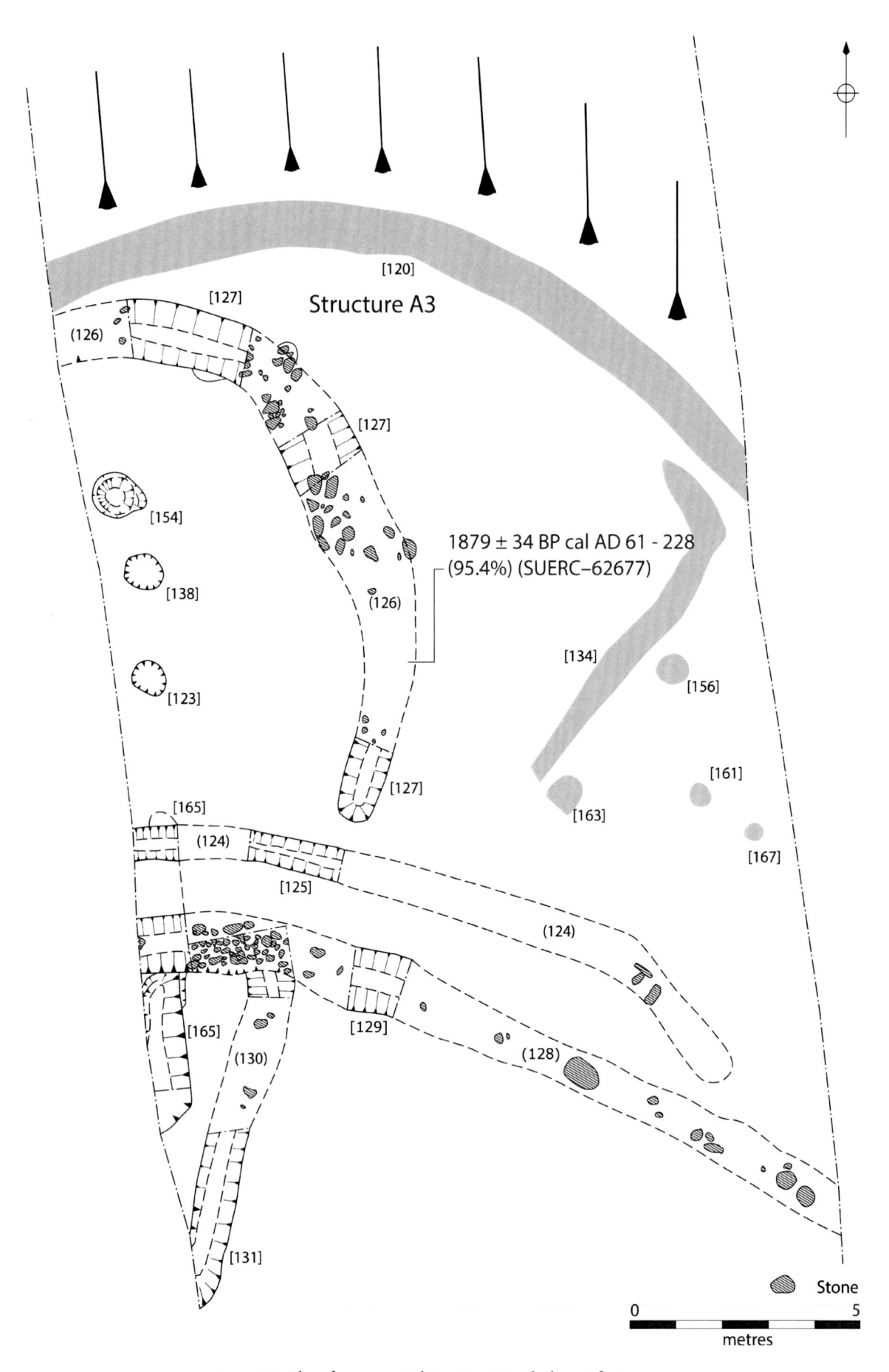

Figure 2.12 Plan of Roman period Structure A3 and adjacent features.

determination from the same deposit, 1879 ± 34 BP, cal AD 61–228 (SUERC-62677), dates the structure to the Roman period and it is possible that the pottery may represent a curated deposit (Chapters 3 and 11). A worked stone **S9**, a sandstone beach cobble with whetstone and hammerstone use, was also recovered from the fill (Quinnell, Chapter 4).

In the space enclosed by ditch [127] was a line of three pits or postholes [123], [138] and [154]. At the southern end of the alignment was cut [123]. This was 0.5m in diameter and 0.5m deep and contained a large quantity of burnt stone. Nine sherds of pottery dating to the early Roman period and a trimmed slate were recovered from its fill (121) (Quinnell, Chapters 3 and 4). Located approximately 2m north of [123], cut [138] was oval in shape and measured 0.73m by 0.8m and was 0.57m deep. Five sherds of pottery dating to the Late Iron Age or early Roman period and a trimmed slate were recovered from its fill (137). What appeared to be packing stones were also present; however, the cut had been disturbed by animal burrowing. Approximately 1m to the north of [138] was cut [154]. This was a shallow feature, irregularly oval in shape, measuring 0.6m in diameter and 0.2m deep. The feature had been disturbed by root activity and there were no finds within it.

Running along the western baulk was gully [165], a shallow feature measuring 0.9m wide by 0.15m deep (Fig 2.12). It was cut by both of the east-west ditches [129] and [125] and appeared to terminate less than 0.5m beyond ditch [125]. It seemed to continue the posthole alignment, and its fill, (164) produced four sherds of Roman period pottery of late first or second century AD date which is consistent with the finds from the other features in this area. It also contained a hammerstone made of porphyritic lava, possibly from a source in the Tintagel area (Quinnell, Chapter 4). However, its relationship with Structure A3 is uncertain and it was too close to ditch [131] to have been contemporary with it.

Ditch [127] produced a few charred macrofossils with grassland weeds and pit [138] produced a small assemblage of hulled wheat and oat grains (J, Jones, Chapter 6), which suggests that some grain processing had been undertaken in the vicinity.

Ditch [131] was located to the south of ditch [127]. It was 1m wide and 0.28m deep and its fill (131) produced a single sherd of Roman period pottery. Ditch [131] was aligned north east – south west. Approximately 13m to the east a second ditch [141] shared the same alignment (below) and although [131] could have been associated with Structure A3, it is possible that they were part of some kind of small enclosed space such as a pen within the larger enclosure formed by ditches [125] and [129] and [201] and [204] (see below).

To the east of Structure A3 was an L-shaped ditch [134]. This feature did not produce any artefacts or other dating evidence. There was also a scattering of pits and postholes – [156], [161], [163] and [167] – in the near vicinity. Unfortunately, with exception of [163], which was associated with Beaker pottery (see above), none of these features produced any artefacts and they cannot therefore be linked with activity in Structure A3. Pit [156], however, did produce a small assemblage of hulled wheat and oat grains similar to that found in feature [138] (J Jones, Chapter 6), and it is possible that it also belonged to the Roman period.

Enclosure Area

The Enclosure Area (Figs 2.13 and 2.17) is defined by parallel east-west aligned ditches [125] and [129] in the north and parallel east-west aligned ditches [204] and [201] in the south, which together with [210] / [212] are likely to form an enclosure. Structure 3 was located inside this enclosure and they are likely to be contemporary with one another. Unfortunately the eastern and western extents of the enclosure lie outside the stripped area and the geophysical evidence is unclear. Ditch [120] may, for example, have formed the northern side of the enclosure at one point in time.

From the northern end of the area the first feature was a single ditch [125], 0.63m wide and 0.63m deep. Four sherds of Roman period pottery, including one from **P12**, a late Cordoned Ware-style vessel, were recovered from the fill (Quinnell, Chapter 3). The date of the pottery would suggest that the ditch was filling during the later first to second century AD.

Less than 2m to the south of [125] was a second ditch [129]. This appeared to run almost parallel to it and was of similar depth, measuring up to 1.1m wide by 0.56m deep. The quantity of stone within its fill (128) was notable and it possibly represents the remnants of a wall or stony bank that had collapsed or been pushed into the ditch. The fill also produced two sherds of pottery of Roman date. There were comparatively few stratigraphical relationships; however, ditch [129] cut the northern end of ditch / gully [131] and both [125] and [129] cut gully [165]. The close spacing of ditches [125] and [129] is similar to [201] and [204], and [210] / [212] to the south (see below) and it is possible that they were not contemporary with one another but represent a redefinition of an enclosure.

Ditch [141] was located to the south of [129] close to the eastern edge of the stripped area. It measured 0.7m wide and 0.11m deep, running from the baulk into the road corridor for approximately 7m before terminating in the middle of the stripped corridor. Six sherds of Roman period pottery were recovered from its fill (140), together with a few charred cereal

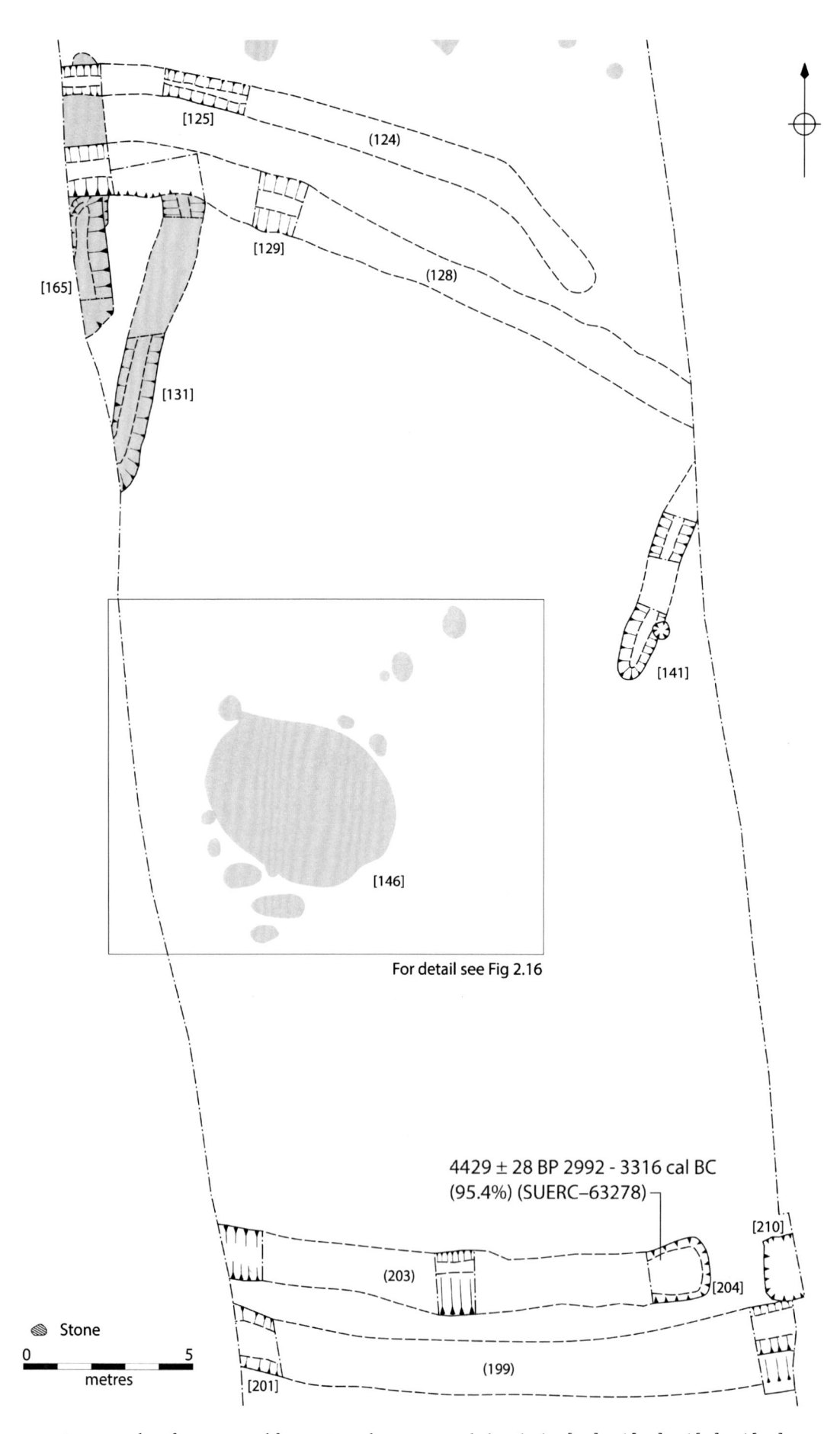

Later prehistoric and Roman sites along the route of the Newquay Strategic Road Corridor

Figure 2.13 Plan of Roman period features in Enclosure Area, including ditches [125] and [129] and [20] and [204].

grains (Quinnell, Chapter 3; J Jones, Chapter 6). A single posthole [169] was cut partially into the eastern side of the gully. It is possible that ditches [131] (above) and [141] were related to one another and were part of a small enclosure or pen within the Enclosure Area.

Ditch [204] was the more northerly of the east-west aligned ditches which formed the southern side of the identified enclosure. It was 1.2m wide and 0.5m deep and terminated approximately 1.2m from the eastern baulk of the excavated area. The upper fill of the ditch, (203) produced a quantity of iron ore and eight sherds of Roman period pottery dating to the second century AD (Quinnell, Chapter 3). Below this, fill (206) produced another sherd of the same date. Fills (203) and (206) both contained assemblages of charred grains and arable weeds (J Jones, Chapter 6). The primary fill (208) contained a significant quantity of hazelnut shell fragments, one of which produced a radiocarbon date of 4420 ± 28 BP, 3316–2992 cal BC (SUERC-62678). This is clearly too early for the ditch and the nutshells must therefore have been redeposited.

Approximately 1.3m to the east of [204] was another ditch terminal or possibly a pit, [210], running under the baulk. When excavated this feature appeared to be similar in shape to [204]. The terminal had been recut by ditch or pit [212], which was filled with a very stony upper layer (213) and (211), a deposit which was rich in iron ore. It is possible that the ore was a deliberate deposit and this is discussed below (Chapter 11). Because it extended beyond the baulk, the feature could not be fully excavated and it is uncertain whether it was a ditch or a pit. However, it is probable that the two features, [204] and [210], were related to one another and of interest that both contained iron ore. It is also probable that the 1.3m wide gap between them represents an entrance into an enclosure during one phase of its use (see discussion below).

Ditch [201] was located approximately 0.5m to the south of ditch [204]. It was steep-sided and measured 1.9m wide and 0.74m deep. The upper fill (199) contained a notched slate and six sherds of pottery of late first or second century AD date. Ditch [201] appeared to contain finds of broadly the same period as ditch [204]. However, it is possible that [204] and [210] / [212] were part of the same boundary, and ditch [201] was of a slightly later date, as there would have been no room for an associated bank and it would have blocked the entranceway into an enclosure (Chapters 10 and 11).

The western and eastern ends of all the ditches comprising the enclosure lie outside the stripped area and it is not entirely certain how they relate to other geophysical anomalies (Figs 1.2, 1.4 and 2.17). Ditches [204] and [210] / [212] and [201], for example, do not appear to be much longer than the stripped area, and there are wide gaps between and the identified geophysical survey anomalies to the east and west of the corridor. This might suggest that there are entrances or, perhaps more probably, the apparent 'gaps' in the ditches are not real but were created by the spaces between the survey areas.

Features north and west of Hollow 1

To the south of ditch [201] and to the north west of Hollow 1 was a complex of linear features. These were hard to disentangle from one another and dating evidence was extremely limited; that available, however, was consistently of the Roman period (Fig 2.14).

On the western side of the road corridor was curvilinear ring-gully [332]. Only part of the arc formed by the feature fell inside the stripped area but it may have enclosed an area approximately 7m in diameter. The excavated portion of the ditch was up to 0.9m wide and 0.25m deep and contained a single fill, (331). The fill produced two residual flints and two sherds of pottery, likely to date to the late first to early second century cal AD. It may have formed a ring-gully around a structure but not enough of the area it enclosed was within the road corridor to be certain of this. Alternatively, ring-gully [332] may have encircled a working area like Hollow 1.

Apart from a short length of shallow ditch [342] located in the northern part of the area enclosed by ring-gully [332], no other features were found inside the space within the ring-ditch. Ditch [342] measured 0.35m wide and 0.09m deep and was filled by (341), which produced a residual flint core (Lawson-Jones, Chapter 5). It appeared to be an earlier feature, as it was cut by [332].

Ditch [322], on the east side of ring-gully [332], measured 1.1m wide and 0.6m deep, and was oriented approximately north west – south east. It was exposed over a length of approximately 11m. At the south east end it appeared to terminate within the Late Iron Age feature Hollow 1 (see above). A small assemblage of cereals was obtained from the fill of [322] (J Jones, Chapter 6). The north west end of ditch [322] was not uncovered, although it probably terminated before ring-gully [332]. The upper fill of [322], (361), produced five sherds of pottery likely to date to the late first to early second century cal AD, and fills (361) and (369) both produced quantities of charred cereal grains (J Jones, Chapter 6). Ditch [322] appears to have cut a shallower narrow gully [360] and then cut curvilinear ring-gully [336], both of which were associated with Hollow 1.

To the south of ring-gully [332] was ditch [311]. This was a small feature measuring 0.5m wide and 0.45m deep which continued under the western baulk. It contained two fills, (310) and (312), which did not produce any finds. Ditch [317] to the east was aligned north east

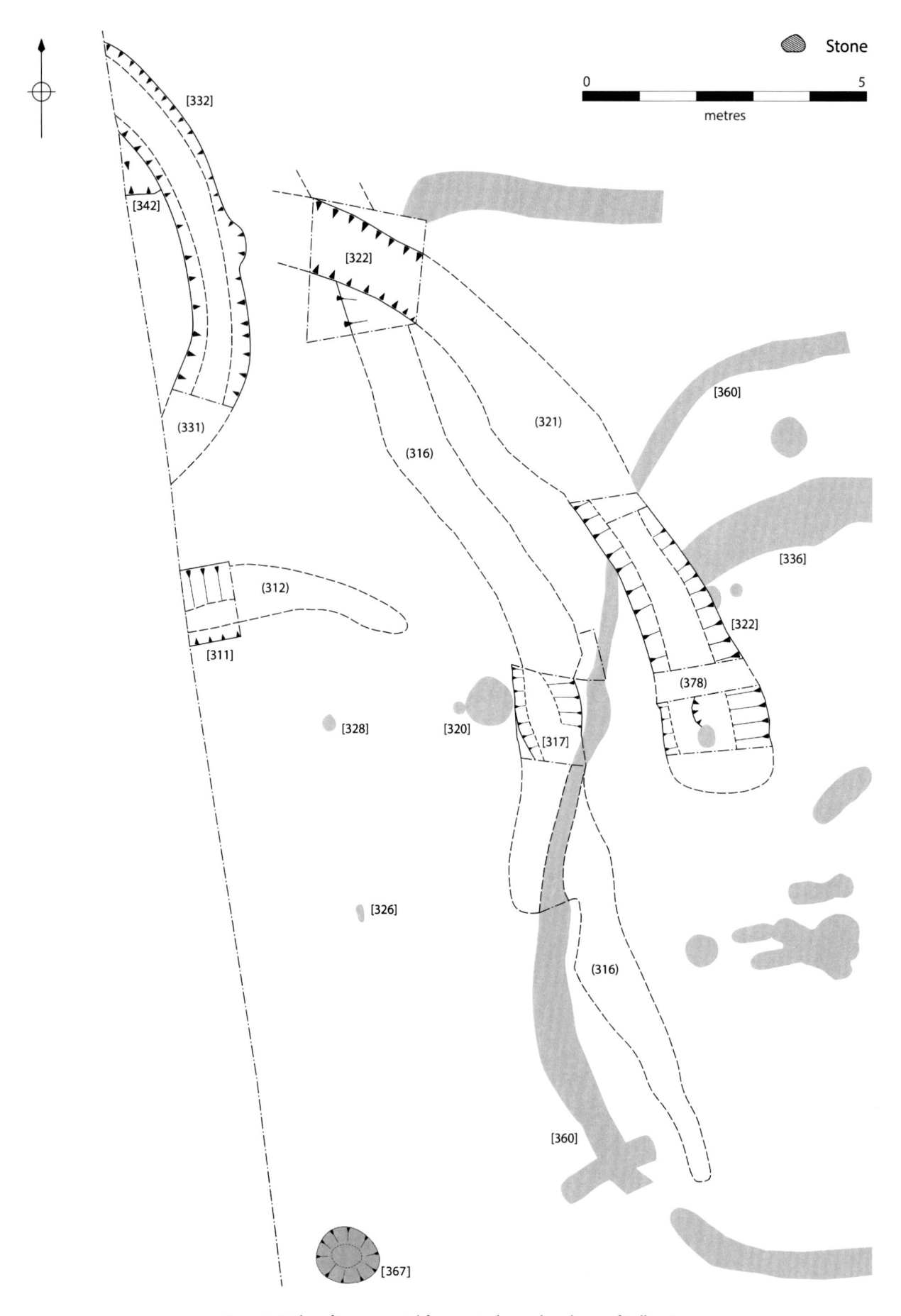

Figure 2.14 Plan of Roman period features to the north and west of Hollow 1.

– south west. It was 0.9m wide and 0.13m deep and appeared to have been cut in the north by ditch [322]. It in turn cut through gully [360] and petered out in the south west corner of Hollow 1.

On the west side of ditch [317] was a circular pit [320], measuring 0.65m in diameter and 0.28m deep. It was filled by (321) which produced 10 sherds of pottery probably dating to the late first to early second century cal AD, and a beach cobble, **S10** showing whetstone and hammerstone use (Quinnell, Chapters 3 and 4).

To the west of pit [320] was posthole [328]. It was shallow, measuring 0.22-0.24m in diameter and 0.15m deep. It was filled by (327), which did not produce any finds. To the south was a small scoop [326], which may not have been a cut feature and to the south of that an oval pit [367]. The cut was over 1.4m long by 0.86m wide and 0.45m deep. It did not contain any artefacts but its basal fill (366) contained a large amount of burnt slate and stone, which appears to have been backfilled into the cut in a single event. Both (366) and upper fill (371) contained a few hulled wheat grains and weeds (J Jones, Chapter 6).

Structure A6

Structure A6 was located at the southern end of Field 1, just to the north of where the stripped corridor widened to accommodate a roundabout. It was found to comprise a semi-circular ring-gully, open to the west, which enclosed a group of six pits and a layer possibly representing an old land surface or occupation deposit (Fig 2.15).

The ring-gully [430] was 0.6m wide by 11m long and reached a maximum depth of 0.4m. It was filled by layer (429), which produced a sherd of amphora likely to date to late in the first century cal AD (Quinnell, Chapter 3).

Three of the pits within the interior of ring-gully [430] were elongated, measuring up to 1.6m long by 0.6m wide; they were steep-sided and up to 0.4m deep. Two of them, [450] and [456], were orientated north west to south east; the third of the elongated pits, [453], was orientated north east to south west. All three pits showed signs of burning and extreme heat. Deposit (454), a fill of pit [456], produced three sherds of pottery of late first to early second century cal AD date (Quinnell, Chapter 3) and (499), the fill of pit [450], produced a small assemblage of charred cereal grains (J Jones, Chapter 6). The radiocarbon determination from (455), 1842 ± 34 BP, cal AD 80–245 (SUERC-62678), the lowest fill within pit [456], spans the first to third centuries AD and is consistent with the date suggested by the pottery.

The remaining three pits [483], [485], and [489], were much smaller, measuring approximately 0.5m by 0.4m and 0.3m deep. None produced any artefacts.

Of note was a layer (487), which extended across the eastern side of the area enclosed by the ring-gully [430]. It was a dark loamy deposit which survived to a depth of 0.2m. A few sherds of pottery of probable second century cal AD date were recovered from it. The layer may have been an old land surface or an occupation layer within Structure A6.

Four further sherds of pottery of probable second century cal AD date or a little earlier were recovered from deposit (492) (not illustrated) to the south east of ring-gully [430]. This deposit was only found in an investigative sondage, and its context and extent is unknown.

Ditch [420] was aligned north east to south west and according to the geophysical, it crossed into Field 3 where it was outside the stripped area (Fig 1.4). It was well-defined, measuring 1.2m wide by 0.4m deep. A fragment from a Trethurgy type stone bowl or mortar, **S7** (Quinnell, Chapter 4) was recovered from fill (423) in the north west terminal of the ditch. The stone bowl is likely to date to the second century AD. Ditch [420] may have been a boundary associated with a Roman period field system. Interestingly, ditch [230], which lay to the south in Field 3, was on a similar alignment and it is possible that both ditches were part of the same field system (Chapter 10).

Just to the south east of ring-gully [430] were a small number of pits and diches which may have been contemporary with it. Two shallow pits [432] and [434], measuring less than 0.1m deep and around 0.4m in diameter were both devoid of finds and cannot be dated. Likewise, a short length of roughly north-south aligned ditch [422], which measured approximately 4m long by 1.2m wide and 0.4m deep was devoid of finds. It did appear to terminate on the northern site of ditch [420], and it is possible that it was associated with this ditch.

Structure 3

Structure 3 was located towards the southern end of Field 2 (Fig 2.16). It was defined by cut [146], an oval-shaped hollow, measuring approximately 5m by 4m and up to 0.32m deep, which had been dug into the shillet natural (105). Several pieces of worked stone and pottery were recovered from the upper loamy deposit (145) which infilled the hollow, including **S6**, a fragment from a Roman period Trethurgy-type stone bowl, which is likely to date to the later second century to early fourth century AD (Quinnell, Chapter 4), and fragments from rotary querns, **S2** and **S3**. A radiocarbon determination 1713 ± 34 BP, cal AD 245–399 (SUERC-62688) was obtained on charcoal from this layer. The lower infill layer within the hollow, (190), especially on the northern side, was made up

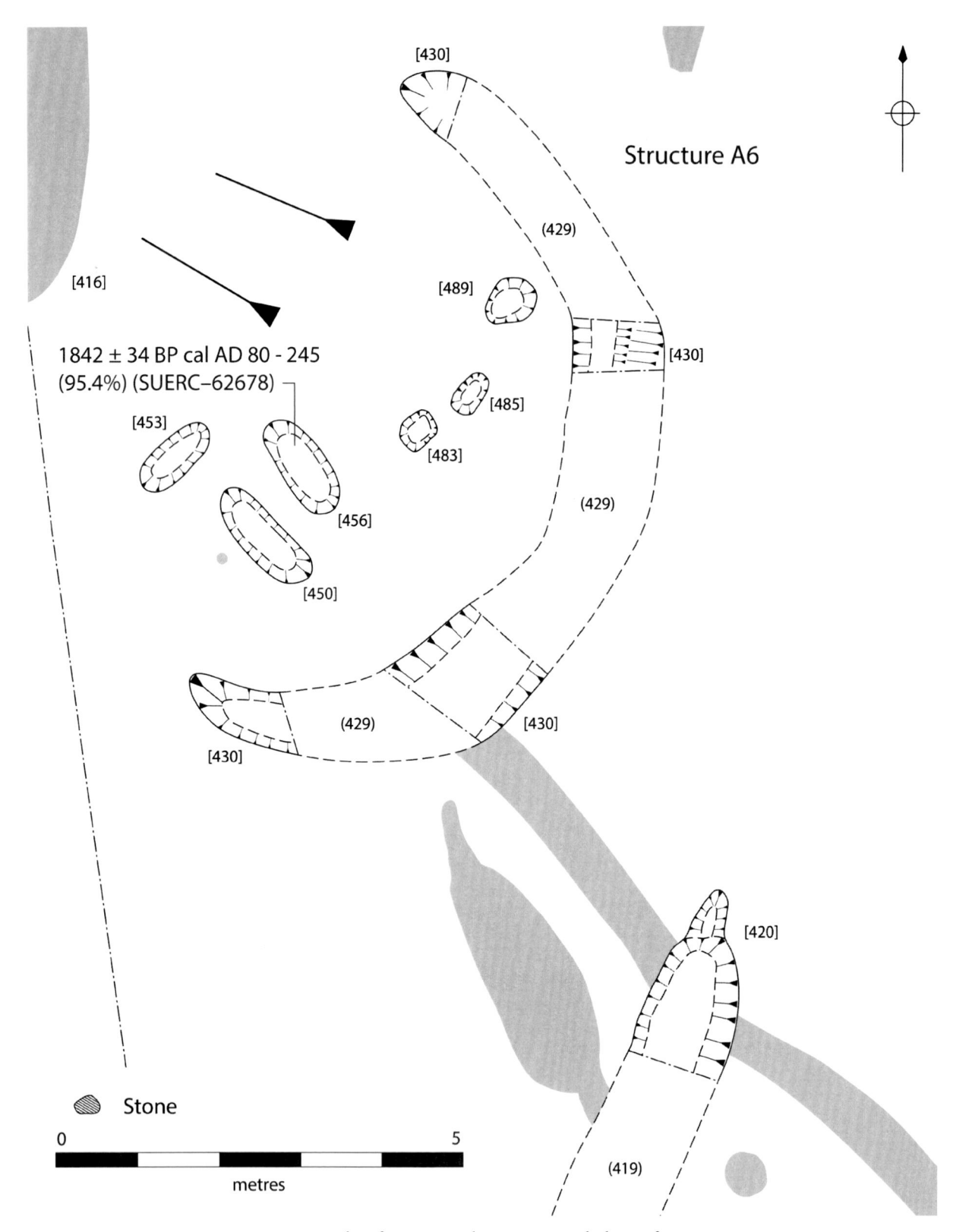

Figure 2.15 Plan of Roman period Structure A6 and adjacent features.

of stones of various sizes, mostly quartz and larger granite blocks; these are not local and must have been introduced into the site, perhaps from Cligga Head on the north coast or from Hensbarrow or Carnmenellis to the south. Both deposits are likely to have been associated with a deliberate infilling of the hollow, and this will be discussed below (Chapter 11). The floor of the structure was pitted and uneven and there was no trace of an occupation deposit. The southern side of the hollow was also uneven and contained a ridge of natural shillet. Only one definite feature was revealed beneath the infilling deposits, a single clearly defined pit [198].

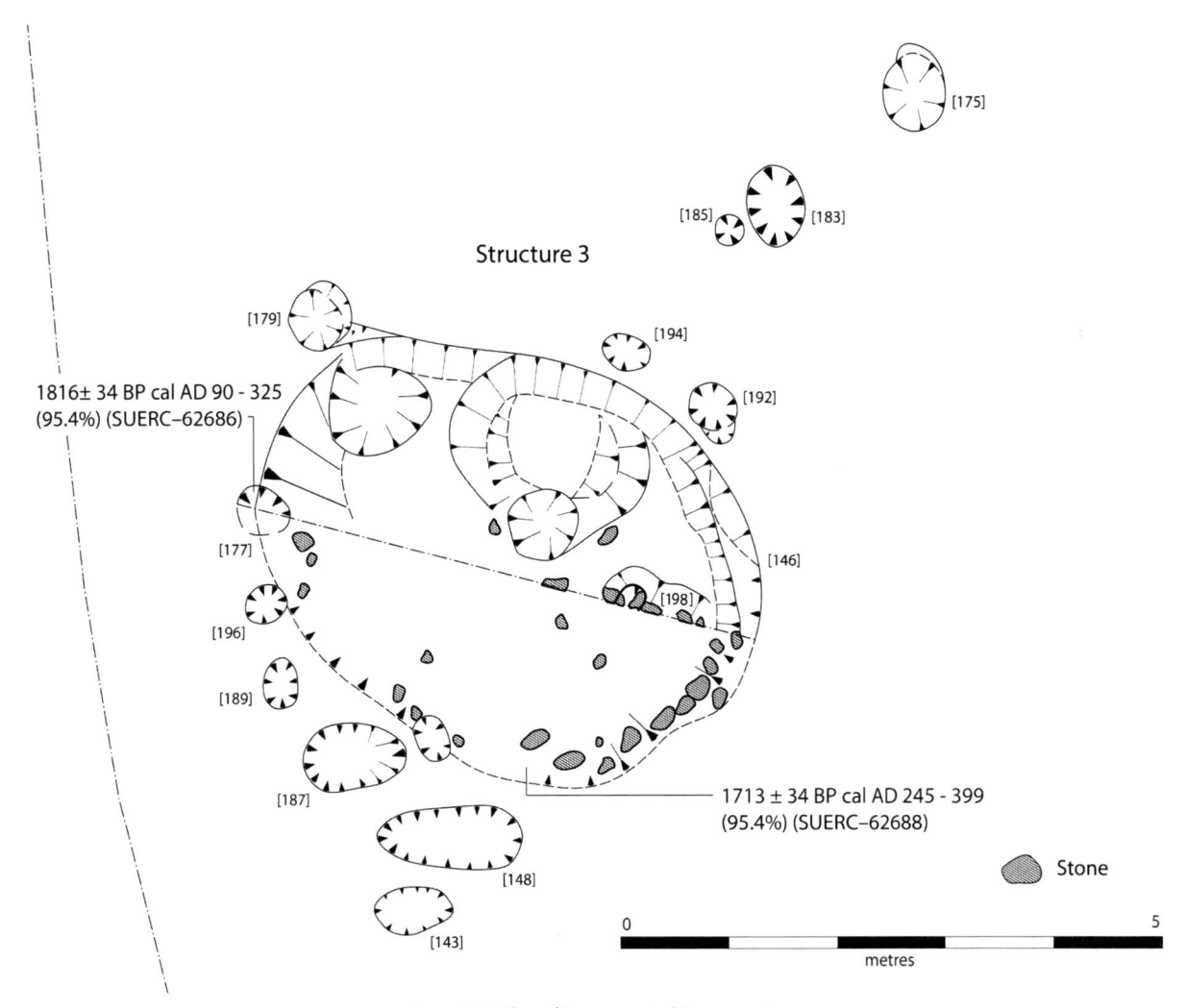

Figure 2.16 Plan of Roman period Structure 3.

The cut measured 0.45m long by 0.3m wide and was 0.23m deep; the fill (197) contained two sherds of later Roman period pottery and two worked slate 'pot lids', **S14** and **S15** (Quinnell, Chapter 4). It also contained a charred macrofossil assemblage which included cereals (J Jones, Chapter 6).

Several of the features on the northern edge of the hollow were initially interpreted as postholes or pits, but some may not have been of an archaeological nature and could have resulted from animal burrowing. The more certain ones included [179], [192] and [194], which all measured approximately 0.4m in diameter by 0.1m deep and were located close to the edge of the hollow. None produced any finds but they may have been part of a structural post-ring.

On the south-western side of the structure the post-ring may have been continued by postholes [177] and [196] and possibly by [189]. None of these postholes produced any finds, although charred cereal remains from fill (176) within posthole [177] and charcoal from this feature produced a date of, 1816 ± 34 BP, cal AD 90–325 (SUERC-62686). The date is earlier than that from the infill above and, together with the artefacts, suggests that the structure may have been in use from the second to fourth century cal AD. The post-ring did not appear to extend beyond [196]. However, the southern edge of the structure was associated with a large amount of stone which could have been structural and derived from a wall. It is also possible that there was an opening on the eastern side of the building, which would account for the lack of postholes in this area.

Just beyond the southern side of the structure there were three sub-rectangular pits [143], [148] and [187]. These were up to 1.2m long, 0.6m wide and 0.3m deep. They were devoid of artefacts but may have been associated with some form of industrial activity involving heat. The fill of pit [187] was full of charcoal and there were signs of scorching around the pit edge. Although there were no finds a small assemblage of charred cereal grains was recovered. The fills of pits [143] and [148] were not especially rich in charcoal; however, the sides of both pits showed signs of heat reddening, implying that *in situ* burning had taken place but that the contents had been emptied out and deposited elsewhere.

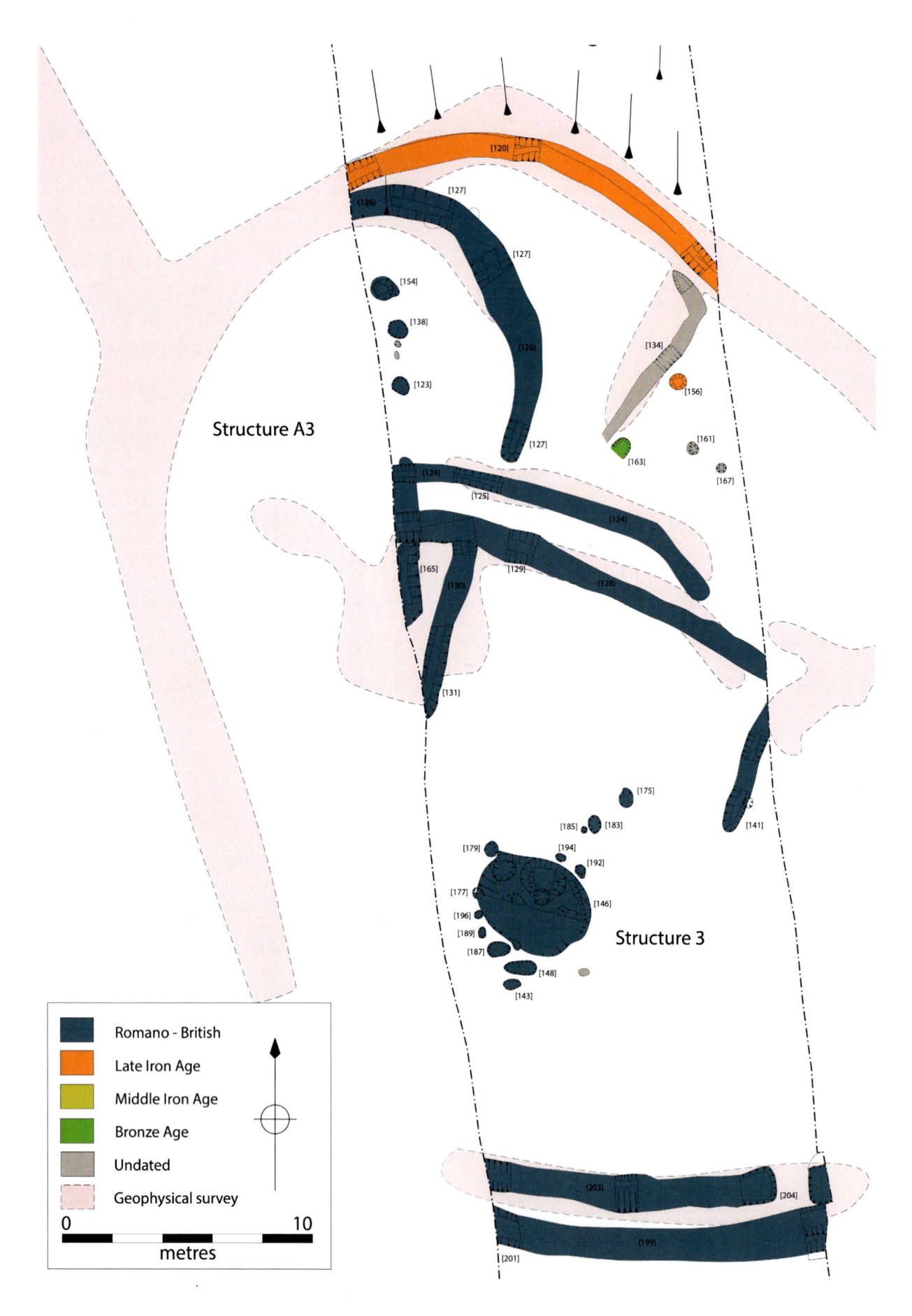

Figure 2.17 Plan showing the location of the Romano-British enclosure, associated features and geophysical features outside the stripped area.

To the north east of the hollow was a cluster of three pits or postholes, [175], [183] and [185]. Cuts [175] and [185] were both circular and approximately 0.3m deep, with [175] being the larger with a diameter of 0.5m. Pit [183] was of a similar diameter to [175], but much shallower, only 0.14m deep. There were few finds from these features but pit [175] produced a cobble with signs of wear and several sherds of Roman period pottery (Quinnell, Chapter 3) and an assemblage of charred cereal grains (J Jones, Chapter 6).

Ditch [230]

Ditch [230] was probably associated with a removed boundary. It was aligned north east – south west and ran diagonally across most of Field 3 (Fig 2.11). The south west end of the ditch was lost in an area of disturbance near a modern water main. The ditch was 0.5m wide and 0.32m deep. It appears to have been cut by a later ditch [223] (below). No artefacts were recovered from it but as noted above it was on a similar alignment to ditch [420] and may be part of a field system of Roman date.

Discussion

Features belonging to the Roman period were found in Fields 1 and 2. Identified activity included three structures, two of which are, on balance, likely to have been associated with industrial processes, amorphous groups of pits and gullies which are not easily interpretable, boundaries associated with ditched field systems, and a probable enclosure.

The structures were different in form from one another and none appear to have been domestic dwellings. The earliest, Structure A3, was roughly oval in shape and could have enclosed a space around 10m in diameter. Too little is known about the overall form of Structure A3, however, to make any comments regarding its original shape or size, beyond saying that a shallow ditch [127] may have encircled a line of three postholes forming one side of a post-built structure, which was possibly extended to the south by a gully on the same alignment. A break in the gully circuit might suggest that there was an entrance on the south east side.

It is possible that the ring-gully around Structure A3 could have held a wall, and this hypothesis is perhaps supported by a large number of stones which may represent survival from the robbing of a wall or were derived from an associated bank. Alternatively, as has been suggested for the earlier Middle Iron Age Structure A1, it is also possible that the ditch encircled a structure and the stones were dumped into the ditch as part of a process of closure. The Structure A3 ring-gully did, however, hold a quantity of Middle Iron Age pottery, which may suggest that the gully had been marked with a 'special', possibly curated, deposit (Chapter 11).

Structure A6 was defined by semi-circular ring-gully [430]. The function of this gully is uncertain, although in this case it is likely that it was structural and that the majority of features in the area around Structure A6 were associated with a building. The gully may, for example, have been intended to hold a screen or walling for a relatively flimsy shed or shelter, open to the west. Several pits inside the area enclosed by the gully bore signs of burning and could have been used for industrial purposes; there was also an occupation deposit within the area defined by the enclosing ring-gully.

Structure 3 was roughly oval in shape and would have enclosed a space of around 4m by 5m. It is uncertain where the entrance into the structure was, although it might have been located on the eastern side of the hollow. Oval working hollows and buildings of Roman period date have been found across Cornwall (Quinnell 2004, 205–206; Lawson-Jones and Kirkham 2009–10; Gossip and Jones 2007). The working hollows at Little Quoit Farm were of a similar size to Structure 3 but these were associated with smithing (Lawson-Jones and Kirkham 2009–10) and the Roman period structure 338 at Tremough was used for both domestic occupation and small-scale metalworking (Gossip and Jones 2007, 23–24) (Chapter 10). The interpretation of Structure 3 is more problematic as it only contained one internal posthole. However, the scorching found in pits just outside the structure might suggest that burning or heating were associated with the use of the building; charred cereal grains from several pits may suggest that food was prepared or processed. Comparanda for and the activities associated with Structure 3 are considered below. Structure 3 does seem to have been deliberately infilled and this is discussed below in Chapter 11.

Too little is known about the majority of the gullies and pits to the north and west of Hollow 1 to say anything meaningful about their extent, overall form or function. Interestingly, the number of features associated with cereal grains shows a marked increase during this period, which perhaps suggests that arable agriculture was gaining in importance. Several substantial ditches were revealed which are likely to form ditched field systems belonging to the Roman period.

The two parallel boundaries [125] and [129] may have formed a substantial barrier, although given their close proximity it is more probable that they may have been sequential in that they represent a renewal or redefinition of an enclosure. To the south a second pair of boundaries, [201] and [204], may have defined another major land division. It is, however, more likely that ditches [125] and [129] and [201] and [204], and [210] / [212] were component parts of an oval enclosure, within which Structure 3 was situated (Chapter 10). As with the northern side of the enclosure it is likely that [201] was not contemporary with [204], and [210] / [212] and the enclosure had two phases.

It is not possible, however, to say which of the ditch circuits are the earliest. Running at roughly right angles to ditches [125] and [129], were the slighter ditches [131] and [141] which may have been internal divisions within the enclosed space or were earlier features which were partly removed by the enclosure.

Ditch [420], near to Structure A6, was on different alignment, but may also represent a boundary of the Roman period. If this were the case, it could be part of a rectilinear field pattern which is indicated by the geophysical survey in the wider area surrounding the road corridor (Chapter 10, below). Ditch [230] was on the same alignment as ditch [420] and it is very possible that they form elements within a rectilinear Roman field system, which had been laid out on a north east to south west axis.

The radiocarbon and artefactual dating allows some temporal separation of features within the Roman period. The oval Structure A3, and the major diches appear to date to the first to second centuries cal AD, and the pits and gullies to the north west of Hollow 1 are also likely to date to the end of this period. Ditch [420] may be a little later and date to the second century, and the same period may also be appropriate for the use of Structure A6. The latest feature in use appears to be Structure 3, which was probably in use between the second and fourth centuries AD.

Undated features

Unsurprisingly, a number of archaeological features which were devoid of finds were partially exposed and / or isolated and were not easily associated with more closely dated features. Undated features include probable unexcavated gullies and possible pits in Field 1, and pits and linear ditches in Field 3. The unexplored features (Smith 2015) will not be considered further and discussion here is limited to those features which were excavated.

Field 1: Ditch [416]

Ditch [416] was visible for approximately 20m, where it ran roughly parallel with the western edge of the stripped area. Neither of the slots excavated through the ditch produced any artefacts, and relative stratigraphic dating is limited to the relationship with Hollow 2, which it cut. Ditch [416] is therefore later than the Late Iron Age phase. It does not appear to fit with the medieval field pattern and it is therefore possible that it is of Roman date.

Field 2: Pit [104]

Pit [104] was an isolated feature situated in Field 2 to the north of the possible 'cemetery area' A2. It was oval in plan, measuring 0.32m by 0.78m and was up to 0.22m deep. It was filled by (103), a dark brown clay loam. There were no finds but the fill was charcoal-rich (Challinor, Chapter 7). It may be of later prehistoric, Roman, or later date, but this was not determined.

Field 3: Ditch [223]

Ditch [223] was a short linear feature, 0.65m wide, 0.48m deep and approximately 6m long. It cut two features, including ring-gully [220] which formed the western side of Middle Iron Age Structure A1. The eastern end of [223] cut into ditch [230] or possibly merged into it. If the latter were the case, it is possible that ditch [223] represented a subdivision within the later Roman period field system. However, this relationship was unclear and the interpretation is therefore uncertain. Its fill (221) contained sherds of Middle Iron Age pottery (Quinnell, Chapter 3) and a burnt flint pebble, but given that it cut or merged into [230], which was of Roman date, it seems probable that these were residual and had been redeposited into the ditch, possibly as a result of it cutting through Structure A1.

Field 3: Features to the east of Structure 1

To the east of Structure 1 were a ditch and three pits, which in the absence of dating evidence cannot be securely placed into the phasing for the site.

Ditch [248] was located approximately 7m to the south east of [230]. It measured 0.6m wide and 0.38m deep and ran north east – south west almost parallel to [230] for approximately 15m. It was clearly defined by its dark fill (246) which contained frequent large stones along its length. The ditch was of a very similar size to [223] and could also have been part of the Roman period field system. However, there was no secure dating evidence.

Three pits were located in the south east part of Field 3. Pit [270] was circular, measuring 0.53m in diameter and 0.34m deep. It contained large quartz blocks, and some stones appeared to have been packed around the sides. The second pit [272] was also circular, 0.95m in diameter and 0.28m deep. Its fill (271) contained a single, possibly nodular waste flake, which is likely to be of Late Neolithic to Early Bronze Age (Lawson-Jones, Chapter 5). It is, however, uncertain if this piece is residual.

A third pit, [260], was also circular, 0.8m in diameter and 0.25m deep. It was marked by burning on the surface and the fill (259) contained heat-reddened granite stones, which suggested that it had been backfilled with burnt material.

**SECTION 3
THE ANALYSES**

Chapter 3

The ceramics

Henrietta Quinnell

Beaker

Contexts (162) and (172), fills of pit [163], contained two sherds weighing 3 grams and five sherds weighing 28 grams respectively, much abraded through bioturbation. These include sherds which have surviving traces of probable comb-stamped horizontal lines and a row of fingernail impressions. Fill (397) of posthole [398] contained one sherd weighing 5 grams which is of the same fabric. The total assemblage comprises eight sherds weighing 36 grams.

Petrology

The fabric is generally oxidized 5YR 5/6 yellowish red and contains sparse inclusions of slate. The fabric is described from examination through a binocular microscope. *Quartz* – white, brownish stained and transparent colourless, angular to sub angular grains, 0.1-2mm; *rock fragments* – slate, light grey finely micaceous sub-rounded fragments, 1.5-2mm, *granite* – fine-grained cream to light buff fragments, one containing a euhedral biotite flake, 0.3mm, sub-angular fragments, 0.5-2mm; *feldspar* – soft white altered grains, 0.1-2.2mm; *mica* – biotite as sparse dark brown cleavage flakes, 0.05-0.8mm; *matrix* – finely sandy and micaceous clay with grains of the main tempering minerals. *Comment.* A granite-derived fabric with the mineral content being an original component of the clay which may have formed to some degree by weathering of fine-grained granite. The nearest source for this clay is the St Austell granite, some 10 kilometres distant. Fairly local sourcing is a general characteristic of Beaker pottery in Cornwall, as elsewhere in Britain (Parker Pearson 1990).

Comment on the Beaker ceramics

It is probable but not certain that the sherds come from one or more vessels in the LN (long-necked) tradition. Fill (162) produced a date of 3635 ± 29 BP (SUERC-64607) on charred hazelnut shell: this calibrates to 2131–2086 (11.7%) and 2051–1912 (83.7%) BC. While this date is the latest associated with Beaker material from Cornwall, nationally it falls well within the span of radiocarbon determinations for LN Beakers (Needham 2005, table 5 and p1 966). Beaker sherds deposited in pits, presumably deriving from domestic activities, are being recognized increasingly on sites in Cornwall. There are now at least 10 such sites known, the latest to be published being near Boscastle, the report on which provides references for the other sites (Quinnell 2014a, 54) except for St Stephen-in-Brannel (Quinnell 2014c). The closest site with Beaker pottery geographically is Trethellan, Newquay, where a few Beaker sherds either precede or are redeposited in contexts from the later Middle Bronze Age settlement (Nowakowski 1991, 12). There is also a small amount of Beaker material from Tregunnel, adjacent to Trethellan, awaiting full analysis (Quinnell 2014b).

Middle Bronze Age

The assemblage consists of 104 sherds weighing 2591 grams; of this, 16 sherds (209 grams) came from old land surface (218) and tended to be abraded. The remainder came from a series of pits (Table 3.1) in the area of Structure 1 and were generally less abraded.

Fabrics

All are gabbroic, varying a little in composition but none with material necessarily added to the clay. All these are therefore gabbroic, rather than gabbroic admixture, and are therefore very unusual in a Middle Bronze Age assemblage. The Middle Bronze Age fabrics at Trethellan Farm, Newquay, include both gabbroic admixture, with greenstone (basaltic or dolerite) additions, and gabbroic fabrics. The proportions of each fabric in the assemblage was not quantified because of difficulties in distinguishing differences (Woodward and Cane 1991, 104).

GAB 1 Identified by microscopic study as a *typical coarse gabbroic fabric*. Full description of the fabric is in the archive.

GAB 2 Petrology: *Feldspar* – soft white altered angular to sub-angular grains, 0.05-5mm, mainly less than 1.5 mm; *amphibole* – a scatter of greenish grey and brown stained fibrous grains and aggregates, 1.1-2.2mm; *quartz* – sparse translucent colourless angular grains, 0.2-0.8mm and two opaque rounded grains, 0.1 and 2mm; *magnetite* – sparse glossy black angular magnetic grains, 0.3-0.4mm; *ferruginous* pellets – common soft brown and black rounded and sub-angular limonitic and manganiferous pellets, 1-4 mm; *matrix* – finely sandy clay with grains of the main tempering minerals less than 0.05mm. *Comment.* A gabbroic fabric with the high content of ferruginous and manganiferous pellets probably indicating a waterlogged clay source.

GAB 3 Petrology: *Feldspar* – off-white soft altered angular grains, 0.05-2mm, some harder, less altered grains show cleavage, 0.4 to 1.5mm; *quartz* – colourless transparent to translucent angular to sub-angular grains 0.1-6mm; *vein quartz* – one elongated rounded pebble, 13mm; *magnetite* – a scatter of black glossy sub-angular to sub-rounded magnetic grains, 0.1-0.6mm; *amphibole* – sparse light grey fibrous sub-angular grains, 0.5-2.1mm; *rock fragments* –fine-grained feldspar/?pyroxene, six weathered sub-angular fragments, probably doleritic, 1-2.3mm; *matrix* – fine sandy clay with some fine mica and grains of the main tempering minerals less than 0.05mm. *Comment.* A gabbroic fabric with a high quartz content. The rock fragments are likely to be associated with the clay rather than an addition.

The fabrics are well made and finished, with common components <1mm, variously fired oxidized to reduced, frequently showing these variations within one sherd.

Illustrated vessels

P1 (Fig 3.1) (299) fill of pit [300]. Flat-topped rim with external expansion, from large vessel, internal rim diameter 210mm, zone with comb stamped in herringbone design bordered by ridges defined by deep grooves above and below. GAB 3, oxidized.

P2 (Fig 3.1) (299) fill of pit [300]. Vessel with irregular flattened out-turned rim, internal rim diameter 180mm, incised slanting decoration below, probably the top of a band of chevrons. GAB 3, variably reduced.

P3 (Fig 3.1) (299) fill of pit [300]. Unusually long squared oblong lug, probably not complete. GAB 1, oxidized.

P4 (Fig 3.1) (218) Old land surface. Square-topped rim with slight groove below. GAB 2, reduced.

Old land surface (218) contained, in addition to **P4**, parts of two different Trevisker vessels, one as **P2** in GAB 3 and another with incised decoration in GAB 1. Pit fill (299) included several sherds with incised lines, probably chevrons, bordered above, in GAB 2, and one with a very eroded bordered comb-stamped design in GAB 2, together with a number of conjoining sherds from a base (not illustrated) in GAB 1, probably not from vessels otherwise represented, and produced a radiocarbon date of 1427–1261 cal BC (SUERC-62689).

Comment on the Middle Bronze Age ceramics

The assemblage belongs with the Middle Bronze Age Trevisker material always found in hollow-set houses of this date in Cornwall. There is a closely comparable vessel to **P1** from the settlement of such houses at Trethellan Farm, some 3 kilometres to the west on the Gannel estuary (Woodward and Cane 1991, fig 42, p12). There are no close comparanda at Trethellan for either **P2** or **P4**, but the square-sectioned lug is longer than but similar in section to P61 from Trethellan (*ibid*, fig 50). A sizeable assemblage of Trevisker pottery awaits publication from the site at Tregunnel which adjoins Trethellan (Quinnell 2014b). It is not unusual to find lack of close comparanda for Trevisker vessels (see comment on the assemblage from a hollow-set house at Tremough (Quinnell 2015, 67)).

The assemblage is too small for useful comment to be made on the size or function of the vessels, although **P1** would be of an appropriate size for storage and **P2** for cooking and eating. The presence of three slightly different fabrics, all without additional inclusions, suggests sourcing of the clays from three different areas of the Lizard gabbro.

Table 3.1 Details of Bronze Age pottery fabrics by sherd numbers and weight in grams. All material comes from Structure 1 except that from the old land surface (OLS) (218).

Context	Description	GAB 1	GAB 2	GAB 3	Total
(218)	OLS across site	6/83	1/26 **P4**	9/100	16/209
(216)	Fill of pit [217]	18/221			18/221
(225)	Fill of posthole [226]		4/69		4/69
(257)	Fill of pit [258]	1/5			1/5
(266)	Fill of pit [267]	2/66			2/66
(276)	Fill of posthole [277]			1/46	1/46
(299)	Fill of pit [300]	31/1129 **P3**	25/572	6/274 **P1, P2**	62/1975
Totals		62/1504	30/667	16/420	104/2591

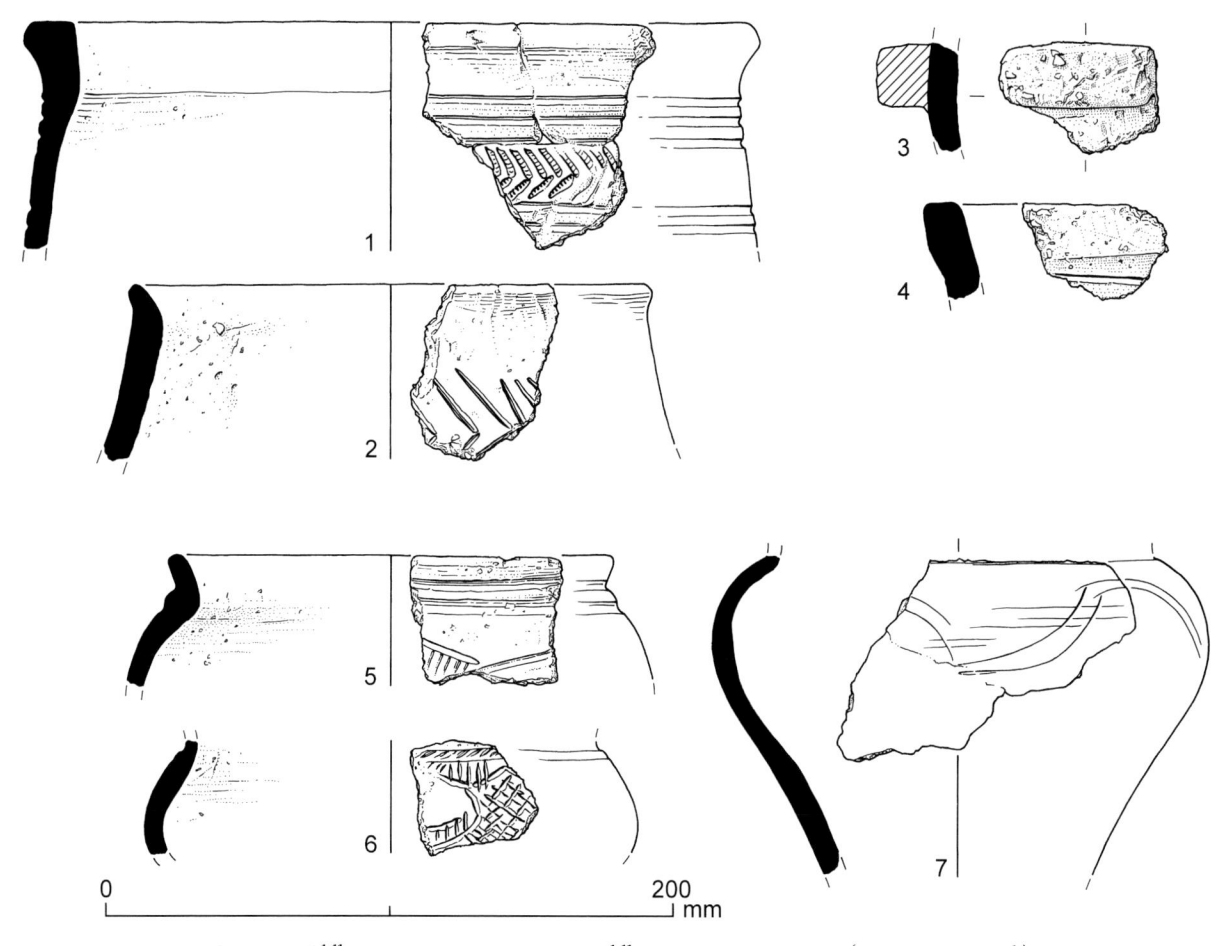

Figure 3.1 Middle Bronze Age pottery P1-P4, Middle Iron Age pottery P5-P7. (Drawing Jane Read.)

There were two radiocarbon determinations from (299), 2995 ± 34 BP, 1382–1117 cal BC (SUERC-62680) on charcoal, and 3081 ± 34 BP, 1427–1261 cal BC (SUERC-62689) on residue from a sherd of the conjoined base. It appears unlikely that the base, with its conjoining sherds, would have survived for very long before deposition in the pit. The general range of these dates is appropriate for the style of the ceramics.

The Middle Iron Age to early Roman period sequence

The total assemblage from these periods is 439 sherds weighing 4843 grams (Tables 3.2 and 3.3). Ceramics from the Middle Iron Age through into the Roman period are made of similar gabbroic fabrics and come from a continuous sequence which gradually changes through time. It is consequently often not possible to date undecorated and formless sherds within the overall period. Abrasion is variable and only commented upon if distinctive.

Cornish fabrics

The 'Well-made' and 'Standard gabbroic' fabrics are as presented in the report on Trevelgue Head cliff castle on the north of Newquay (Quinnell 2011a, 148). 'Well-made' fabrics tend to be better quality than 'Standard' fabrics and are finished by external burnish, whereas 'Standard' typically has a 'wiped' outer surface.

Non-local fabric: South Devon ware

A small sherd of this probable Devon fabric (Holbrook and Bidwell 1991, 177) was found within pit [198], Structure 3.

Non-local fabric: amphora

There are six sherds of similar fabric, one 50 grams from gully [430] Structure A6 and five totalling 225 grams, unstratified from Field 1. Paul Bidwell and Alex Croom provide the following comment on the sherd from [430].

Sherd in an orange–red fabric, with a variety of small inclusions. Prominent amongst them are grains of 'black sand' which suggest that the amphora in question was a Dressel 2-4 in the Campanian fabric (Class 10, Peacock and Williams 1991, 87–88, 105–106, fig 39). This type of amphora, the principal contents of which were wine, occurs in small numbers at several Roman military sites in the south west; its production was in decline by the late first century AD. It is also known from Iron Age sites in Britain from the late first century BC, and the same fabric was used for the slightly earlier Dressel 1A and 1B (Classes 3 and 4, Peacock and Williams 1991, 86–90, figs 26–28). For Roman amphorae in Iron Age Britain see Fitzpatrick (2003).

Middle Iron Age

The assemblage is characterized by South Western Decorated ware (SWD) fully described in the report on the assemblage from Trevelgue Head cliff castle (Quinnell 2011a). The decoration was applied by heavy pressure from a burnishing tool rather than by incision. The style was in use in the area from the fourth to the first centuries cal BC. Vessel forms follow the BD6 subdivisions used for the Trevelgue assemblage (*ibid*, 163–164). It should be noted that the upright or slightly out-turned rims of vessels in this style continue in use with subsequent Late Iron Age Cordoned ware and these rims, where no lower sherds are present, are described below as 'Later Iron Age'.

Structure S2 and adjacent ditches

The material present is all, even if in small quantity, entirely consistent with the radiocarbon determination from pit [298], fill (297), 2100 ± 34 BP, 337–40 cal BC (SUERC-62685).

Structure A1

P5 (Fig 3.1) (236) fill posthole [237]. Standard gabbroic. Unusual short out-turned SWD rim, tooled cordon below, traces of shoulder decoration with infilled areas, abraded. The vessel is not paralleled at Trevelgue Head but is by no 11 from Carloggas, St Mawgan-in-Pydar, a little further to the north east (Threipland 1956, fig 14).

P6 (Fig 3.1) (236) fill posthole [237]. Well-made gabbroic. Shoulder of SWD vessel of BD6.2, cordon with incised lines below neck, curvilinear design below, with very untidy criss-cross infill.

All the distinctive pottery is of Middle Iron Age date, consistent with radiocarbon determinations on charcoal from posthole [233], fill (232), 2114 ± 34 BP, 346–321 cal BC (4.1%) and 206–45 cal BC (91.3%) (SUERC-62677), and from gully [220], fill (219), 2179 ± 34 BP, 365–161 cal BC (94%) and 131–119 cal BC (1.4%) (SUERC-62695). The style of **P5** and **P6** are 'Standard' and 'Accomplished' SWD respectively, with areas of decoration infilled by diagonal lines or cross-hatching, and are not likely to date before the third century cal BC (Quinnell 2011a, 170–171, 176–178).

Curated or redeposited material in Structure A3

P7 (Fig 3.1) (126) fill of ditch [127]. Upper body of SWD vessel with fine incised curvilinear paired lines, fine fabric, well burnished. All 12 sherds (190 grams) from Slot 2 across ditch [127] are from this vessel. The vessel is of the less common BD6.2 type, more frequent towards the end of SWD currency. The decoration is currently unparalleled in its sparse simplicity. Ditch [127] produced determination 1879 ± 34 BP, cal AD 61–228 (SUERC-62677) suggesting infill in the second century AD. Given the unusual character of the vessel and its probable late Middle Iron Age origin, it is possible that this was curated rather than redeposited.

Late Iron Age Cordoned Ware

The initial classification of Cordoned ware is by Threipland (1956) in her report on the excavations at Carloggas, St Mawgan-in-Pydar. This used a series of alphanumeric Types, for example Type D, and the classification has generally stood the test of time (Tables 3.4 to 3.6). However, recent work has allowed more understanding of the chronology for the introduction of new vessel forms. Importantly, it has now been shown that serving / drinking vessels Types F and G were introduced in the late second century BC, together with storage jars Types H and J (Quinnell 2011b). Both these forms were absent in South Western Decorated Ware, but they were then used with it for perhaps a century. At a date in the first century BC the decorated SWD cooking vessels were replaced by plain but burnished Type D and E jars. Type O jars, small but with everted rims, and Type C vessels with a variety of rim-set lugs were introduced either at the same time or a little later but before the arrival of Rome. This Late Iron Age use of Cordoned ware, with at least two stages, has been termed First Phase Cordoned ware (Quinnell 2011b, 239; 2004, 110). Second Phase Cordoned ware runs from the arrival of Roman influence until a date in the second century AD, with well-made gabbroic fabrics still common. The most distinctive features of this phase are the introduction of Type R serving dishes (see Fig 3.2, **P12**) and the manufacture of a range of copies in gabbroic fabric of imported Roman styles, including samian.

At a date in the second century AD well-made gabbroic fabrics gradually pass out of use. This is most clearly shown by the replacement of the Type D cooking pots with those in standard fabric of Type 4. The numeric series of Roman period styles was developed for the report on Trethurgy Round, and this covers all known material from this date onward (Quinnell 2004, 110).

Hollow 1

P9 (Fig 3.2) (308) fill of pit [309]. Well-made gabbroic. Body of well-made Cordoned ware vessel probable Type H; sherds have split so that most of interior not present.

Table 3.2 Details of ceramic fabrics from Structure 2 by sherd numbers and weight in grams.

Context	Description	Standard gabbroic	Well-made gabbro	Totals	Comment
(273)	Fill of ditch [274]		2/10	2/10	Slight traces of SWD decoration.
(296)	Fill of ditch [293]		4/20	4/20	Fragment later IA rim.
(297)	Fill of pit [298]	5/7		5/7	
Totals		5/7	6/30	11/37	

Table 3.3 Details of ceramic fabrics from Structure A1 by sherd numbers and weight in grams.

Context	Description	Standard gabbroic	Well-made gabbroic	Totals	Comment
(219)	Fill of gully [220]		11/95	11/95	SWD cordon below neck with slanting lines.
(221)	Fill of gully [223]		2/32	2/32	
(236)	Fill of posthole [237]	1/32	1/18	2/50	**P5, P6**
(238)	Fill of posthole [239]	1/24		1/24	
Totals		2/56	14/145	16/201	

Table 3.4 Details of ceramic fabrics from Hollow 1 by sherd number and weight in grams.

Context	Description	Standard gabbroic	Well-made gabbro	Totals	Comment
(308)	Fill of pit [309]		13/270	13/270	**P9**
(329)	Fill of posthole [330]	2/10	1/2	3/12	
(335)	Fill of ditch [336]	6/30	28/429	34/459	**P11**
(345)	Fill of pit [346]	3/142	9/92	12/234	Well-made gabbroic part of burnished Type D jar. **P10**
(363)	Fill of pit [364]	3/15		3/15	Rim of Type O jar
(379)	Fill of pit [380]		25/265	25/265	Small sherds from Type M/O jar and from a lid.
(381)	Fill of pit [382]		40/131	40/131	Small sherds.
(446)	Fill of ditch [360]	6/30		6/30	
(447)	Fill of ditch [317]	2/12		2/12	
(412)	Layer	3/12		2/12	Part of Type D jar rim.
(441)	Fill of gully [442] west of H1	3/65		3/65	
Totals		28/316	116/1189	144/1505	

P10 (Fig 3.2) (345) fill pit [346] Well-made gabbroic. Rim of Type H storage jar.

P11 (Fig 3.2) (335) fill ditch [336] Well-made gabbroic. Rim of Type C bowl with perforate lug extending horizontally from rim top, unusual extension to the perforation on outer side of lug. Good burnish. Two perforations either side of lug with iron *in situ*, indicating mending of extensive breaks. The practice of mending broken pottery with iron clamps is well documented in Middle and Late Iron Age assemblages from sites in north Cornwall and Trevelgue Head, The Rumps and Carloggas, more so than sites further south and closer to the source of gabbroic clays (Quinnell 2011a, 183).

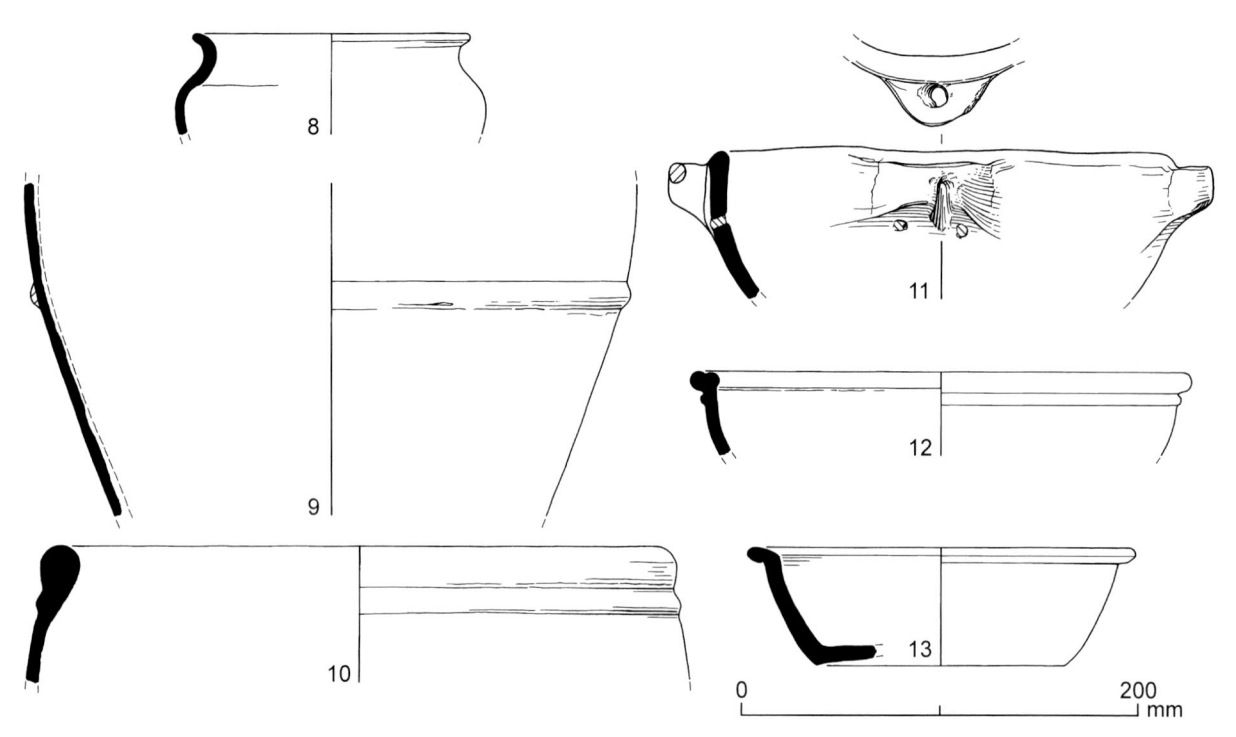

Figure 3.2 Pottery of Late Iron Age and Roman date P8–P13. (Drawing Jane Read.)

The pottery present suggests a date somewhere in the first century cal BC until broadly the arrival of Rome. With this the four radiocarbon dates are in good accord: (345) 2028 ± 34 BP, 159–134 cal BC (4%) and 116 cal BC – cal AD 55 (91.4%) (SUERC-62679); (345) 2077 ± 34 BP, 189–20 cal BC (93.2%) and 12–1 cal BC (2.2%) (SUERC-62694); (335) 1981 ± 34 BP, 52 cal BC – cal AD 85 (SUERC-62690); (308) 1984 ± 29 BP, 46 cal BC – cal AD 74 (SUERC-63279). The Cornish mortar **S5** from [334] (Chapter 4, Fig 4.1) should not date before the arrival of Rome and may extend the use of Hollow 1 until at least the later first century AD.

Hollow 2

The pottery is consistent with the determination from layer (457), 2065 ± 34 BP, 179 cal BC – cal AD 5 (SUERC-62684), but the presence of Type O rims is interesting. The date, if typical of the hollow-associated activity as whole, pins the introduction of the small Type O jars before the change of era.

Area A2

The minimal pottery only situates activity sometime before the earlier second century AD.

Roman period

The numerical Type series (Tables 3.7 to 3.12) follows that developed for the report on Trethurgy Round (Quinnell 2004).

Structure A3

Middle Iron Age **P7** is suggested above as possibly curated. The radiocarbon determination from ditch [127] 1879 ± 34 BP, cal AD 61–228 (SUERC-62677) suggests infill in the second century AD. The quality of the Type D rim sherds in pit [123] indicates that these were not made after the early part of that century (Quinnell 2004, 111). The pottery would all be appropriate for either the first centuries BC or AD, although the amount is too small to draw definite conclusions.

Enclosure Area (north)

P12 (Fig 3.2) (124) in ditch [125]. Well-made gabbroic. Rim and upper part of bowl with flat-topped rim, grooves below. Cordoned Ware Type R, Roman Type 19. This has a date range spanning the later first to second century AD. The other sherds from the area would be appropriate for this date.

Enclosure Area (south) ditches

The pottery from Enclosure Area (south) includes a Type 4 jar rim which should not date before the second century AD. The fragment of a copy of a Dr 27 cup post-dates the arrival of Rome and should be before the middle second century AD, while the Type R bowl has a slightly longer date within the Roman period. Overall the material is probably late first to early second centuries AD. The date from fill (208) from ditch [204],

Table 3.5 Details of ceramic fabrics from Hollow 2 by sherd numbers and weight in grams.

Context	Description	Standard gabbro	Well-made gabbro	Totals	Comment
(417)	Fill of pit [418]		2/8	2/8	
(424)	Fill of pit [435]	22/310		22/310	Small sherds, fragment Type O rim.
(436)	Fill of pit [437]	7/93	2/7	9/100	Well-made gabbroic fragment Type O rim.
(440)	Fill of pit [437]	3/45		3/45	Rims Type O, Type H.
(443)	Fill of pit [445]	2/11		2/11	
(457)	Layer		9/113	9/113	Body sherd Type G.
(470)	Fill of pit [471]	1/13		1/13	
(479)	Fill of posthole [480]	2/22		2/22	
(476)	Fill of pit [478]	1/8		1/8	
(490)	Fill of pit [491]	1/15		1/15	
Totals		39/517	13/128	52/645	

Table 3.6 Details of ceramic fabrics from Area A2 by sherd numbers and weight in grams.

Context	Description	Standard gabbro	Well-made gabbro	Totals	Comment
(106)	In pit [108]	1/9		1/9	
(119)	In ditch [120]		6/75	6/75	Part of rim of plain jar either SWD or Type D.
Totals		1/9	6/75	7/84	

Table 3.7 Details of ceramic fabrics from Structure A3 by sherd numbers and weight in grams.

Context	Description	Standard gabbroic	Well-made gabbro	Totals	Comment
(121)	In pit [123]		9/82	9/82	Type D rim well-made gabbroic.
(126)	In ditch [127]	20/209	12/190	32/399	**P7** (see above).
(137)	Fill of pit [138]	3/18	2/9	5/27	
Totals		23/227	23/281	46/508	

Table 3.8 Details of ceramic fabrics from Enclosure Area (north) by sherd numbers and weight in grams.

Context	Description	Standard gabbroic	Well-made gabbro	Totals	Comment
(124)	In ditch [125]	1/8	3/68	4/76	Type R bowl **P12**.
(128)	Fill of ditch [129]	1/20		1/20	Type 4 rim.
(173)	Fill of ditch [129]	1/53		1/53	Base angle.
(130)	Fill of ditch [131]	1/6		1/6	
(140)	Fill of ditch [141]	6/84		6/84	Rim sherds from Type J storage jar.
(164)	Fill of gully [165]	4/18		4/18	
Totals		14/189	3/68	17/257	

Table 3.9 Details of ceramic fabrics from Enclosure Area (south) ditches by sherd numbers and weight in grams.

Context	Description	Standard gabbroic	Well-made gabbro	Totals	Comment
(199)	Fill of ditch [201]	6/114		6/114	Includes rim sherds Type 4 jar.
(203)	Fill of ditch [204]	1/13	7/32	8/45	Well-made sherds include Type O rim and fragments from copy of Dr 27.
(206)	Fill of ditch [204]		1/17	1/17	Part of another Type O jar.
Totals		7/127	8/49	15/176	

4420 ± 28 BP, 3316–2992 cal BC (SUERC-63278), was obviously on redeposited material.)

Features north west of Hollow 1

P8 (Fig 3.2) (361) fill ditch [322]. Well-made gabbroic. Upper part of Type M / Type 1 small jar, of first century BC to early second century AD date.

P8 together with the Roman period introduction Type R would be best accommodated in the earlier second century AD.

Structure A6

All the gabbroic sherds were of Standard type. Type H continues right through the Roman period, Type M probably ceased somewhere during the second century AD. The amphora sherd was of a fabric ceasing production in the later first century AD but was markedly abraded. The sherds fit reasonably well with the radiocarbon determination from fill (455), below (454) in pit [456], 1842 ± 34 BP, cal AD 80–245 (SUERC-62678), but on the sherds alone a date in the earlier second century might be suggested. However, the presence of a piece of probable Trethurgy bowl S7 from [420], in the adjacent group of features, would support continuance to around AD 200 if contemporaneity of these with Structure A6 is accepted.

Structure 3

P13 (Fig 3.2) (174) fill pit [175] Structure 3 Standard gabbroic. Flat-rimmed bowl Type 20, second to late third centuries.

The limited amount of pottery from the structure makes chronology difficult. The radiocarbon determination from posthole [177], fill (176), 1816 ± 34 BP, cal AD 90–325 (SUERC-62686) was from a feature within the structure. It should pre-date that from infill layer (145), 1713 ± 34 BP, cal AD 245–399 (SUERC-62688). Together these dates suggest a structure built in the second to

Table 3.10 Details of ceramic fabrics from features north west of Hollow 1 by sherd numbers and weight in grams.

Context	Description	Standard gabbroic	Well-made gabbro	Totals	Comment
(321)	Fill of pit [320]	9/55	1/3	10/58	
(331)	Fill of ring-gully [332]	2/2		2/2	Sherd probably from Type R bowl.
(361)	Fill of ditch [322]		5/45	5/45	**P8**
Totals		11/57	6/48	17/105	

Table 3.11 Details of ceramic fabrics from Structure A6 by sherd numbers and weight in grams.

Context	Description	Standard gabbroic	Amphora	Total	Comment
(429)	Fill of gully [430]		1/50	1/50	Body sherd.
(454)	Fill of pit [456]	3/24		3/24	Rim Type H storage jar.
(487)	Layer	6/8		6/8	
(492)	From sondage in Field 1	4/43		4/43	Rim Type M.
Totals		13/75	1/50	14/125	

Table 3.12 Details of ceramic fabrics from Structure 3 by sherd numbers and weight in grams.

Context	Description	Standard gabbroic	S Devon ware	Totals	Comment
(145)	Fill of cut [146]	11/140		11/140	Storage jar, body sherds.
(174)	Fill of pit [175] outside structure	5/120		5/120	Flat-rimmed Type 20 bowl. **P13**
(197)	Fill of pit [198]	1/8	1/6	2/14	Storage jar rim as Type J.
Totals		17/ 268	1/6	18/268	

Table 3.13 Totals of sherds by fabric, sherd numbers, weight and period.

	Standard gabbroic	Well-made gabbroic	Amphora	South Devon ware	Totals
Middle Iron Age	7/63	32/365			39/428
Late Iron Age	68/842	135/1392			203/2234
Roman period	85/943	40/446	1/50	1/6	127/1435
Unstratified	54/465	11/56	5/225		70/746
Totals	214/2313	218/2259	6/275	1/6	439/4843

early third centuries AD and going out of use in the earlier fourth century. This date would fit that of the Type 20 bowl **P13**, if this is considered to fall within the structure. The presence of a small piece of South Devon ware is consistent with this later Roman date (Quinnell 2004, 107). An earlier fourth century AD date would be appropriate for the stone Trethurgy bowl fragment **S6** (Fig. 4.1).

Comment on the Middle Iron Age to Roman period ceramics

The unstratified material included sherds of Late Iron Age Type G and of early Roman period Type R.

In general, there is only a small quantity of pottery present from all these periods, perhaps because contexts such as middens were not present. The range of forms and fabrics is very much as would be expected. The percentage of gabbroic fabrics present, 98 per cent by sherd numbers and 94 per cent by weight, is very high. Such fabrics generally form some 90 per cent of Cornish assemblages (Quinnell 2004, 108). The large quantity may be partly due to the small size of the assemblage, partly to over half being of Iron Age date, before imports from outside Cornwall generally occur.

A summary of the probable chronology of the pottery is presented in Tables 3.13 and 3.14.

Table 3.14 Suggested chronology for the ceramics of different structures and areas, presented in broad sequence.

Structure / Area	Probably chronological range represented
Structure S2 and adjacent ditches	Middle Iron Age
Structure A1	Middle Iron Age
Hollow 1	Late Iron Age; 1st century BC extending up to *circa* AD 100.
Hollow 2	Late Iron Age, restricted to 1st century BC.
Area A2	Late Iron Age to early Roman.
Structure A3	1st century BC to 2nd century AD.
Enclosure Area (north)	Later 1st to 2nd centuries AD.
Enclosure Area (south)	Later 1st to early 2nd centuries AD.
Features north west of Hollow 1	Centring on earlier 2nd century AD.
Structure A6	Broadly 2nd century AD.
Structure 3	Late 2nd to early 4th centuries AD.

Chapter 4

The stonework

Henrietta Quinnell

with petrological comment by Roger Taylor

The stonework assemblage, as with the ceramics, is not numerous, considering the length of activity and the range of contexts. All is much as would be expected. Where appropriate, detailed comment is given below under individual artefact groups. Both of the mortars / bowls and the spindle whorl extend the range of known data for these classes of artefact.

Bronze Age

Saddle quern

S1 (Fig 4.1) (299) in pit [300], within Structure 1. 230mm+ x 120mm+ x 130mm. Part of saddle quern with unusually sharp angle between heavily worn side and edge; rough trimming on outer side. Surface fragment of mica / biotite granite, probably from an inclusion or xenolith, sourced from an area of granite and brought into the structure from at least 8 kilometres away.

Also from context (299) is a roughly trimmed square slab 255mm x 230mm x 40mm of slightly tuffaceous slate probably split from a local outcrop. Context (289), the fill of posthole [290], produced a piece of local slate 70mm x 56mm x 20mm with a notch 20mm across.

Later Iron Age and Roman period

For the probable dating of the various areas and structures see Table 3.14 and Chapter 8.

Sourcing

Most of the material used is fairly local. All artefacts described as cobbles could derive from beaches around Newquay while slate comes from the immediate locality, either weathered deriving from the surface or else split from of local outcrops. Similarity between the elvan used for artefacts suggests a common source, especially for the pieces used for bowls. Kaolinisation indicates a possible source within the St Austell granite some 10 kilometres distant. The granite of **S3** could come from the same area. The possible hammerstone from (164) possibly comes from an inland source of porphrytic lava in the Tintagel area, some 30 kilometres distant, and is the only stone artefact to source outside a 10 kilometre radius. Fairly local sourcing for stone used in artefacts is usual in other settlements within this date range (Quinnell 2011c). About 150 pieces of stone, beach cobbles, slate and weathered elvan were recorded but discarded. The elvan differs from that of the artefacts and was probably collected from a dyke which lies some 0.5 kilometres east of the site.

Rotary querns

S2 (Fig 4.1) (145) fill cut [146] Structure 3. Diameter 360mm, 85mm thick. Part of lower rotary quern. Heavily worn, rough trimming to circumference, central pivot hole rather than full perforation which would enable tentering (adjustment of the size of the gap between the stones). Probably deliberate breakage. Porphrytic elvan with quartz and mica phenocrysts, subject to metasomatic action, probably kaolinisation, giving a very porous texture. Lower rotary querns with both pivot holes and central perforations are known in Cornwall during the Roman period, a time when a wide range of cereal processing equipment was in use (Quinnell and Watts 2004).

S3 (not illus) (145) fill cut [146] Structure 3 Diameter *circa* 500mm, *circa* 110mm thick. Part of a large thick upper rotary quern, with part of rectangular eye, broken during manufacture. Biotite granite with small well-formed feldspar crystals up to 20mm, sourced from a granite area. Its presence indicates on-site manufacture of some lithic pieces.

Spindle whorl

S4 (Fig 4.1) (490) in pit [491] Hollow 2. Spindle whorl, 30mm across, cylindrical perforation 7mm wide, 14+ grams, local surface slate probably weathered, broken. Form biconical with concentric grooves. This spindle whorl should be of Late Iron Age date. Its biconical grooved form is more elaborate than any found in Middle Iron Age contexts at Trevelgue Head (Quinnell 2011c, fig 11.7). Carloggas, St Mawgan-in-Pydar, with substantial Late Iron Age activity, had a number of biconical spindle whorls with a variety of decoration but none with concentric grooves (Threipland 1956, fig 38).

Stone bowls

S5 (Fig 4.1) (333) fill of pit [334] in Hollow 1. Side of Cornish mortar, internal diameter 220mm, with slightly

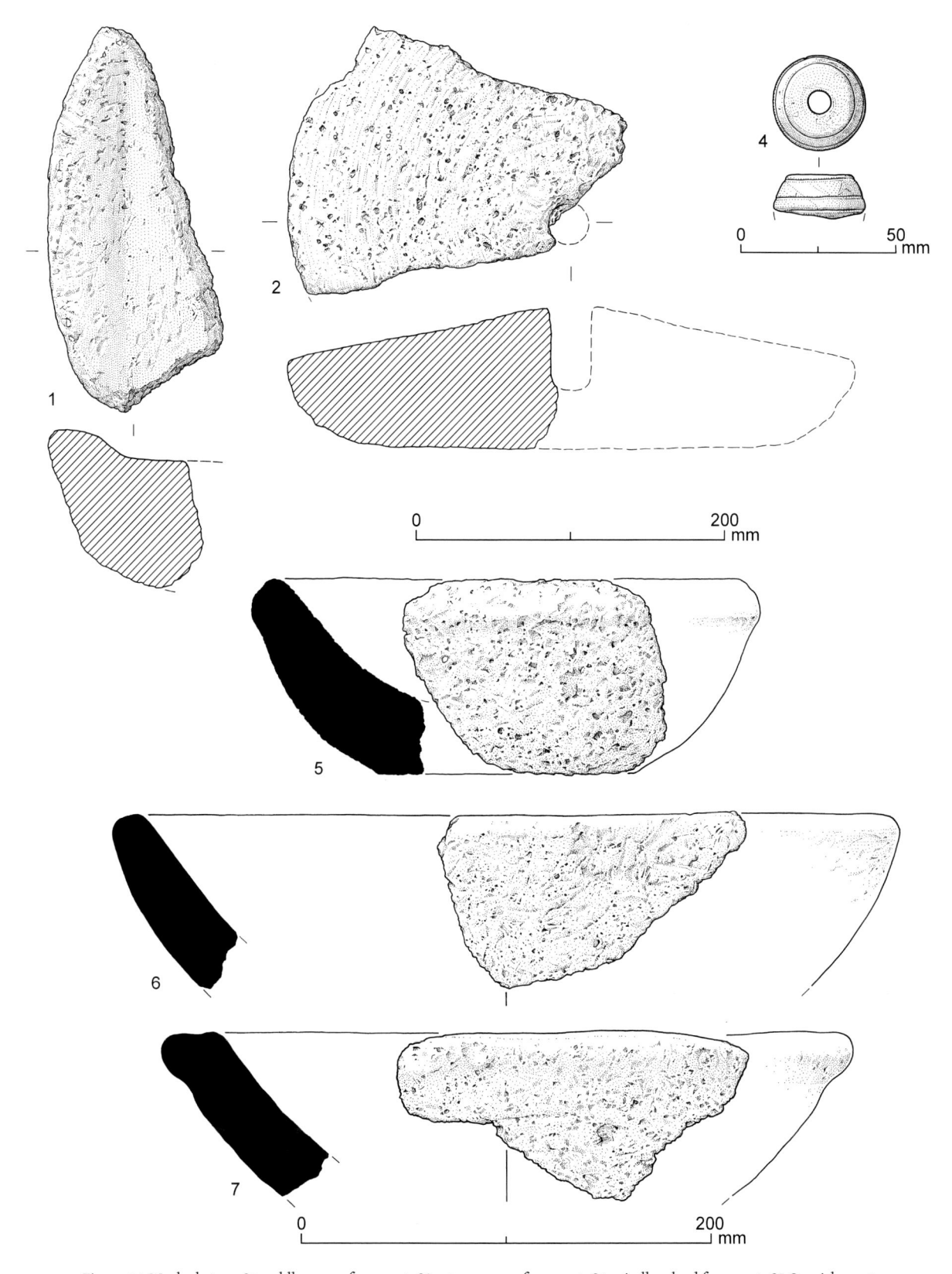

Figure 4.1 Worked stone S1 saddle quern fragment, S2 rotary quern fragment, S4 spindle whorl fragment, S5 Cornish mortar, S6–S7 large Cornish mortars or small Trethurgy bowls. (Drawing Jane Read.)

expanded rim. Porphrytic elvan with quartz and mica phenocrysts; subject to metasomatic action, probably kaolinisation, leaving a very porous texture; probably local. The interior is unworn and the exterior shows pecking which suggests that it was unfinished.

S6 (Fig 4.1) (145) fill of cut [146], Structure 3. Simple rim of Trethurgy bowl, internal diameter 360mm. Elvan with phenocrysts of quartz and mica subject to metasomatic action, probably kaolinisation, leaving a very porous texture; probably local. Interior worn.

S7 (Fig 4.1) (423) fill of ditch [420], Structure A6. Rim of either small Trethurgy bowl or large Cornish mortar, internal diameter 290mm, with expansion and slight groove in rim top. Porphrytic elvan with quartz and mica phenocrysts; subject to metasomatic action, probably kaolinisation, leaving a very porous texture; probably local. Interior worn.

Cornish mortars, with diameters of 200–300mm, appear in the early Roman period, copying, as does **S5**, the rims of mortaria, introduced in the later first century AD initially by the Roman army. Previously the earliest dated example was that from Trevisker, deposited with later second century pottery (Quinnell 1993, 70). It is difficult to extend the use of Hollow 1, in which **S5** was found, beyond the later first century AD. Even this pushes back the date of Cornish mortars by nearly a century. The mortar appears to have broken during manufacture, presumably on site. There is already data on the production of these mortars, especially common in elvan, on settlement sites (Quinnell 2004, 135). Cornish mortars continued to be made and used into the early post-Roman period.

Larger stone bowls, with diameters generally between 400 and 500mm, are generally found in contexts from the fourth to the sixth centuries AD and the more complete examples have paired skeuomorph handles apparently copied from metal vessels (Quinnell 1993; 2004, 136). Such handled examples are termed 'Trethurgy bowls' after the site on which they were identified, and cannot be definitely dated before the fourth century AD. These also were used as mortars, but their size and general elegance of form suggests some social function beyond the kitchen. In the absence of handles, and with their small size, **S6** and **S7** may be seen either as large Cornish mortars or small Trethurgy bowls. **S6** from Structure A6 may be second century, **S7** from Structure 3, later second century to early fourth. These two vessels may be demonstrating the emergence of vessels larger than Cornish mortars in the second and third centuries, showing that handled Trethurgy bowls were at the end of a sequence not only of vessel form but of social practices which underpinned them.

All three examples were very probably deliberately smashed and are represented by fragments which form less than 10 per cent of the original vessels.

Whetstones

The five examples are described below, all using cobbles of suitable materials. Two also have some use as hammerstones.

S8 (Fig 4.2) (214) fill of pit [215], Structure A1. 132mm+ x 43mm x 35mm. Whetstone, elongated beach cobble, hard finely micaceous siltstone, end broken, one side

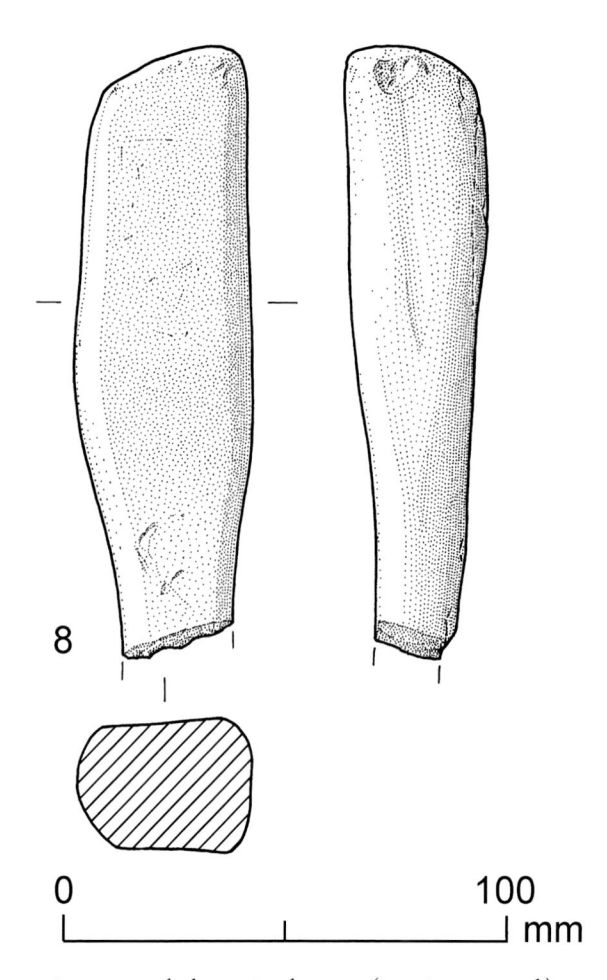

Figure 4.2 Worked stone S8 whetstone. (Drawing Jane Read.)

worn flat and glossy by whetstone use; some use of the other three faces.

There is also the tip of a hard tourmalinized slate blade beach cobble from [220] Structure A1 with whetstone wear on its side.

S9 (not illus) (139) fill of ditch [127] Structure A3. 110mm x 95mm x 25mm. Tabular beach cobble, fine micaceous sandstone, one narrow edge with whetstone facet, some hammerstone use on corners.

S10 (not illus) (321) fill of pit [320]. 70+mm x 65mm x 22mm. Tabular beach cobble micaceous siltstone / fine-grained sandstone, broken, one narrow edge with whetstone facet, possible hammerstone use on end.

S11 (not illus) unstratified Field 1, north end. Flat volcanic tuff beach cobble with whetstone use on both long edges.

Rubbing stones (not illus)

There are three of these from Hollow 1 on substantial beach cobbles, with slight traces of wear on the flattest surface. One from (381), fill of pit [382], 105mm x 84mm x 52mm is of vein quartz and another from the same context, 120mm x 115mm x 75mm, is a beach cobble of hard micaceous siltstone, one surface used as rubber with subsequent hammerstone use, possibly burnt leading to exfoliation. Another from (403), the fill of pit [404], is of hard micaceous siltstone.

A fragment of a bladed cobble of altered igneous basic rock with some wear comes from (174) fill of ditch [175] Structure 3.

Figure 4.3 Worked stone S12 Beach cobble with slight peck marks from anvil or hammerstone use. (Photograph: Gary Young.)

Hammerstones

S12 (Fig 4.3) (381) fill of pit [382] Hollow 1. 110mm x 105mm x 56mm. Elvan beach cobble with peck / anvil marks from occasional hammer use.

Context (164) fill of gully [165] had a very weathered surface fragment of porphrytic lava, possibly from an inland source in the Tintagel area, with some possible hammerstone use, 130 x 95 x 80mm. Context (232) in posthole [233], Structure A1, produced a triangular hard fine sandstone beach cobble, measuring 115mm x 84mm x 57mm, with some hammerstone use on one corner.

Slate discs: 'pot lids'

S13 (Fig 4.4) (335) fill of ditch [336] Hollow 1, 74mm x 68mm x 10mm.

S14 and **S15** (Fig 4.4) (197) fill of pit [198] Structure 3. **S14** measured 76mm x 75mm x 11mm and **S15** was 135mm x 125mm x 14mm.

These are all of soft grey slate probably from small local quarry / extraction pit and all are very slightly worn.

Chopper

S16 (Fig 4.5) (381) fill of pit [382] Hollow 1. The chopper measures 124mm x 104mm x 45mm. Split

Figure 4.4 Worked stone S13 Slate discs, S13 top right, S14 bottom right, S15 left. (Photograph Gary Young.)

Figure 4.5 Worked stone S16 split tuffaceous slate beach cobble trimmed as chopper. (Photograph Gary Young.)

piece of a beach cobble with a quartz lens within tuffaceous slate; trimmed as a rough chopper on one side.

Notched slates (not illus)

Deposit (199) fill of ditch [201]. 190 x 110 x 30mm, two notches, not worn, both 45mm across, adjacent on one side. These are the only examples and were from local slate.

Trimmed slate (not illus)

There are five other pieces of local grey slate, some slightly tuffaceous, trimmed to rough shapes: (121) fill of pit [123], Structure A3: rectangle 150mm x 1105mm x 9mm; (137) fill of pit [138], Structure A3: rectangle 125mm x 85mm x 9mm with slight anvil pecking on one surface; (339) fill of posthole [340], Hollow 1: triangle 165 x 125 x 25mm and rectangle 152mm x 142mm x15mm; (424) fill of pit [435] Hollow 2: oval 165mm x 155mm x 23mm.

Iron ore from ditch [204] and ditch / pit [212]
Comment by Roger Taylor

Several 40 litre sample bags were filled with what was thought to be slag from ditch [204] and ditch / pit [212]. Processing revealed the material to be iron ore.

Limonitic iron fragments shot through with narrow quartz veins and probably from the upper gossan region of a metalliferous lode, potentially a low-grade iron ore. The pieces have smooth surface areas which appear 'glossy and glassy looking'. This is actually a form in which limonite can take. This appearance can cause confusion with slag, and indeed the iron ore was originally identified as slag during the archive phase of the project (Smith 2015).

The only major recorded local occurrence is the Perran Iron Lode which crops out at the northern end of Perran Beach (SW764585). There may well have been other minor occurrences in the area which did not attract later working, as with the lode at Trevelgue Head (Nowakowski and Quinnell 2011, chapter 9).

Chapter 5

The flint

Anna Lawson-Jones

A total of 64 pieces of flintwork were recovered during the excavations. Of these, 26 came from stratified contexts and 38 are unstratified pieces, largely collected from the exposed subsoil. Few pieces are closely diagnostic tool forms.

The assemblage

The assemblage as a whole is mixed, of variable quality, condition and date, and attests to prolonged activity on and around the site, pre-dating the many Iron Age and Roman period features excavated. It reflects Neolithic and Bronze Age activity within the immediate vicinity, which is likely to extend well beyond the confines of the investigated area. Where Iron Age and later activity is less concentrated, Late Neolithic and Early Bronze Age features might well be expected to survive *in situ*. No clearly Mesolithic material was identified.

Much of the flintwork appears to have been residual prior to redeposition during later Iron Age and Roman period activity. This is most clearly demonstrated by the non-fresh condition of flint excavated from undisturbed (later) contexts, with the wear and tear reflecting exposure and disturbance of old land surfaces. Much more recent ploughing has also left its mark on the assemblage, with pieces being uprooted from surrounding subsoil layers and the tops of formerly undisturbed features and deposits being truncated, resulting in multi-period intermixing. Less resilient prehistoric finds will undoubtedly have been destroyed by later activity, making flintwork the sole representative of early site use.

Most of the corticated material is local beach pebble flint. There are also a small but significant number of imported nodular flint pieces. The imported material is likely to have come from Devon where nodular flint exists at several mainland sources (Newberry 2002), including Beer Head (Tingle 1998). An alternative source might possibly be west Cornwall, where some beaches produce nodular flint washed up from offshore deposits (Rogers 1923). Although some of the nodular cortex shows abrasion, it is at such a low level that surface disturbance as opposed to a beach source is more likely to account for it.

Neolithic and Early Bronze Age flintwork

The majority of the flintwork (48 pieces) belongs to the broadly dated Late Neolithic to Early Bronze Age period (see Table 5.1). None of the pieces are strongly diagnostic to either period, although a number of tool types and / or uses have been identified including a hammerstone, cores, scrapers, simple knives and used blades, possible composite tool pieces including a number of miscellaneously used flints, and 17 pieces of waste (including small debitage pieces). Many of these forms were identified from the 31 unstratified pieces, collected from all fields from the stripped topsoil and the resultant mechanically exposed surface (including pockets of the old land surface).

There are no complete, heavily retouched classic tool forms, and no tools directly associated with contemporary finds, or original *in situ* contexts. The technology and basic character of day-to-day flintwork during this period varies little (Butler 2005, 155; Edmonds 1995, 122), and is seen in this assemblage. As a result, the identification of distinct areas of activity (by even broad date) has not been possible. Occasional pieces more strongly suggest one period than the other, but never unquestionably so.

Twenty of the Late Neolithic to Early Bronze Age pieces were excavated from specific contexts; however, with the exception of four flints from pit [163], which were associated with Beaker pottery (Quinnell, Chapter 3), most of the features post-dated the flintwork. The significant pieces are summarized below. As can be seen, the excavated flintwork is essentially indistinguishable from the unstratified material:

Deposit (145), the upper infill within Structure 3, a Roman period building in Field 2, produced three flints. These include an undiagnostic hammerstone, which could realistically belong to any period, a rejuvenation flake and a used cortical flake.

(162), the fill of pit [163] in Field 2, produced four flints: a smashed cortical waste flake; a small dark flakelet; a notably large, pale, comfortable to hold cutting flake or unmodified knife, **L1** (Fig 5.1), and a pale grey, sharp, fresh, hard-hammered, squat flake with a large ventral removal.

L1 **L2**

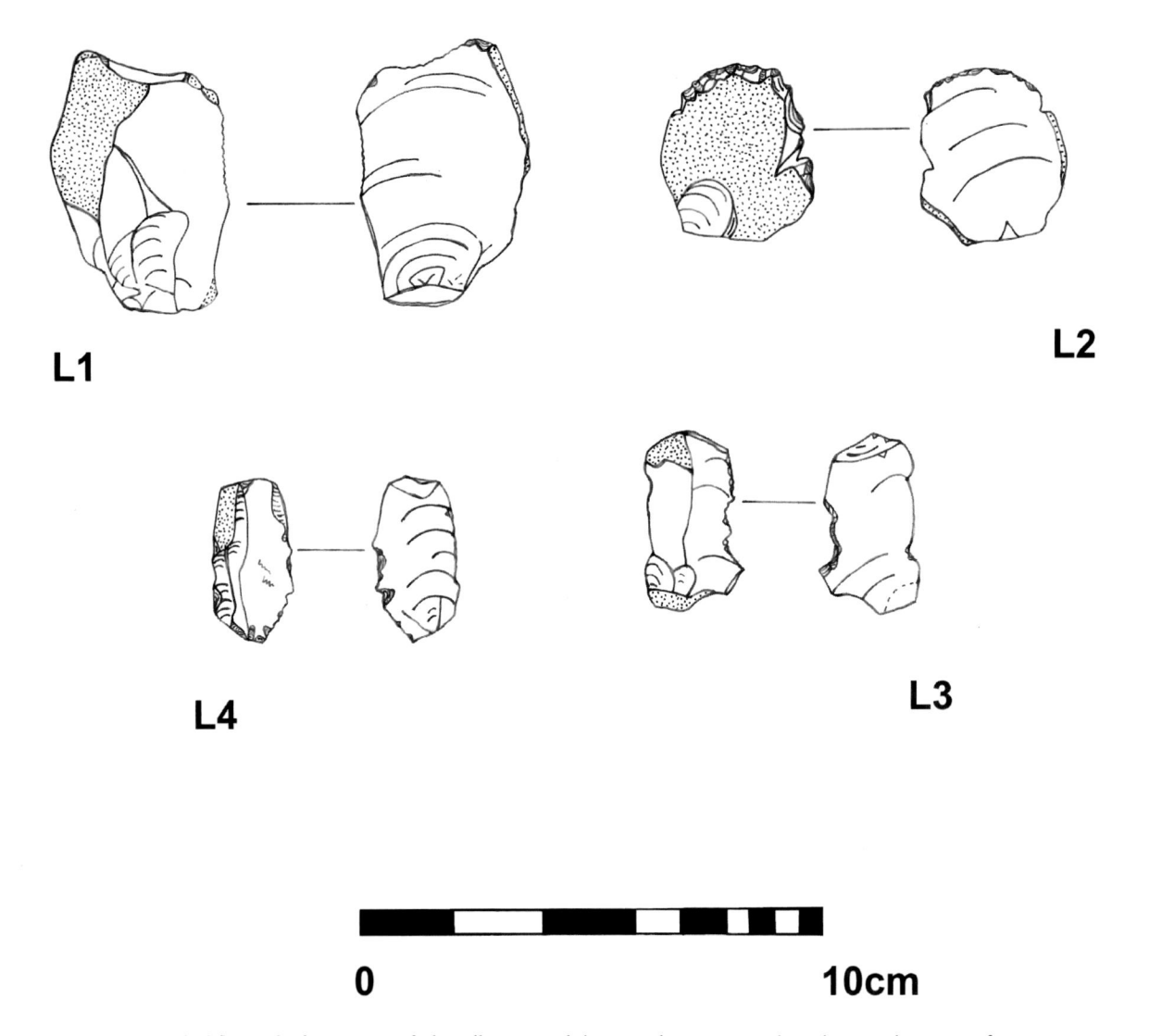

L4 **L3**

0   10cm

Figure 5.1 Four worked flints. The first two are of a broadly Late Neolithic to Early Bronze Age date, the second two came from Bronze Age Structure 1. L1 is a cutting flake or simple knife flake from pit fill (162); L2 is a cortical flake scraper from curvilinear gully fill (219), L3 is a slightly denticulated blade from Structure 1 stone lined pit fill (257) and L4 is a short, utilized blade from central pit fill (299).

(218), a remnant old land surface layer in Field 3, produced three soft-hammered small flakes, one possibly used. All were thin and relatively fresh giving the impression of having been largely undisturbed.

(219), the fill of [220], a curvilinear ditch or ring-gully associated with Structure A1 in Field 3, produced a single used cortical scraper, **L2** (Fig 5.1), as well as a small, heavily abraded broken blade.

(221), the fill of [223], a ditch in Field 3, contained a single burnt pebble. This could be of any date.

(238), the fill of posthole [239] in Structure A1 in Field 3, produced a triangular sectioned, small, probable mounted but broken tool which was possibly made from nodular flint.

(271), the fill of pit [272] in Field 3, produced a single possibly nodular waste flake.

(296), the fill of ditch [293] in Field 3, contained a single burnt, incomplete but originally well-made partially retouched flake tool.

(331), the fill of ring-gully [332] located in Field 1, produced two flints, a miscellaneously used cortical flake and a broken possible borer / engraver?

(335), the upper fill of ditch [336] and part of Hollow 1 in Field 1, produced a single tried pebble.

(441), the fill of gully [442] in Field 1, contained one keeled core with subsequent chopping / slashing use.

Eight pieces were strongly cortical with a more than 75 per cent corticated dorsal surface. In total 26 pieces had a pebble cortex, three black pieces had a nodular cortex and the remaining 19 did not retain any cortex. The non-corticated pieces show a variety of colours, including a number of near-black fine quality flint flakes, implying the presence of some further nodular imported material. Six pieces were so burnt that damage through blistering and / or fracturing had occurred. The date for the burning is not known. It may relate to hearths or fires contemporary with the use and discard of the flint, or it may have been significantly later and caused by activity during the Iron Age or Roman periods.

The alteration of flint by the controlled use of heat is, however, a recognized later Mesolithic and Neolithic technique designed to improve the knapping property and (possibly indirectly) the colour of the flint being treated. Seven pieces within the assemblage may suggest heat treatment, identified via a soapy surface texture and slight alteration in colour as compared to other similar pieces. Incipient patination is the more likely cause of surface changes seen in nine other pieces.

Related to the multi-period use of this site, with later disturbance and upheaval or exposure of previously *in situ* material, four pieces were recorded as notably abraded and 13 were identified as unintentionally broken. Few of the pieces exhibited sufficient use wear to suggest breakage through use, with most of the breaks reflecting post-use damage. Three pieces were deliberately snapped as a part of the tool making process Six pieces appeared fresh and undamaged, suggesting there were pockets of surviving Neolithic or transitional contexts. Three of these pieces came from layer (218), an old land surface of probable prehistoric origin. It is tempting to suggest that this may have been the source of a number of the unstratified pieces, particularly the material in better condition.

The Bronze Age flintwork

Sixteen pieces of Bronze Age flintwork have been identified, 11 on broad characteristics and five through character and association with features inside Structure 1, a Middle Bronze Age roundhouse (see Table 5.2).

Structure 1 was only partially revealed by the excavations, but elements identified included a deeply cut pit [300], the fill (299) of which contained deliberately deposited decorated pottery (Quinnell, Chapter 3) plus two pieces of worked flint. There were also four substantial postholes, one of which [283], fill (282), produced a single flint blade. An irregular stone-lined pit [258], fill (257), produced two pieces of flint. Other features were also associated with this structure, but none produced further flints. This is not in itself unusual since few Middle Bronze Age roundhouses in Cornwall have produced a notable flint component; the paucity of flint in Cornish roundhouses is demonstrated by excavated sites at Scarcewater, Trevisker, and Poldowrian (Jones and Taylor 2010; ApSimon and Greenfield 1972; Smith and Harris 1982).

The following three contexts were all associated with Structure 1:

(257), the fill of stone-lined pit [258], produced a single near-black burnt piece and a distinctive mid-brown, soft-hammered broad blade of good quality flint with use wear along one slightly denticulated edge and probable haft or hand-held damage along the opposing edge, **L3** (Fig 5.1). Possible glossing at the bulbar end is likely to be attributable to hafting. The distal end appears to have broken off in use. This piece is interesting because it may well have come from the same core as a piece from context (299).

(282), the fill of posthole [283], contained a single small, thin, broken, pale blade with significant ventral glossing of uncertain origin.

(299), the fill of pit [300], produced a small, thin, broken, dark blade. In addition, a soft-hammered blade was found with an opposing partially corticated long edge with damage probably caused via hafting, **L4** (Fig 5.1). The distal end is missing. This piece in many ways resembles the design and use of the denticulated piece from (257). It may well have come from the same distinctively coloured, soft-hammered, good quality flint core. If so, then these pieces were not only made and used for very similar tasks, but also deposited within features that were open at the same time.

One other piece of probable Bronze Age date came from the following later context (Table 5.3). Layer (341), the fill of ditch [342] within Field 1, produced a single near exhausted multi-platform core with numerous removals. Removals appear haphazard and hard-hammered, producing squat, variable flakes. This piece has all the prerequisites for identification as a late prehistoric core and is very similar to another slightly smaller, near rhombus-shaped example found as an unstratified core (in bag E, Table 5.3, below). Both pieces are dark and in the process of incipient repatination.

The general unstratified material includes 11 pieces of probable Middle to Later Bronze Age date (including the multi-platform rhombus-shaped core referred to above). The other pieces (from bag E) include two single platform cores, one of which has been inverted and had its platform used as a scraper; a potential small projectile made on a diagonally split flake; a waste flake; and a sharp, angular, difficult to hold flake with a short straight edge showing miscellaneous retouch. Bag G (Table 5.3) produced two similar split pebble single platform scrapers, both with apparent scraper use of the platform following inversion; a small thumbnail-shaped, barely retouched, lightly-used scraper, and a small retouched triangular projectile with retouch around the angular tapered distal end.

As with the probable earlier Late Neolithic to Early Bronze Age assemblage, this material includes a very similar range of elements. Two nodular, ten pebble and three unknown raw material sources have been recorded.

Concluding comments

This multi-phased assemblage from the Newquay Strategic Road corridor is predominantly residual in character. With two exceptions, even where flint has been found within secure contexts, its creation and use significantly pre-dates the features in which it was found. The exceptions to this are the small flint assemblage from pit [163], which was associated with Beaker pottery, and that from Structure 1, a roundhouse of Middle Bronze Age date.

In the case of Structure 1, the flint was recovered from a central pit, as well as other associated pits and postholes. This material was probably contemporary with the structure's use, including a stone-lined pit [258], which is likely to have been an entrance feature, and a particularly large posthole [283] within the post-ring. None of the flint from these contexts is categorically diagnostic of the period, but none would be out of place, and none appears to have been notably battered, implying that these pieces had not been 'kicking around' as residual waste but rather came from more carefully controlled feature contents. This deliberation implies contemporaneity for the flint and pottery content of the Structure 1 central pit at least.

The longevity of general occupation of the site from at least the Middle to Late Neolithic, through Bronze Age, Iron Age and Roman periods has ensured a very thorough mixing of contexts and finds, making close dating difficult.

Although residual flint can be reused by later peoples when found on a site, this has not been identified within this assemblage. The abundance of locally available flint within walking distance of the site is likely to have negated the need for either reuse or frugality. Pebble flint can be found along the length of Newquay's active beaches, while large quantities of flint exist within the Fistral Beach raised beach exposures.

Most of the assemblage is thoroughly mixed, of varied date, assorted use and variable condition. The range of tool forms, including simple knives, scrapers, mounted composite pieces, flakes and blades, some used, some not, attests to a wide range of different tasks which are likely to have included the preparing and processing of foodstuffs, working of leather, wood and bone, and probably indirectly in the production of artefacts associated with other processes such as weaving and the making of matting and basketry (*cf*, for example, Hurcombe 2014, 152). The presence of a core rejuvenation flake and the probable use of heat as a pre-knapping treatment in a small number of pieces reflect the care taken in routine tool production, particularly for the Neolithic period. The range of tools, presence of use-wear and scattering of burnt pieces all imply domestic occupation within the immediate vicinity. We might therefore expect pits, postholes and hearths to be found nearby.

Table 5.1 Late Neolithic and Early Bronze Age flint. NOTE: the bags of unstratified material have been individually distinguished by letters A to G. Bag D came from Field 1, bag C from Field 2 and bag F from Field 3. Bags A, B, E and G include material from all fields.

Context no	Form	Source /colour	Fresh / Abraded Heated / Broken	Detailed description
(145)	Hammer stone?	Pebble / mottled greys	A	Flint pebble hammer stone with single ?accidental flake removal with focused percussive damage around the abraded flake scar. Abandoned. Not used as a core.
(145)	Cortical flake – used	Pebble / mottled greys	burnt	Thin flat cortical flake. Heat fractured with partial survival of possibly utilized edge.
(145)	Rejuvenation flake – used	Pebble / mottled greys	H	Partial cortical flake with thin primary flake / blade removal scars. Cutting use wear on one edge. Distal dorsal cortex and thick bulb facilitate hand held use.
(162)	Cutting flake / knife – used	Pebble / uniform pale grey		Well-formed, large hard hammered cortical flake with cortex backing and opposing straight edge showing cutting use wear. Comfortable to hold. (**L1**)
(162)	Cortical waste flake	Pebble / Dark grey, flecked	B	Part of formerly large cortical flake showing rubbed surface with cortex thinned / partially removed. Part of a cobble tool? Edges all around flake have been smashed off.
(162) <15>	Waste flake	Unknown / dark brown	F	Small, thin amorphously shaped waste flakelet. No use-wear. Debitage. Controlled dorsal scar ridge.

(162)	Flake – waste	Pebble / mottled pale grey	F	Core on a flake. Sharp and unused with distinctly undulating hard hammer removals.
(218)	Small waste flake	Unknown / near black	F?, H, B	Soft hammered hinged, broken flakelet. Probable debitage from tool manufacture. Heat treatment.
(218)	Flake – miscel. use	Unknown / mottled mid greys	F?	Soft hammered, triangular shouldered flake with use wear (cutting?) along both tapered edges. Distal tip missing.
(218)	Waste flake	Dark mottled greys	F?	Small, soft hammered near cortical flake. Tear-shaped with sharp, un-used lateral and platform edges.
(219)	Cortical end scraper – used	Pebble / mottled pale greys	-	? Soft-hammered cortical flake with steep, rough distal retouched scraper and use wear, plus slight use / wear on one side; probable wear caused during scraper use. (**L2**)
(219)	Point? – used	Unknown / mottled greys	A, H, B	Small dark, heat treated (?), probable point / awl with distal cortex. Tapered proximal end missing / severely abraded through use.
(221)	Burnt pebble	Pebble / grey	Burnt, B	One end of a long, thin beach pebble. One end missing / tried, but largely lost through heat damage. Only one small part of previously knapped edge is still visible. Quite distinctive and very comfortable to hold – so may have had a tool worked at one end?
(238) <48>	Bladelet – used	Unknown / near black	-	Proximal end of narrow, well formed, soft-hammered blade. Triangular section, distal end missing with use-wear on one straight edge and very slight wear on broken end. Too small for hand held use – must have been mounted, possibly part of composite tool.
(271)	Waste flake	Nodular / black	-	Small / squat soft-hammered flakelet. Possibly heat treated debitage from tool manufacture.
(296)	Former tool – used	?Nodular / near black	Burnt, B	Burnt, blistered former large flake tool with remnant use-wear / uncertain retouch on one edge and distal end. Appears soft-hammered, originally well formed. Probably Late Neolithic
(331)	Cortical flake – used	Pebble / mottled dark grey	-	Flake with a broad triangular working edge which shows light (slightly abraded through-use) fine nibbled retouch. Miscellaneous use.
(331)	Cortical flake – used?	Pebble / black	B	Small cortical flake. Distal end missing / broken off. Proximal end shows some possible use as borer / engraver?
(335)	Tried pebble	Pebble / mid grey	burnt, B	A tried pebble or core (?) which has seen subsequent burning? Severely blistered.
(341)	Keeled core?	Pebble / mottled grey	H	Split pebble / flake core with sharp edge showing possible slight slashing / chopping use.
U/S (A)	Split cortical flake	Pebble / mottled grey	-	Diagonally split thick cortical flake with distal end and part of side missing. Sharp (non-corticated) edge shows probable slight use-wear as a cutting flake.
U/S (B)	Waste flake	Unknown / dark grey	-	Small partially cortical, thin, round flake removed as a part of core preparation.
F2 U/S (C)	? Knife	Pebble / speckled grey	A, B	Chert. Proximal half of well-formed thick flake with cortex backing, use-wear / possible retouch on opposing edge (partially around platform – probably softening of sharp edges for hand held use / hafting?) Distal end broken off, possibly deliberately snapped since the degree of use-wear is not pronounced.
F1 U/S (D)	Misc. flake – used	Unknown / speckled grey	B	Thin flake with distal end missing and remnant probable wear along edges.
F3 U/S (F)	Cutting flake – slight use	Pebble / pale grey	-	Hard-hammered flake. Remnant cortex at dorsal distal edge. Slight use as cutting flake on one edge.
F3 U/S (F)	Flake – waste	Unknown / mottled dark grey	F	Small, thin, tapered waste from a multi-platform flake / blade core.
F3 U/S (F)	Misc. flake – used	Unknown / speckled dark grey	H	Small, rounded, soft-hammered, well-formed flake which has an all-over gloss. One very short side has steep retouch; opposite side has tiny use-wear removals around the convex edge and extending along distal end.

F3 U/S (F)	Unmodified knife – used	Pebble / mottled greys	B	Broken, long, partly cortical flake. Cortex backing, opposing sharp edge shows cutting use-wear. Would have been fairly comfortable to hold: long, thick flake with razor-sharp edge. Deliberately snapped?
F3 U/S (F)	End scraper / knife? – used	Pebble / brown	-	Bulbar end of a soft-hammered flake with thick corticated dorsal surface at bulbar end. Comfortable to hold, with opposing end steeply retouched to form a short, straight scraper-like edge.
F3 U/S (F)	Cutting flake – used	Unknown / mottled dark grey	F	Well-formed flake with light use-wear and slight retouch along one edge and damaged distal end. Comfortable to hold cutting flake.
F3 U/S (F)	Flake scraper – used	Pebble / dark grey	-	Cortical flake with slight scraper use at distal side and proximal side. Largely opportunistic use rather than modification for use.
F3 U/S (F)	Scraper – used	Pebble / very dark grey	A	Soft-hammered cortical flake with variable scraper retouch around edges, crushed platform and an abraded slight notch.
F3 U/S (F)	? Composite knife blade – used	Unknown / mottled grey	F	Narrow, slightly curved blade-like piece with tiny removals along one edge. Opposite long edge was almost certainly hafted. Probably one of several mounted pieces forming a sickle-like tool.
U/S (G)	Cortical flake – used	Pebble / dark grey	-	Thick cortical flake with pressure flakes removed from all sides via levering? Opportunistic use?
U/S (G)	Flake – used	Nodular / black	-	Flake with distal dorsal cortex and probable backing retouch on one edge and slight cutting use along opposing unmodified edge.
U/S (G)	Flake – waste	Pebble / dark grey	-	Small flake possibly showing re-use of an earlier core / tool? This piece has not been used.
U/S (G)	Flake – waste	Unknown / dark grey	burnt, B	Small burnt piece with edges fractured away and hairline crazing of the surface.
U/S (G)	Flake – waste	Unknown / grey brown	-	Small, unused debitage piece from tool manufacture.
U/S (G)	Flake – waste	Pebble / grey brown	-	Small, unused waste flake from tool manufacture. Soft hammered.
U/S (G)	Flake – waste	Unknown / grey brown	-	Small, thin unused waste flake from tool manufacture. Soft hammered.
U/S (G)	Flake – waste	Unknown / near black	-	Small, thin waste flake or debitage. Soft hammered. Post deposition damage on one thin side?
U/S (G)	Flake – waste	Unknown / grey brown	-	Small, thin unused waste flake from tool manufacture. Soft hammered. Thinning flake
U/S (G)	Flake – used	Unknown / brown	H	Small, thin, rounded waste flake. Soft hammered. Thinning flake with uncertain wear around edges suggesting very fine use-wear. Thumbnail scraper-shaped, but much thinner.
U/S (G)	Rejuvenation flake – waste	Unknown / black	H	Burin-like removal from the distal end of a well-managed alternate, single platform core. Very fine dark, good quality nodular-looking flint. Soft hammered.
U/S (G)	Split pebble core – used	Pebble / mid-pale grey	A	A split pebble core with very bashed / abraded angular edge from probable use as chopper, which saw subsequent abrasion through wear and tear.
U/S (G)	Cortical waste flake	Pebble / mottled grey	-	Long, complete cortical flake. No obvious use; small damage along edge may be either effect of cortex or post-depositional.
U/S (G)	Waste blade	Unknown / mid-pale grey	burnt, B	Proximal end of a small blade-like piece. Triangular sectioned, with much hairline crazing and distal end blistered off. Uncertain if a former tool.
U/S (G)	Misc. tool – used	Pebble / grey tan	B	Well-formed thick flake which has been split / snapped lengthways. Un-split edge shows wear along its short straight length – cutting / scraping.

Table 5.2 Bronze Age flint from Structure 1.

Context No	Form	Source /colour	Fresh / Abraded Heated / Broken	Detailed description
(257)	Burnt waste	Nodular? near black	Burnt, B	Remains of a thick black cortical flake. Heavily burnt, blistered and fractured.
(257)	Denticulate – used	Pebble / mid grey brown	H B	Soft-hammered long flake. Distal end missing. Heat treated. One side denticulated / used. Opposing edge has slight probable backing / hafting damage. Comes from a well-managed core. Possibly from same core as (299). **(L3)**
(282)	Flake – waste	Pebble / pale grey	B	Distal part of very thin soft-hammered piece. Abrasive glossing on ventral face is of uncertain origin since it is difficult to envisage how use of such a thin piece could have generated sufficient wear.
(299)	Unmodified knife – used	Pebble / mid grey brown	-	Soft-hammered long flake with denticulated use-wear on one edge and probable hafting damage along the opposing, partially corticated edge. Possibly from same core as (257). **(L4)**
(299)	Flake waste	?Nodular / near black	B	Small mid-section flake / blade. Very thin; both ends are missing. Some slight post-depositional damage but no obvious use.

Table 5.3 Other probable Bronze Age material. NOTE: the bags of unstratified material have been individually distinguished by letters A to G. Bag D came from Field 1, bag C from Field 2 and bag F from Field 3. Bags A, B, E and G include material from all fields.

Context No	Form	Source /colour	Fresh / Abraded Heated / Broken	Detailed description
(341)	Multi-platform core	Pebble / mottled dark grey	A? / H?	A rhombus-shaped multi-platform core with a slightly abraded, partially repatinated, possibly heated surface. Mostly hard hammer removals. Probable use as an unmodified (?) core-scraper tool? Very similar to a piece from U/S bag E).
U/S (E)	Multi-platform core	Unknown / near black with white speckles	A? / H?	Small rhombus-shaped multi-platform core with one crushed / abraded edge of uncertain function? Hard hammer removals. Possible heat treatment. Very similar to a piece from (341). Possible source of projectile-like flake below?
U/S (E)	Single platform core / core tool – used?	Pebble / pale grey tan	A	Split pebble with single platform removals on one side. Abandoned, perhaps because of poor-quality flint. Slightly fluted platform too abraded to be sure of post-core scraper use.
U/S (E)	Single platform core / core tool	Pebble / dark mottled greys	A	Small split pebble with single platform removals on one side. Abandoned. Slightly fluted platform. Post-core scraper use visible.
U/S (E)	?Projectile – used flake	Unknown / near black with white speckles	B?, F	Small, sharp, soft hammered proximal end of a diagonally split / broken (?) flake with one side showing use-wear and possible working on platform edge. Possibly a small projectile? Possibly from multi-platform core above?
U/S (E)	Flake – waste	Unknown / mottled greys	-	Soft-hammered flake with platform preparation but no use of the flake.
U/S (E)	Misc. tool – used?	?Nodular / mottled greys	F	Sharp, angular, uncomfortable to hold flake from a poorly managed multi-platform core. Platform has been retouched as short scraper, but appears not to have been used? Alternatively, may have been an engraver / point with tip missing and opposing retouch represents softening rather than scraper?

U/S (G)	Split pebble scraper – used	Pebble / mottled greys	-	A split pebble with steep, short retouched scraper edge and slight use-wear. Comfortable to hold possible core tool.
U/S (G)	Split pebble scraper – used	Pebble / grey	H?	Thickly corticated, waterworn nodular cortex, possibly from raised beach deposits Exposed flint shows heat treatment. Three removals with steep scraper-like use of platform.
U/S (G)	Thumbnail –like scraper-used	Pebble / pale browns	-	Small circular flake with remnant distal dorsal cortex and slight use wear around approximately half of the convex edge.
U/S (G)	Small triangular arrowhead?	Unknown / grey brown	H?	Small triangular flake with retouch / wear along both short, near straight tapered edges. Probable arrowhead?

Chapter 6

The plant macrofossils

Julie Jones

A total of 62 bulk samples was taken during the excavations, from a range of features including pits, postholes and ditch fills, for the recovery of charred plant remains and charcoal. The samples were processed by the flotation method with residues collected on a 500 micron mesh and flots on a 250 micron mesh.

The dried flots were then sorted under illuminated low-powered magnification with a stereo-binocular microscope with magnifications between x10 and x45. The charred cereal remains were identified with reference to Jacomet (2006), with seeds and fruits identified with the aid of the author's reference collection and consultation with Cappers *et al* (2006) and Bertsch (1941). Details of all 62 samples are shown in Table 6.1. Of these, 26 samples contained charred plant remains, the results of which are shown in Table 6.2. One of these samples is associated with an Early Bronze Age pit, with the remainder likely to be of Late Iron Age or Roman date.

All remains refer to fruits and seeds unless otherwise stated and plant nomenclature and habitat information follows Stace (1997). Many of the floats were very small ranging in size from <1 to 81ml. As a result many of the charred assemblages are limited, with the cereal grain in particular of variable preservation with some grains highly vacuolated suggestive of high temperatures.

Crop plants and weed assemblages

Cereal remains

No cereal remains occurred in the Middle Bronze Age or Middle Iron Age features. The archaeological evidence suggests industrial activity from several areas during the Late Iron Age and Roman period, notably from Hollow 1 and the ring-gullied Structure A6. However, the charred plant remains were fairly limited from the 24 samples from this phase, with cereal grains occurring most frequently with a total of 143 hulled wheat, 3 free-threshing wheat, 53 oat (*Avena* sp.) and 18 barley (*Hordeum* sp.) grains. These, together with other chaff components such as wheat glume bases, including 4 identified as spelt wheat (*Triticum spelta*), barley rachis internodes and oat awns and floret bases, together with a small but recurring weed assemblage, suggest that these are the remains of crop cleaning waste that has been distributed around the site into ditch, pit and posthole fills.

Although only four glume bases were well enough preserved to confirm the presence of spelt this is likely to be the crop cultivated here, as spelt is the most commonly occurring species of the Roman period, although there is also some bread-type wheat (*Triticum aestivo-compactum*-type), with several of the more rounded grains characteristic of this type in two features. Barley is clearly a minor component, only occurring in four features. Oats appear to be second in importance to wheat; unfortunately there were only two poorly preserved floret bases, which did not allow confirmation of whether these were from cultivated or wild varieties. There were almost three times as many brome (*Bromus* spp.) caryopses as oat grains and, due to poor preservation and the difficulties in differentiating oats from brome species, a further 66 individuals were identified as oat / brome (*Avena/Bromus*).

Weeds

Although not a crop in its own right, *Bromus* species are a frequent weed of cereal crops as indeed are wild oats (*Avena fatua*). Brome, a large-seeded grass, is the most frequent of a small, but recurring arable weed assemblage, many also having bigger seeds including cleavers (*Galium aparine*), black-bindweed (*Fallopia convolvulus*), docks (*Rumex*) and vetch (*Lathyrus/Vicia*). Also notable are the substantial pods of wild radish (*Raphanus raphanistrum* ssp. *raphanistrum*), with 85 recovered from eight contexts and onion couch (*Arrhenatherum elatius*) bulbils present in the fills of six features.

Food / wild plants

There is limited evidence for hedgerow plants which may have been collected as fuel or as food plants. Charred hazelnut shells only appear in two features, particularly notable in the basal fill (208) of ditch [204], where 472 fragments were the only macrofossils present, and pit [163] fill with 42 fragments.

Other woody taxa include bramble (*Rubus* sect *Glandulosus*), a Rosaceous thorn, a single gorse (*Ulex*) spine and fragment of an Ericaceous flower, all of which seem likely to have come from gathered fuel. The only other food item is a single Celtic Bean (*Vicia faba*) from the fill of pit [175] in Structure 3.

Results

Early Bronze Age

Pit [163]

The Beaker-associated pit [163] produced a small assemblage of hulled wheat and oat grains, and 42 hazelnut fragments.

Late Iron Age

Hollow 1

The interior of this feature contained 24 pits and postholes, of which only three produced sparse plant remains. Posthole [340], pit [373] and postholes [351] / [352] incorporated a total of 7 wheat grains and a single oat, with 4 wild radish pods.

On the northern side of Hollow 1 was pit [309], which included small quantities of hulled wheat grain, occasional oats and a weed assemblage incorporating wild radish pods, cleavers, black-bindweed and dock seeds.

Ditch [120]

The single fill (119) of a steep-sided curvilinear enclosure or boundary ditch [120] and the fill of pit [163] produced a small assemblage of hulled wheat and oat grains, with a Rosaceae thorn and Ericaceae (heather family).

Roman period

The charred remains dating to this period include assemblages from Structure A3, the Enclosure Area, Structure 3, Structure A6 and features to the north west of Hollow 1.

Structure A3

Structure A3 was comprised of pits and postholes and a ditch [127]. Two samples from (126), the fill of [127], had very small floats, containing grassland weeds including ribwort plantain (*Plantago lanceolata*), selfheal (*Prunella vulgaris*) and various grasses such as meadow-grass / cats'-tails (*Poa/Phleum* spp.), heath-grass (*Danthonia decumbens*), an onion couch bulbil (*Arrhenatherum elatius*) and a charred grass (Poaceae) stem and culm node.

The fills of pit / posthole [138] produced a small assemblage of hulled wheat and oat grains, as did the nearby pit [156], although the latter could not be directly linked with Structure A3.

Features near to Structure 3

Four samples from three pits and one posthole fill included charred remains. Pit [175] was one of a number of pits and postholes on the northern edge of Structure 3; it had a slightly larger charred assemblage than the other features which included 20 hulled wheat grains, a single barley and 10 oat / brome grains, plus a single Celtic Bean (*Vicia faba*). Posthole [177] and pit [187] on the western perimeter of the hollow included 38 wild radish pods with other weeds such as cleavers, narrow-fruited cornsalad (*Valerianella dentata*), several vetches (*Lathyrus/Vicia* spp.) and two wheat grains in fill (176) of posthole [177]. There were only a few hulled wheat, oat and brome grains with an onion couch bulbil in the fill (186) of pit [187].

Enclosure Area

Ditch [204] was one of two steep-sided flat-bottomed ditches in this area. An assemblage of 472 hazelnut fragments was all that occurred in the basal fill (208), which were found through radiocarbon dating to be residual and of Middle to Late Neolithic date (below). The two overlying fills (206) and (205) had larger cereal assemblages than elsewhere around the site. These were largely oat and brome with poorly preserved examples identified as oat / brome. Unfortunately, the single oat floret base recovered was too poorly preserved to help determine if these were cultivated or wild oats. There were also hulled wheat grains and fragmented glume bases, including a single spelt. Arable weeds included cleavers, dock and common chickweed. A single gorse spine may have been brought in with gorse brushwood for fires.

Features north and west of Hollow 1

There was only one feature to the west of Hollow 1 with charred remains, oval pit [367], although both the basal (366) and overlying fill (371) had a few hulled wheat grains with small weed assemblages.

To the north of Hollow 1 was ditch [322]. The assemblage from it included small quantities of hulled wheat grains, barley, occasional oats and a weed assemblage including wild radish pods, cleavers, black-bindweed and dock seeds.

Structure A6

Pit [450] was one of three pits within the interior of ring-gully [430], all of which showed signs of burning. The charred assemblage here was poor with only two hulled wheat grains and few weed seeds.

Discussion

The only prehistoric charred remains were associated with Beaker pit [163], ditch [120] and the Late Iron Age – early Roman period Hollow 1, and these were largely limited to small assemblages of hulled wheat and oat grains.

The Roman period Structure A3 was limited to a small grassland assemblage including ribwort plantain, selfheal and grasses that may have occurred as weeds from recently ploughed fields, although there was no evidence from cereal remains to suggest any indication of Roman period cultivation around Structure A3. Several onion couch bulbils and a heath-grass (*Danthonia decumbens*) caryopsis suggest these may have originated from turves burnt as fuel (Hall 2003).

The remaining spread of Roman period features examined across the site, mostly ditch and pit fills, shows some plants of economic importance. These occur as low densities of charred cereal grains, with limited accompanying chaff and arable weeds. Their mode of preservation comes from contact with fire, perhaps from accidental parching during crop processing, from cooking, from use as fuel or several of these factors combined. They can, however, be used to indicate the resources available to the people living on the site and provide evidence on the local economy.

Overall, charred grains were the most numerous component found. Hulled wheat accounted for 33 per cent, with occasional well-preserved glume bases suggesting this was spelt, the variety mostly cultivated during the Roman period, although there are occasional examples (<1 per cent) of the more rounded grains more typical of bread wheat, a variety that begins to make its appearance at this time. It is possible that bread wheat may be under-represented here since parching is not required in processing as with hulled wheat and therefore the small quantities that occurred here were probably deliberately burnt waste. While its presence as a crop can be suggested its relative importance to spelt, or barley (accounting for 4 per cent of grain present), cannot be determined. Oat and grains identified as oat / brome formed 27 per cent, with brome 35 per cent so these are clearly an important component. There were only two oat floret bases from the entire site, although these were not well enough preserved to confirm whether they were from cultivated or wild oats. However, oats would have been able to tolerate the local acid soils and high rainfall of the south-west, conditions not conducive to large-scale cultivation of wheat and barley. Celtic Bean would also have been a useful plant resource providing valuable protein although there was only a single charred bean from pit [175].

The occurrence of 85 wild radish capsules from eight samples is interesting as this may also have been a food plant. Wild radish is claimed to be the ancestor of the edible radish (*Raphanus sativus*), although unlike modern varieties, wild radish has a single long white taproot; both this and the leaves are edible and have the spicy flavour of radish. Greig (1991, 306) lists *Raphanus* as one of a group of typical cornfield weeds that first appeared in the Iron Age. Wild radish would have been suited to the acidic sandy soils around Newquay, as indeed are oats, which are a useful crop on poor acid soils where rainfall is high. Oats, usually spring sown, can also be harvested before fully ripe and have the ability to dry in the sheaf. This may suggest that cereal cultivation was local, with the oats and brome perhaps used as fodder or animal bedding, with wheat and barley for human consumption. Brome has been suggested as a famine food and it is possible that this and wild oats may have been harvested to boost yields in times of need or as animal feed (Greig 1991).

The growth habit of cleavers and black bindweed, both twining species that could have grown around cereal stems, meant they could easily have been gathered at the cereal harvest, together with the upright medium to tall annual wild radish, perhaps by uprooting. The *Raphanus* pods and other larger seeds may have been retained through less thorough grain cleaning, or used to supplement animal consumption, but in view of the low densities and spread of this material around the site in secondary contexts definite interpretations of crop processing activities are not possible.

The highest concentration of charred material occurred in the Enclosure Area from ditch [204], with two of the secondary fills incorporating grains of oat, oat / brome and brome, with rare oat chaff. There are also a few hulled wheat grains, with rather more glume bases. Hollow 1, south of ditch [204], accommodated a number of pits and postholes, although here plant remains were few with a similar range of wheat, oats and barley grain and weed seeds that occurred elsewhere around the site. Structure 3 had a slightly bigger charred assemblage. It is, however, perhaps not surprising that concentrations of cereal grains, chaff and weeds are low from features around the site if many were associated with industrial activity and may indicate that the main centre of domestic occupation and crop cleaning activities was located elsewhere.

Hazelnut fragments were concentrated in two features, pit [163] and ditch [204], where the primary fill (208) showed an abundance of hazel shell. These may have provided a further food resource or result from fuel collection. Interestingly, the hazelnuts in (208) have been dated to the Middle to Late Neolithic period and those from pit [163] to the Early Bronze Age. Gorse spines and a heather flower fragment seem likely to relate to fuel gathered from heathland habitats.

Industrial activity associated with burning and iron ore was found in a ditch and a pit. It seems possible, therefore, that the low concentrations of charred remains found at Newquay represent a spread of material from an area of domestic occupation and that crop processing activities were located in an area of the site not yet investigated.

Oats may have been the most important crop used as animal fodder or bedding, although cereal waste was often used as tinder in hearths, fires / or perhaps furnaces, although no evidence was found for these at the site. Although later in date a site at Hemyock in Devon did provide evidence for the use of cereals, particularly oats, in association with iron smelting activities dating from the ninth to tenth centuries AD (Jones 2014). Mikkelsen (1998) also analysed material from many sites associated with iron smelting in Denmark from the first to eighth centuries AD, which showed the use of straw to support charcoal and iron ore before smelting commenced.

Evidence from other sites

Plant remains from a site at Atlantic Road in Newquay excavated in 1998 by Cornwall Archaeological Unit were examined by Wendy Carruthers (Carruthers 1998). Occupation here was dated to the Roman period when it appears attempts were made to cultivate the sandy soil (Carruthers 1998).

Although mostly dated to the Middle Bronze Age the site at Trethellan, further along the coast from Newquay produced mostly naked barley with emmer, spelt and a few oats, although it is interesting that wild radish capsules were also present, suggesting continuity from this earlier period of cultivation of these acidic sandy soils, a characteristic of this northern Cornwall coast (Straker 1991).

There was also evidence for crops along with industrial activity at the Roman period site at Duckpool (Straker 1995), which is also located on the north Cornish coast, albeit to the east and close to the Devon border. The dominant taxon here was oats recovered from occupation / rubbish layers of mid fourth century AD date although numbers were low and there was no diagnostic chaff to suggest whether these were from a cultivated crop. Straker suggested that as there was so little evidence for wheat or barley that the oats were crop remains. Oats were also important at Tintagel only 20 miles to the south of Duckpool also on the exposed Atlantic coast (Straker 1997) although occupation here was of a later fifth to sixth century AD date.

Conclusion

Overall, the amount of cereal grain recovered from Newquay is small and therefore it is difficult to give a real impression of the importance of arable cultivation here, although we can show the presence and variety of crops available for consumption, whether by humans or animals. However, there is also the added variable of a possible industrial use of crop processing waste as fuel.

Table 6.1 Bulk samples from the Newquay Strategic Road corridor.

Sample	Context	Cut	Feature	Weight (g)	Flot vol (ml)	Plant remains	
1	(103)	[104]	pit	103.8	100	None	
2	(109)	[110]	linear	2.1	<1	Arrhenatherum elatius (bulbil)	1
3	(106)	[108]	linear	22.7	16	None	
4	(117)	[118]	pit	5.9	<1	None	
5	(119)	(120)	ditch	12.3	10	cf Triticum sp. (hulled grain) Triticum sp. (glume base) Triticum spelta (glume base) Ericaceae indet (flower fragment) Rosaceae (thorn)	1 1 1 1 1
6	(133)	[134]	ditch	4.3	3	None	
7	(137)	[138]	pit	7.1	3	Arrhenatherum elatius (bulbil)	2
9	(126)	[127]	ditch	10.6	3	Arrhenatherum elatius (bulbil) Danthonia decumbens Plantago lanceolata Poa / Phleum spp. Rumex sp.	5 1 1 2 1
10	(121)	[123]	pit	10.6	8	None	
11	(126)	[127]	ditch	9.6	6	Lathyrus / Vicia spp. Poaceae indet. (stem and culm node) Prunella vulgaris Valerianella dentata	2 1 1 1

The plant macrofossils

12	(155)	[156]	pit / posthole	9	5	*Triticum* sp. (hulled grain) *Avena* sp. (grain) *Arrhenatherum elatius* (bulbil) Poaceae indet.	1 1 1 1
13	(140)	[141]	ditch	43.3	32	*Triticum* sp. (hulled grain) *Avena*/Poaceae *Arrhenatherum elatius* (bulbil)	3 1 1
15	(162)	[163]	pit	64.7/5.6	50	*Triticum* sp. (hulled grain) cf *Triticum* sp. (grain) *Avena* sp. (grain) *Corylus avellana* (nut fragments) *Fallopia convolvulus*	2 1 1 42 1
17	(124)	[125]	ditch	1.6		None	
18	(128)	[129]	ditch	1.6		Charcoal fragments only	
19	(124)	125]	ditch	1.5	<1	None	
21	(164)	[165]	ditch	1.6		Charcoal fragments only	
22	(147)	[148]	pit	2.6		Charcoal fragments only	
23	(174)	[175]	pit	3.4	2	*Avena/Bromus* spp. (grain) *Hordeum* sp. (grain) *Triticum* sp. (hulled grain) *Triticum* sp. (free-threshing grain) cf *Triticum* sp. (wheat) *Triticum* sp. (glume base) *Bromus* sp. cf *Bromus* spp. *Vicia faba*	10 1 20 1 6 1 1 3 1
24	(176)	[177]	posthole	7.7	7	*Triticum* sp. (hulled grain) *Galium aparine* *Lapsana communis* *Lathyrus / Vicia* spp. *Raphanus raphanistrum* (pods) *Valerianella dentata*	2 6 1 4 38 5
25	(142)	[143]	pit	11.6		charcoal fragments only	
27	(186)	[187]		9.6	5	*Avena* sp. (grain) *Triticum* sp (hulled grain) *Arrhenatherum elatius* (bulbil) *Bromus* sp.	1 1 1 1
28	(145)	[146]		1.9	<1	none	
30	(197)	[198]		2.4	6	*Avena/Bromus* sp. *Triticum* sp. (hulled grain) *Galium aparine* *Raphanus raphanistrum* (pod)	1 1 1 1
31	(199)	[201]		9	10	*Rubus* sect. *Glandulosus*	1
32	(202)	[201]		14.2	13	None	
33	(203)	[204]		4.4		Charcoal fragments only	
34	(199)	[201]		4.6	5	None	
35	(205)	[204]		10.6	10	*Avena* sp. (grain) *Avena* sp. (awns) *Avena/Bromus* spp. *Triticum* sp. (hulled grain) *Triticum* sp. (glume base) *Triticum spelta* (glume base) Cereal indet. *Bromus* spp. cf *Bromus* spp. *Galium aparine*	22 2 40 2 19 2 7 60 33 1

36	(206)	[204]		25.3	10	Avena sp. (grain) Avena/Bromus spp. Avena sp. (floret base fragment) Avena sp. (awns) Hordeum sp. (grain) Hordeum sp. (rachis internode base) Triticum sp. (hulled grain) Triticum sp. (glume base) Triticum spelta (glume base) Bromus spp. cf Bromus spp. Galium aparine Rumex spp. Silene dioica Stellaria media Ulex sp. (spine)	12 14 1 4 1 2 3 25 1 21 28 1 3 1 1 1
37	(208)	[204]		66.3	81	Corylus avellana (nut fragments)	472
42	(222)	[223]		5.2	5	None	
44	(219)	[220]		25.3	70	None	
45	(225)	[226]		2.8	3	None	
46	(227)	[228]		5.8	<1	None	
48	(232)	[233]		7.8	4	None	
49	(234)	[235]		5.3		Charcoal fragments only	
52	(259)	[260]		22.6	23	None	
57	(282)	[283]		1.4		Charcoal fragment only	
61	(291)	[292]		3.1		Charcoal fragment only	
63	(297)	[298]		12.6	5	None	
64	(299)	[300]		15.9	5	None	
66	(308)	[309]		57.8	40	cf Avena sp. (grain) Avena/Poaceae spp. (grain) Avena sp. (floret base) Avena sp. (awns) Hordeum sp. (rachis internode) Triticum sp. (hulled grain) cf Triticum sp. (grain) Triticum sp. (glume base) Bromus spp. Rumex spp.	2 3 1 6 1 11 2 1 3 2
68	(299)	[300]		8	8	None	
69	(319)	[320]		6.3	12	None	
70	(321)	[322]		14.5	8	Avena/Bromus sp. (grain) Triticum sp. (hulled grain) Triticum sp. (free-threshing grain) cf Triticum sp. (grain) Triticum sp. (glume base) Cereal indet. (grain) Carex spp. Fallopia convolvulus Galium aparine Plantago lanceolata Raphanus raphanistrum (pods)	1 4 2 1 1 5 2 1 1 fragment 1 13
71	(325)	[326]		13.5	18	None	
73	(333)	[334]		5.8	7	None	
74	(339)	[340]		3.1	5	Triticum sp. (hulled grain) Bromus sp. Raphanus raphanistrum (pods)	5 4 1
75	(353)	[351]/ [352]		1.9	1	Triticum sp. (grain) Lathyrus/Vicia sp.	1 1 fragment
76	(345)	[346]		14	2	None	

The plant macrofossils

77	(363)	[364]		5	1	None	
78	(361)	[332]		3.8	2	Avena/Poaceae indet. (grain) Hordeum sp. (grain) Hordeum/Triticum spp. (grain) Cereal indet. (grain) Raphanus raphanistrum (pods)	1 3 3 2 2
79	(369)	[332]		4.6	2	Avena sp. (grain) cf Avena sp. (grain) Hordeum sp. (grain) cf Hordeum sp. (grain) Triticum sp. (hulled grain) cf Triticum sp. (grain) Triticum sp. (glume base) Cereal indet. (grain) Atriplex spp. Fallopia convolvulus Galium aparine Raphanus raphanistrum (pods)	7 5 11 2 47 19 1 31 12 1 2 4 + fragments
80	(366)	[367]		39.2	35	Triticum sp. (hulled grain) Avena sp. (awn) Arrhenatherum elatius (bulbil) Bromus sp. Plantago lanceolata Raphanus raphanistrum (pods)	5 1 1 2 2 1
81	(371)	[367]		10.7	3	Avena sp. (grain) Triticum sp. (grain)	1 1
82	(372)	[373]		5.6	4	Avena sp. (grain) Triticum sp. (hulled grain) Galium aparine	1 1 1
87	(417)	[418]		7.3		sample retained for charcoal ID	
94	(449)	[450]		9.3	1	Triticum sp. (hulled grain) Galium aparine Raphanus raphanistrum (pods) Valerianella dentata	2 2 2 1
95	(452)	[453]		7.5	1	None	
96	(455)	[456]		69.5	95	None	
97	(457)			13.1		sample retained for charcoal ID	

Table 6.2 Charred plant remains from the Newquay Strategic Road corridor.

Sample	Context	Cut	Feature	Weight (g)	Flot vol (ml)	Plant remains	
EARLY BRONZE AGE							
Beaker pit [163]							
15	(162)	[163]	pit	64.7/5.6	50	Triticum sp. (hulled grain) cf Triticum sp. (grain) Avena sp. (grain) Corylus avellana (nut fragments) Fallopia convolvulus	2 2 1 42 1
IRON AGE							
Hollow 1 Iron Age							
66	(308)	[309]	pit	57.8	40	cf Avena sp. (grain) Avena/Poaceae spp. (grain) Avena sp. (floret base) Avena sp. (awns) Hordeum sp. (rachis internode) Triticum sp. (hulled grain) cf Triticum sp. (grain) Triticum sp. (glume base) Bromus spp. Rumex spp.	2 3 1 6 1 11 2 1 3 2

74	(339)	[340]	posthole	3.1	5	*Triticum* sp. (hulled grain)	5
						Bromus sp	1
						Raphanus raphanistrum (pods)	4
75	(353)	[351]/[352]	Postholes	1.9	1	*Triticum* sp. (grain)	1
						Lathyrus/Vicia sp.	1 fragment
82	(372)	[373]	pit	5.6	4	*Avena* sp. (grain)	1
						Triticum sp. (hulled grain)	1
						Galium aparine	1
	Area A2
2	(109)	[110]	pit	2.1	<1	*Arrhenatherum elatius* (bulbil)	1
5	(119)	[120]	ditch	12.3	10	cf *Triticum* sp. (hulled grain)	1
						Triticum sp. (glume base)	1
						Triticum spelta (glume base)	1
						Ericaceae indet (flower fragment)	1
						Rosaceae (thorn)	1
	ROMAN PERIOD
	Structure A3
9	(126)	[127]	ditch	10.6	3	*Arrhenatherum elatius* (bulbil)	5
						Danthonia decumbens	1
						Plantago lanceolata	1
						Poa/Phleum spp.	2
						Rumex sp.	1
11	(126)	[127]	ditch	9.6	6	*Lathyrus/Vicia* spp.	2
						Poaceae indet. (stem and culm node)	1
						Prunella vulgaris	1
						Valerianella dentata	1
7	(137)	[138]	pit	7.1	3	*Arrhenatherum elatius* (bulbil)	2
12	(155)	[156]	pit	9	5	*Triticum* sp. (hulled grain)	1
						Avena sp. (grain)	1
						Arrhenatherum elatius (bulbil)	1
						Poaceae indet.	1
	Structure 3
23	(174)	[175]	pit	3.4	2	*Avena/Bromus* spp. (grain)	10
						Hordeum sp. (grain)	1
						Triticum sp. (hulled grain)	20
						Triticum sp. (free-threshing grain)	1
						cf *Triticum* sp. (wheat)	6
						Triticum sp. (glume base)	1
						Bromus sp.	1
						cf *Bromus* sp.	3
						Vicia faba	1
24	(176)	[177]	posthole	7.7	7	*Triticum* sp (hulled grain)	2
						Galium aparine	6
						Lapsana communis	1
						Lathyrus/Vicia spp.	4
						Raphanus raphanistrum (pods)	38
						Valerianella dentata	5
27	(186)	[187]	pit	9.6	5	*Avena* sp. (grain)	1
						Triticum sp (hulled grain)	1
						Arrhenatherum elatius (bulbil)	1
						Bromus sp.	2
30	(197)	[198]	pit	2.4	6	*Avena/Bromus* spp.	1
						Triticum sp (hulled grain)	1
						Galium aparine	1
						Raphanus raphanistrum (pod)	1
	Enclosure Area
31	(199)	[201]	ditch	9	10	*Rubus* sect. *Glandulosus*	1

The plant macrofossils

35	(205)	[204]	ditch	10.6	10	*Avena* sp. (grain)	22
						Avena sp. (awns)	2
						Avena/Bromus spp.	40
						Triticum sp. (hulled grain)	2
						Triticum sp. (glume base)	19
						Triticum spelta (glume base)	2
						Cereal indet.	7
						Bromus spp	60
						cf *Bromus* spp.	33
						Galium aparine	1
36	(206)	[204]	ditch	25.3	10	*Avena* sp. (grain)	12
						Avena/Bromus spp.	14
						Avena sp. (floret base fragment)	1
						Avena sp. (awns)	4
						Hordeum sp. (grain)	1
						Hordeum sp. (rachis internode)	2
						Triticum sp. (hulled grain)	3
						Triticum sp. (glume base)	25
						Triticum spelta (glume base)	1
						Bromus spp.	21
						cf *Bromus* spp.	28
						Galium aparine	1
						Rumex spp.	3
						Silene dioica	1
						Stellaria media	1
						Ulex sp. (spine)	1
37	(208)	[204]	ditch	66.3	81	*Corylus avellana* (nut fragments)	472
13	(140)	[141]	ditch	43.3	32	*Triticum* sp. (hulled grain)	3
						Avena/Poaceae	1
						Arrhenatherum elatius (bulbil)	1
Features north west of Hollow 1
70	(321)	[322]	ditch	14.5	8	*Avena/Bromus* sp. (grain)	1
						Triticum sp. (hulled grain)	4
						Triticum sp. (free-threshing grain)	2
						cf *Triticum* sp. (grain)	1
						Triticum sp. (glume base)	1
						Cereal indet. (grain)	5
						Carex spp.	2
						Fallopia convolvulus	1
						Galium aparine	1 fragment
						Plantago lanceolata	1
						Raphanus raphanistrum (pods)	13
79	(369)	[332]	Ring-gully	4.6	12	*Avena* sp. (grain)	7
						cf *Avena* sp. (grain)	5
						Hordeum sp. (grain)	11
						cf *Hordeum* sp. (grain)	2
						Triticum sp. (hulled grain)	47
						cf *Triticum* sp. (grain)	19
						Triticum sp. (glume base)	1
						Cereal indet (grain)	31
						Atriplex spp.	12
						Fallopia convolvulus	1
						Galium aparine	2
						Raphanus raphanistrum (pods)	24 + fragments
80	(366)	[367]	pit	39.2	35	*Triticum* sp (hulled grain)	5
						Avena sp. (awn)	1
						Arrhenatherum elatius (bulbil)	1
						Bromus sp.	2
						Plantago lanceolata	2
						Raphanus raphanistrum (pods)	1
81	(371)	[367]	pit	10.7	3	*Avena* sp. (grain)	1
						Triticum sp. (grain)	1

						Structure A6 ROMAN PERIOD	
94	(449)	[450]	pit	9.3	1	*Triticum* sp. (hulled grain) 2 *Galium aparine* 2 *Raphanus raphanistrum* (pods) 2 *Valerianella dentata* 1	2 2 2 1

Chapter 7

The charcoal

Dana Challinor

Thirty eight of the samples taken during the excavations at Newquay merited some analysis of the charcoal. The majority were assigned to the Late Iron Age and Roman periods and represented material from a series of settlement features, including ditches, postholes and pits. The charcoal offered the potential to examine the use of wood for fuel in this phase and to explore the availability and selection of local woodland resources. Additionally, some material from Early Bronze Age, Middle Bronze Age and Middle Iron Age phases was analysed for comparison. The results of identifications made in advance of radiocarbon dating are also included in this report.

Methodology

Standard identification procedures were followed using identification keys (Hather 2000; Schweingruber 1990) and modern reference material. The charcoal was fractured and examined at low magnification (up to x45), with representative fragments examined in longitudinal sections at high magnification (up to x400). Where there were abundant fragments a representative sample was identified (between 20 and 50 fragments, depending upon diversity). For all sparser assemblages, 100 per cent of the identifiable material (>2mm) was examined. Observations on maturity and other features were made where appropriate. Classification and nomenclature follow that of Stace 1997. The results are presented below by period and feature type.

Results

The condition of the charcoal was very variable, ranging from excellent preservation of large fragments of roundwood to small, scrappy, heavily sediment infused pieces. A total of 863 fragments were examined from which 11 taxa were positively identified:

Fagaceae:

Quercus spp., (oak), large tree, two native species, not distinguishable anatomically.

Betulaceae:

Betula spp. (birch), trees or shrubs, two native species, not distinguishable anatomically.

Alnus glutinosa, Gaertn., (alder), tree, sole native species.

Corylus avellana L., (hazel), shrub or small tree, only native species.

Salicaceae:

Salix spp. (willow) and / or *Populus* spp. (poplar), several native species, rarely possible to separate. Both are trees although there is variation within the genera.

Rosaceae:

Rosa spp. (rose), shrubs, several native species

Prunus spp., trees or shrubs, including *P. spinosa* L. (blackthorn), *P. avium* L. (wild cherry) and *P. padus* L. (bird cherry), all native, which can sometimes be separated on the basis of ray width. Only *P. spinosa* was positively identified, but the variability in ray width suggests that another taxon (probably *P. avium* as *P. padus* had a more northern distribution) is also represented. Later phases may also include *P. domestica* (cultivated plum), a Roman introduction, which is difficult to distinguish from *P. spinosa*.

Maloideae, subfamily of various shrubs and small trees including several genera, *Pyrus* (pear), *Malus* (apple), *Sorbus* (rowan / service / whitebeam) and *Crataegus* (hawthorn), which are rarely distinguishable by anatomical characteristics.

Fabaceae:

Cytisus/Ulex, broom / gorse, shrubs, several native species, are not distinguishable anatomically. The presence of *Ulex* spines in a couple of the samples suggests that this species is likely to be represented.

Celastraceae:

Euonymus europaeus L., (spindle tree), shrub or small tree, native.

Aquifoliaceae:

Ilex aquifolium L., (holly), evergreen tree or shrub, native.

The results are presented by phase, with discussion of individual features (Tables 7.1 to 7.6 below).

Early Bronze Age

Pit [163] (Table 7.1)

Pit [163] was associated with Beaker pottery (Quinnell, Chapter 3) and an Early Bronze Age radiocarbon date on a hazelnut shell (Chapter 8). The charcoal from context (162) was abundant, with a mixed assemblage of *Quercus* sp. (oak) and *Corylus avellana* (hazel), and rare fragments of Maloideae (hawthorn / apple group). Some of the hazel charcoal exhibited asymmetrically shaped insect tunnels, indicating that the wood had been either deliberately seasoned or collected as deadwood prior to burning. This suggests that it was deliberately taken for fuel rather than related to collection practices for hazelnuts, of which a large quantity was recovered (J Jones, Chapter 6). Evidence for roundwood was recorded in both the Maloideae and the hazel charcoal. The oak was, in many fragments and highly vitrified, which obscured the evidence for maturity; only one fragment was confirmed as heartwood and one as roundwood.

The charcoal from this feature is consistent with the type of wood that would have been readily available in Late Neolithic / Early Bronze Age Cornwall; oak-hazel woodland and margin or hedgerow types. The use of small diameter roundwood and some mature oak is appropriate for general domestic fuel use and could have been sourced from managed or unmanaged woodlands. The evidence from the insect tunnels may suggest stockpiling of fuel supplies, but the absence of additional comparanda prohibits any firm interpretation.

Middle Bronze Age

Structure 1 (Table 7.1)

Two samples from the Middle Bronze Age roundhouse in Field 3 were examined. Other postholes from this area (such as [228] and [283]) produced only rare fragments or flecks of charcoal which were not analysed. Posthole [226] contained a fairly sparse assemblage, although with some large fragments, which was all identified as *Quercus* sp. (oak). Strong infusion of sediment into the pores prohibited examination of maturity but the general ring curvature appearance suggested trunkwood rather than roundwood. It is possible that the material represents the burnt remains of an oak post, but there was no on-site evidence for burning *in situ*, so the charcoal may represent unrelated burnt debris which accumulated in the feature post-abandonment of the building.

By contrast, pit [300] produced an abundant quantity of charcoal which, although dominated by *Quercus* sp. (oak), evidenced a range of other taxa, including *Betula* sp. (birch), *Corylus avellana* (hazel), Maloideae (hawthorn group), *Cytisus/Ulex* (broom / gorse), *Euonymus europaeus* (spindle tree) and *Ilex aquifolium* (holly). Much of the charcoal, including the oak, derived from small diameter roundwood, including some young stems of 3-4 years growth. The presence of broken pottery and worked stone in the pit suggests that it may have been deliberately backfilled (Chapter 11, below) and the charcoal probably derived from domestic fuel waste. The character of the wood is appropriate for domestic waste and indicates that a variety of taxa from mixed

Table 7.1 Charcoal from Early and Middle Bronze Age features.

	Phase	EBA	MBA	
	Feature type	Pit	Posthole	Pit
	Cut Number	[163]	[226]	[300]
	Context Number	(162)	(225)	(299)
Quercus sp.	Oak	24 (hr)	18	30 (rs)
Betula sp.	Birch			1
Corylus avellana L.	Hazel	21 (r)		5 (r)
Alnus/Corylus	Alder / hazel			2
Maloideae	Hawthorn group	4 (r)		2
Cytisus/Ulex	Broom / gorse			1r
Euonymus europaeus L.	Spindle			2r
Ilex aquifolium L.	Holly			2
Indeterminate		1		5rb
Total		50	18	50

r=roundwood; b=bark; h=heartwood; s-sapwood; (brackets denotes recorded in some fragments only or *cf* identification).

deciduous woodland, hedgerow, scrub and heathland habitats was utilized.

Middle Iron Age

Structure 2 (Table 7.2)

The sample from pit [298] produced a rich assemblage of charcoal, with a diverse range of taxa, including *Quercus* sp. (oak), *Betula* sp. (birch), *Corylus avellana* (hazel), *Prunus* sp. (cherry / blackthorn), Maloideae (hawthorn group), *Cytisus/Ulex* (broom / gorse), *Euonymus europaeus* (spindle tree) and *Ilex aquifolium* (holly). Much of the material derived from roundwood, with moderate to strong ring curvature evident (although whole stems were not preserved). The assemblage was strikingly similar to that of Middle Bronze Age pit [300], to the extent that it is surprising that they came from such different phases, confirmed by radiocarbon dating as well as the pottery evidence. It is notable that these two samples were more taxonomically diverse than any others in either phase and contained the only identifications of spindle wood. This taxon was, as the name suggests, commonly used for turning and artefact making, but it also makes a good charcoal fuel (Edlin 1949).

Structure A1 (Table 7.2)

This area contained various associated features bounded by a possible structure from which charcoal from ring-gully [220] and posthole [233] was examined. Both assemblages were dominated by *Quercus* sp. (oak), with rare fragments of *Prunus* sp. (blackthorn / cherry) and *Cytisus/Ulex* (broom / gorse) from [233]. Most of the oak fragments from ring-gully [220] came from heartwood, but maturity was difficult to determine in posthole [233] since the charcoal was exceptionally comminuted. The charcoal presumably represents fuel waste from the activities that were occurring within the structure, but the absence of associated finds makes interpretation difficult. The assemblage of mature oak would be consistent with burnt structural remains or charcoal fuel (for industrial activities), rather than typical of domestic waste.

Late Iron Age to early Roman period

Hollow 1 (Table 7.3)

Several features in Hollow 1 produced Late Iron Age cordoned ware and the radiocarbon dates indicated activity within the first century BC, extending into the first century AD. The quantity of charcoal in the hollow was generally low, with rich assemblages from only two pits; [309] (sample 66) and [346]. Both of these were dominated by *Quercus* sp. (oak), with some *Corylus avellana* (hazel), *Prunus spinosa* (blackthorn) and Maloideae (hawthorn group). Additional taxa were recorded in the sparser assemblages from features [322], [340] and [373], including *Populus/Salix* (poplar / willow) and *Cytisus/Ulex* (broom / gorse). The single fragment of *Ulmus/Cytisus/Ulex* is probably an additional broom or gorse, but there was <1 ring to confirm the identification.

The majority of the charcoal derived from roundwood fragments, with strong ring curvature and a minimum

Table 7.2 Charcoal from Middle Iron Age features.

	Group	S2	Structure A1	
	Feature type	Pit	Ring-gully	Posthole
	Cut Number	[298]	[220]	[233]
	Context Number	(297)	(219)	(232)
Quercus sp.	Oak	16 (hrs)	30 (h)	24 (r)
Betula sp.	Birch	2		
Prunus sp.	Cherry type	6r		3
Maloideae	Hawthorn group	11r		
Cytisus/Ulex	Broom / gorse	4r		3r
Euonymus europaeus L.	Spindle	5r		
Ilex aquifolium L.	Holly	1		
Indeterminate	Diffuse	5r		
Total		50	30	30

r=roundwood; b=bark; h=heartwood; s-sapwood; (brackets denotes recorded in some fragments only or *cf* identification).

Table 7.3 Charcoal from Late Iron Age features.

Group	Feature type	H1					H2	
		Pit	Ring-gully	Posthole	Pit	Pit	Pit	Layer
	Cut Number	[309]	[322]	[340]	[346]	[373]	[418]	NA
	Context Number	(308)	(321)	(339)	(345)	(372)	(417)	(457)
Ulmus/Cytisus/Ulex	Elm / broom / gorse					1		
Quercus sp.	Oak	20 (hsr)			21 (hsr)		8 (sr)	
Corylus avellana L.	Hazel	7r	3r		4r		3	
Alnus/Corylus	Alder / hazel		2r					
Populus/Salix	Poplar / willow			4				
Prunus spinosa L.	Blackthorn		5r		3r			9
Prunus sp.	Cherry type			1r			3r	21r
Maloideae	Hawthorn group	1r			2r			
Cytisus/Ulex	Broom / gorse		18r			4r	11r	
Indeterminate		2b	2r					
Total		30	30	5	30	5	25	30

r=roundwood; b=bark; h=heartwood; s-sapwood; (brackets denotes recorded in some fragments only or *cf* (identification).

age of 6 years. Some of the oak heartwood in fill (308) in pit [309] was relatively slow grown, with a radius of 11mm and age of 26+ years. Fragments of hazel showed evidence for insect tunnels, with some charred fungal hyphae also observed. In common with the wood-boring beetles, this indicates a significant duration of time between cutting / gathering and combustion, in which the wood was subject to fungal attack.

The evidence suggests that the pit assemblages represent deposits of spent fuel waste, in which oak was the main fuel used, with a range of supplementary taxa of understorey (hazel) or woodland margins (hawthorn, blackthorn). Charcoal from the other features, being sparser, derived from more dispersed material, but indicates that fuel was additionally sourced from heathland (broom / gorse) and wetland type (willow / poplar) habitats.

Hollow 2 (Table 7.3)

Two samples from Hollow 2 were examined, from pit [418] and layer (457). Neither sample was particularly rich, with *circa* 100 per cent of the identification material identified. Layer (457) was composed exclusively of *Prunus* charcoal, some of which was confirmed (on the basis of ray width) as *Prunus spinosa* (blackthorn), but the majority could not be positively distinguished and it is possible that another cherry species may also be present. The character of the wood was predominantly young stems of 4-7 years. The charcoal from pit [418] was more varied, with *Quercus* sp. (oak), *Corylus avellana* (hazel), *Prunus* sp. (blackthorn / cherry) and *Cytisus/Ulex* (broom / gorse). The results, though lesser in quantity, are comparable to the pattern of fuelwood use indicated by the charcoal from Hollow 1.

Pit [104] (Table 7.4)

This feature produced an abundant assemblage, chiefly comprising *Quercus* sp. (oak) and *Corylus avellana* (hazel), with traces of *Populus/Salix* (poplar / willow) and Maloideae (hawthorn group) (Table 7.4). The hazel derived mostly from roundwood of small diameter. This feature was not, however, dated.

Area A2 and Structure A3

The features from these areas spanned the Late Iron Age to the early second century AD and it is notable that they were generally sparse in charcoal. The samples examined from A2 'cemetery' area and Structure A3 produced scant identifiable fragments from which *Quercus* sp. (oak), *Alnus glutinosa* (alder), Maloideae (hawthorn group) and *Cytisus/Ulex* (broom / gorse) were detected. In common with the other assemblages of Late Iron Age / early Roman period date, fuelwood was drawn from oak-hazel woodland, with traces of taxa drawn from other habitat types such as hedgerow / scrub, and heathland. Ditch [127] produced the only confirmed identification of alder, which prefers wet ground, adjacent to streams. Given the paucity of evidence for it, alder was probably not growing in the near vicinity of the site.

Table 7.4 Charcoal from Area A2, Structure A3 and Enclosure Area (north).

	Group		A2	Structure A3		Enclosure Area (north)
	Feature type	Pit	Ditch	Pit	Ditch	Ditch
	Cut Number	[104]	[120]	[123]	[127]	[141]
	Context Number	(103)	(119)	(121)	(126)	(140)
Quercus sp.	Oak	22 (hs)	3r	10		30 (hsr)
Alnus glutinosa Gaertn.	Alder				1	
Corylus avellana L.	hazel	26r				
Populus/Salix	Poplar / willow	1				
Maloideae	Hawthorn group	1r			3r	
Cytisus/Ulex	Broom / gorse			5r		
Indeterminate					2r	
Total		50	8	10	6	30

r=roundwood; b=bark; h=heartwood; s=sapwood; (brackets denotes recorded in some fragments only or *cf* (identification).

Roman period

Enclosure Area (north) (Table 7.4)

Only one sample from this area merited analysis. Ditch [141] produced an abundant assemblage, which was all *Quercus* sp. (oak). Evidence of maturity was largely obscured by high levels of vitrification, but traces of heartwood as well as younger roundwood were noted. The assemblage was similar to that of pit [320].

Enclosure Area (south) (Table 7.5)

This area produced the largest assemblage of charcoal, although it included some multiple samples from the same features, which were examined to determine if there were any differences within features. The features were generally phased to the later first to second century AD. Preservation was generally good, although there was some vitrification in oak fragments.

Ditch [201] contained a deposit of burnt branches of *Cytisus/Ulex* (broom / gorse), including a very large fragment recovered from context (199); this was roundwood with pith but no bark, 43mm in length, with a radius of 10mm and 12+ years in age. Ditch [204] also produced a quantity of burnt broom / gorse roundwood, with *Quercus* sp. (oak) from the richer assemblages, and lesser components of *Betula* sp. (birch), *Corylus avellana* (hazel), *Rosa* sp. (rose) and probable *Ilex aquifolium* (holly). Taxonomic variations within the contexts of this ditch indicate several discrete episodes of deposition, which is supported by the plant evidence: large quantities of burnt redeposited hazelnut shells of Neolithic date in the primary fill (208), with assemblages of cereal grains in the upper fills (205 and 206) (J Jones, Chapter 6). Clearly the fuel associated with the burning of the hazelnut shells was mostly oak and hazel, while the burning of cereal waste was associated with the use of broom / gorse as fuel.

Broom / gorse was also dominant in the assemblages from pit [367]. By contrast, the assemblages from pit [320] and scoop [326] were dominated by oak, with some *Alnus/Corylus* (alder or hazel) and *Prunus* sp. (cherry type) in [326]. The presence of burnt *Ulex* spines in (20), fill of ditch [204] (J Jones, Chapter 6) and also noted in (366), the bottom fill of [367] strongly suggest that gorse is the charcoal represented in [204] and [367], and probably across the whole site assemblage. However, the distinction from broom is not possible on anatomical grounds alone. Individually, none of the features from Enclosure Area (south) produced diverse assemblages, which suggests that they represent deliberate deposits of burnt fuel waste rather than generally dispersed material. It is clear that oak and gorse were the main wood types utilized for fuel.

Structure A6 (Table 7.6)

The charcoal from the second century AD features associated with Structure A6 was limited to relatively small assemblages from pits [450], [453] and [456]. Only the latter produced abundant charcoal, but it was clear that all three were dominated by *Cytisus/Ulex* (broom / gorse), with rare fragments of *Quercus* sp. (oak). This picture is consistent with the broadly contemporary features of Enclosure Area (south).

Structure 3 (Table 7.6)

This group represents the latest material examined from Newquay, with features of late second to early fourth

Table 7.5 Charcoal from Enclosure Area (south) features.

	Group	Enclosure Area (south)								
	Feature type	Ditch					Pit	Scoop	Ring-gully	Pit	
	Cut Number	[201]	[204]				[320]	[326]	[332]	[367]	
	Context Number	(202)	(203)	(205)	(206)	(208)	(319)	(325)	(331)	(366)	(371)
Quercus sp.	Oak		8r	3r	9 (hr)	17 (hr)	30 (sr)	15 (hr)	5		
Betula sp.	Birch			1r							
Corylus avellana L.	Hazel						8		3		
Alnus/Corylus	Alder / hazel						4	5r	(1)		
Rosa sp.	Rose			3r							
Prunus sp.	Cherry type							5r			
Cytisus/Ulex	Broom / gorse	30r	1r	23r	21r				4r	20r	20r
cf *Ilex aquifolium* L.	Holly						1				
Indeterminate									3		
Total		30	9	23	30	30	30	20	16	20	20

r=roundwood; b=bark; h=heartwood; s=sapwood; (brackets denotes recorded in some fragments only or *cf* identification).

Table 7.6 Charcoal from Roman period features.

	Group	Structure A6			Structure 3					
	Feature type	Pit	Pit	Pit	Pit	Posthole	Pit	Pit	Hollow	Pit
	Cut Number	[450]	[453]	[456]	[148]	[177]	[143]	[187]	[146]	[198]
	Context Number	(449)	(452)	(455)	(147)	(176)	(142)	(186)	(145)	(197)
Quercus sp.	Oak	1		1r	11 (r)		11r			
Corylus avellana L.	Hazel				6r		5r			
Populus/Salix	Poplar / willow				3r		3r		1	
Rosa sp.	Rose					1r				1r
Prunus sp.	Cherry type				(1)					3r
Cytisus/Ulex	Broom / gorse	9r	20r	19r	11r	4r	9r	10r		3r
Indeterminate									2	
Total		10	20	20	32	5	28	10	3	7

r=roundwood; b=bark; h=heartwood; s=sapwood; (brackets denotes recorded in some fragments only or *cf* identification).

centuries AD date. Of the six samples from Structure 3, all were relatively sparse in material and 100 per cent of the identifiable charcoal was examined. In common with the earlier Roman period samples, *Cytisus/Ulex* (broom / gorse) was well represented, present in all but one sample. Other taxa included *Quercus* sp. (oak), *Corylus avellana* (hazel), *Populus/Salix* (poplar / willow), *Rosa* sp. (rose) and *Prunus* sp. (blackthorn / cherry).

The majority of the material came from roundwood, including the oak, indicating the use of branch or stem wood of small diameter.

Discussion

Provenance of the charcoal

There was scant direct evidence at Newquay for specialized activities involving fire: no furnaces, hearths or cremations. In general, the charcoal assemblages would have derived from spent firewood, either deliberate dumps, which are usually associated with other waste products (for example, crop processing debris, broken pottery, slag or butchery waste), or from longer-term accumulation of charcoal into open or partially infilled features. The latter assemblages tend to be smaller in quantity and fragment size and may have had multiple origins. Differentiation of deposit type and likely provenance of assemblages at Newquay was generally difficult to determine. However, some areas of Late Iron Age and Roman period features (including Hollow 1, Hollow 2 and Structure A6) were interpreted as working, cooking or storage areas. Hollow 1 was the only area where the evidence of burning *in situ* was a direct connection for the charcoal assemblages, although it is unclear exactly what function was served. The recovery of dispersed iron ore in ditches across the site indicates that some smelting is likely to have occurred in the vicinity. Some of the charcoal, therefore, may have originated in metalworking activities and represent the spent remains of charcoal, rather than wood fuel.

Charcoal assemblages associated with iron smelting or smithing are commonly dominated by oak, with supplementary taxa used for kindling. The results from pits [309] and [346] (which evidenced *in situ* burning) are consistent with this model, but the other assemblages were composed of other, diverse taxa, predominantly comprising roundwood. If associated with metalworking, this would indicate that roundwood was collected from a range of taxa for conversion to charcoal for use as fuel. The use of gorse in metalworking contexts is unusual, as it provides a high but fast heat suitable for some purposes but not others. It was commonly used to heat medieval bread ovens, for instance (Gale and Cutler 2000, 260), and is frequently found in domestic type assemblages of Roman date. Nonetheless, industrial fuels at Little Quoit Farm, St Columb Major, consisted principally of oak and broom / gorse (Gale 2009–10). Its presence in the hollow areas at Newquay suggests that either it was used as kindling or supplementary fuel for charcoal fires, or the assemblages include mixed domestic type waste.

Given the limitations in sourcing the origins of the charcoal assemblages, little interpretation on activity types can be made, except to say that there was no clear evidence for context-related variation; deposits from pits compared to ditches, for example, did not yield any patterns. Generally, assemblages were not very diverse; across the Late Iron Age and Roman period phases, there was a mean of 2.2 taxa per deposit. Of greater interest, however, is using the data to examine the exploitation of the local environment for fuelwood supplies.

Local resources

It is not surprising that three taxa (oak, hazel and gorse) dominate the charcoal assemblage from Newquay. These taxa commonly occur in charcoal records from sites in Cornwall. They occur on sites from the Early Bronze Age, as at the Lower Boscaswell Beaker burnt mound (Gale 2006) and Beaker pits at Sennen (Challinor 2012), the Iron Age, with settlement evidence from Camelford (Challinor 2015a) and Trevelgue Head (Gale 2011), and Roman period, with, for instance, domestic and industrial fuels at St Newlyn East (Gale 2004) and Penhale Round (Challinor 2015b). At the nearby Middle Bronze Age roundhouse settlement at Trethellan Farm, Vanessa Straker (1991) pointed out that, in a coastal location, the possibility that driftwood may have been collected for use as fuel means that not all of the wood may have been locally grown and there is some evidence for this at the Roman period settlement at Atlantic Road, Newquay, where non-native taxa were found in the charcoal (Gale, forthcoming). However, at this site, there is nothing to suggest unusual taxa and, as seen above, the results here are consistent with those from other sites, reflecting the landscape of oak-hazel woodland prevalent in the early prehistoric period (Straker *et al* 2008a). Clearance and a consequent rise in heathland is thought to date to the second millennium BC, with pollen evidence from Bodmin Moor indicating intense pasture from the Middle Bronze Age (*ibid*). Of course, some local variations should be allowed for, but the evidence from multi-disciplinary studies indicates that Roman period impact on the woodland vegetation of the area was minimal (Straker *et al* 2008b), so the greatest episodes of landscape change had occurred by the later prehistoric phases.

The charcoal evidence from Newquay shows an appreciable increase in the exploitation of heathland resources by the Roman period (Fig 7.1). Although the Bronze Age dataset is limited, it appears that broom / gorse is a minor component of the fuel supplies, with most wood sourced from oak-hazel woodland. Oak, although with less hazel and more hedgerow type taxa, still represents more than 65 per cent of the charcoal assemblage in the Middle Iron Age. This suggests that either widespread clearance of the native woodland had not occurred at Newquay by the Middle Iron Age, or that there were enough remnants of oak-hazel woodland surviving on sheltered hillslopes to supply adequate fuel. The chronological gaps in evidence for these phases limit the interpretation, but it is clear that the definite Roman period phases see a rise in the use of gorse and the pattern is confirmed by ubiquity analysis. Overall, there is little evidence for the use of wetland resources, with some presence of poplar or willow and only a trace of alder, but hedgerow / woodland margin taxa are present, in varying quantities, throughout the record.

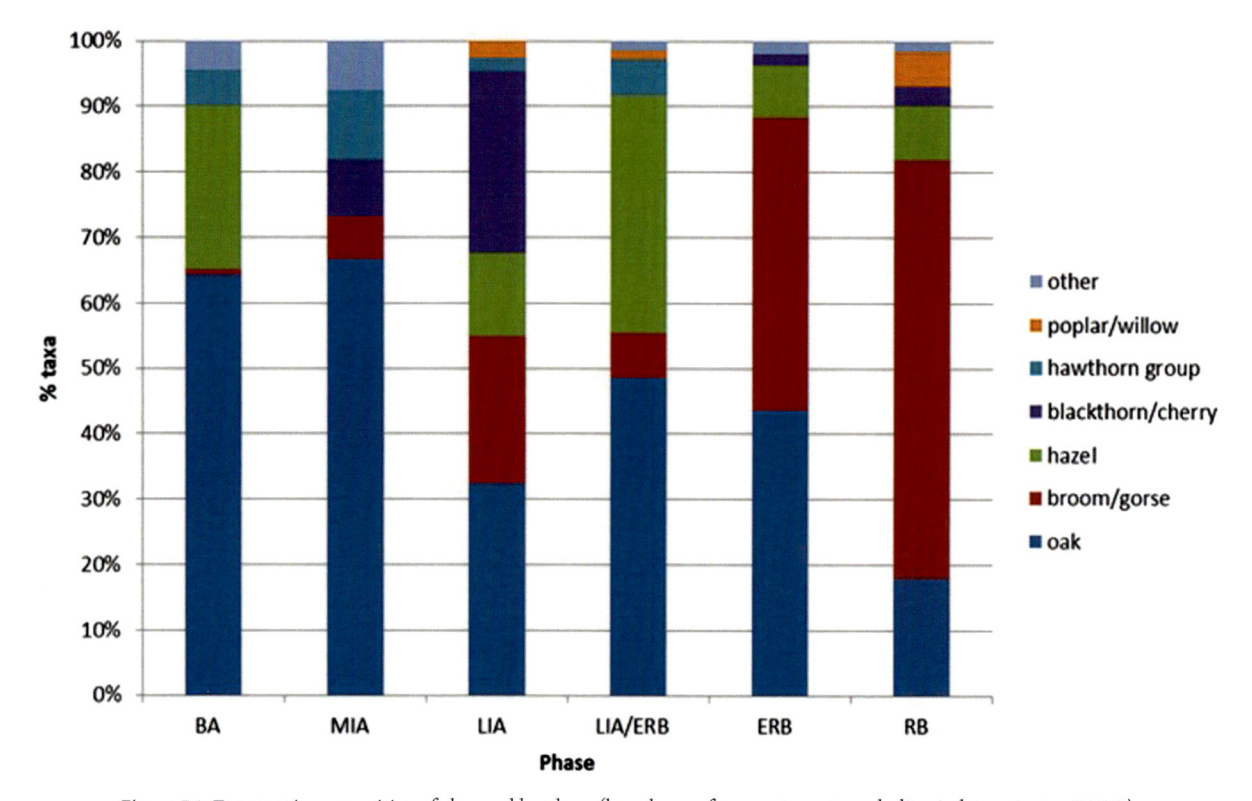

Figure 7.1: Taxonomic composition of charcoal by phase (based upon fragment count, excluding indeterminates; N=841).

Chapter 8

The radiocarbon dating

Andy M Jones

The aim of the dating strategy was to obtain determinations from key features and contexts which would support and enhance the data obtained from the stratigraphic and artefactual analyses to help provide a chronological framework for activity within the project area. Secure dating was essential as the linear nature of the investigations meant that most of the archaeological features were only partially captured in the confines of the road corridor and wider stratigraphical relationships could not be investigated. Furthermore, although a large number of features were uncovered, many did not contain any artefacts or none that were closely datable (for example, Structure 2), which meant that their phasing was essentially 'floating'.

All of the samples were submitted for accelerator mass spectrometry (AMS) dating to the Scottish Universities Environmental Research Centre (SUERC) at Glasgow.

A total of 16 samples were submitted. These consisted of residue from potsherds, charred plant macrofossils, including cereal grains, and charcoal from short-lived species such as gorse and from oak roundwood (Table 8.1 and Fig 8.1).

Results

Neolithic Period

Ditch [204]

A single radiocarbon date was obtained from the primary fill of ditch [204]. The determination from ditch fill (208), 4420 ± 28 BP, 3316–2992 cal BC (SUERC-62678), was on a charred hazelnut shell. The date falls in the Middle to Late Neolithic period. This is a period for which few monuments are known in the

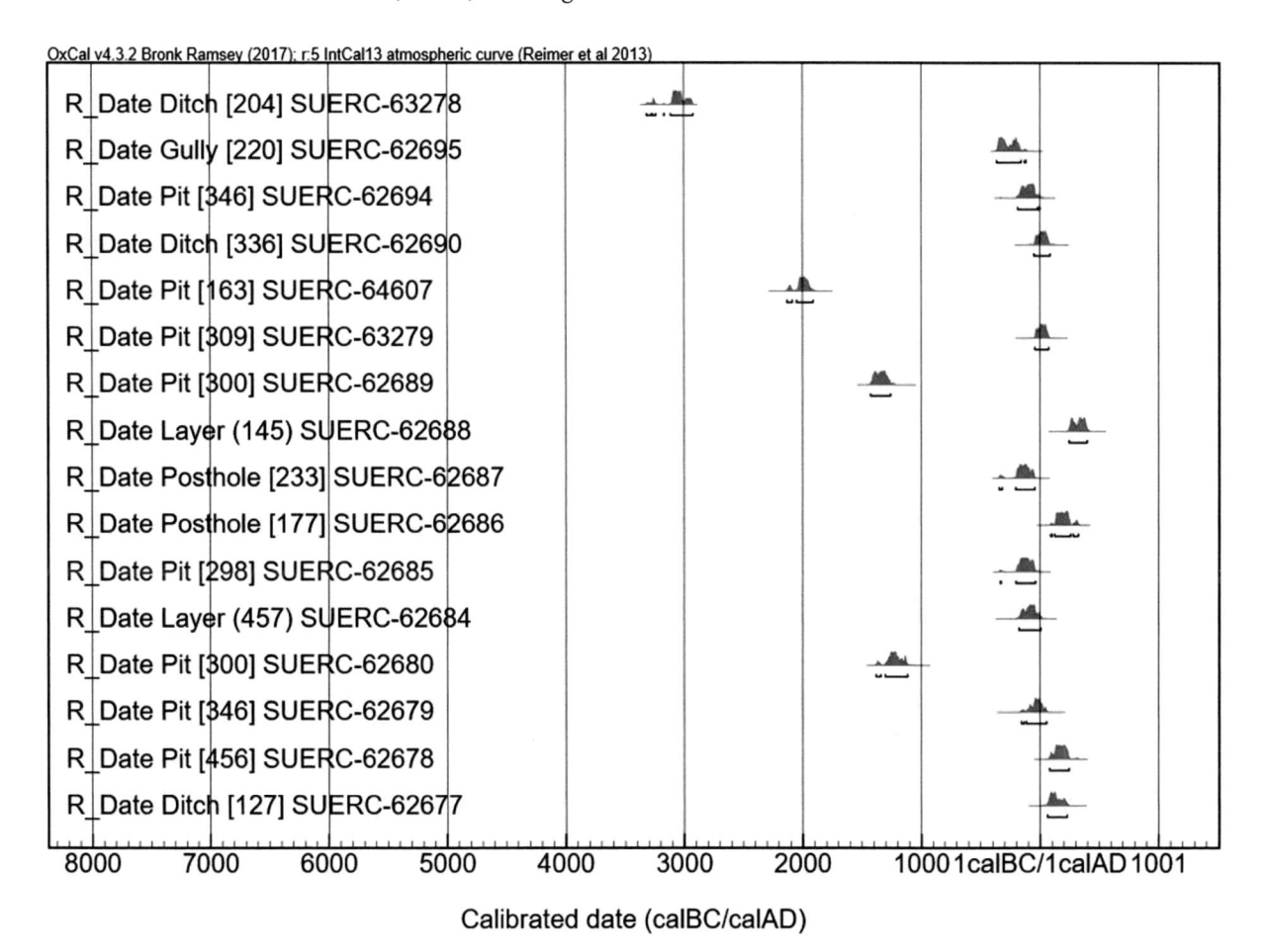

Figure 8.1 Radiocarbon date ranges from the Newquay Strategic Road corridor.

south west and ceramics, especially in Cornwall, are generally scarce (Jones, forthcoming c). However, in this case the presence of much later finds means that the radiocarbon date is unlikely to relate to the actual age of the ditch and, like the majority of the flintwork (Lawson-Jones, Chapter 5), the nutshell is likely to have been redeposited into a much later feature.

Early Bronze Age

Pit [204]

A single radiocarbon date was obtained from the upper fill of pit [163]. The determination from fill (162), 3635 ± 29 BP, 2131–1912 cal BC (SUERC-64607) was obtained on a charred hazelnut shell. The date falls in the first centuries of the second millennium cal BC, the Early Bronze Age. Until recently there were very few dates associated with Beaker pottery in Cornwall (Jones and Quinnell 2006a). The last ten years, however, has seen an increase in the number of Beaker-associated dates, especially in relation to pits. The significance of the date is discussed below in Chapter 10.

Middle Bronze Age

Structure 1

Two radiocarbon determinations were obtained from this structure. Both were from samples within pit [300], a large feature just inside the entranceway.

The determination from pit fill (299), 2995 ± 34 BP, 1382–1117 cal BC (SUERC-62680) was on charcoal. It is consistent with the anticipated date of Structure 1, a hollow-set roundhouse of Middle Bronze Age type. The second determination, 3081 ± 34 BP, 1427–1261 cal BC (SUERC-62689) was obtained on residue from the pottery within the pit. The determination on the residue appears to be earlier than that from the charcoal and one possibility is that the pottery is older than the pit into which it was placed (see Chapter 10).

Middle Iron Age

Structure 2

The determination from pit [298], fill (297), 2100 ± 34 BP, 337–40 cal BC (SUERC-62685) is consistent with the Middle Iron Age pottery which was present in small quantities. It is the earliest of the Iron Age structures. The lack of features, occupation deposits or evidence for recutting, suggests that it may not have been a long-lived structure.

Structure A1

Structure A1 comprised a group of postholes and pits enclosed to the east by a gully [220]. The gully may have defined the perimeter of a building, and the postholes may have been a structural component. All the distinctive pottery was of Middle Iron Age type. Two radiocarbon determinations were obtained, one from a posthole and the other from the ring-gully.

The determination on charcoal from posthole [233], fill (232), 2114 ± 34 BP, 346–45 cal BC (SUERC-62687), was from a feature located within the area defined by the ring-gully. The second radiocarbon determination from ring-gully [220], fill (219), 2179 ± 34 BP, 365–119 cal BC (SUERC-62695) was on ceramic residue. Both determinations confirm that the structure was associated with Middle Iron Age activity and that the posthole is likely to be associated with the ring-gully.

Late Iron Age to Roman period

Hollow 1

The area defined as Hollow 1, comprised a slight depression which was associated with intercutting ring-gullies, ditches and a concentration of pits. Two of the ring-gullies [335] and [408] may have formed an oval structure, within which the majority of pits were found. The features in this area produced finds of Late Iron Age pottery, none of which need date after the arrival of Rome. Four radiocarbon determinations were obtained on features within or close to hollow 1.

The earliest determinations are those from pit [346]. Charcoal from fill (345) produced a date of 2028 ± 34 BP, 159 cal BC – cal AD 55 (SUERC-62679), and a second on ceramic residue of 2077 ± 34 BP, 189–1 cal BC (SUERC-62694). These dates are broadly consistent with one another. This pit lay outside the space defined by ring-gullies [335] and [408] and is probably associated with a Late Iron Age, first century cal BC phase of activity. A third determination on charred hulled wheat was obtained from pit [309], 1984 ± 29 BP, 46 cal BC – cal AD 74 (SUERC-63279). The date from the pit spans the Iron Age–Roman transition period.

The final determination from ditch [336], fill (335), 1981 ± 34 BP, 52 cal BC – cal AD 85 (SUERC-62690) was obtained on ceramic residue. This date is slightly later than the others but the pottery suggests it was deposited before the arrival of Roman influence: it might suggest that an oval structure was located on the site of earlier Iron Age activity.

Hollow 2

The determination from layer (457), 2065 ± 34 BP, 179 cal BC – cal AD 5 (SUERC-62684) was obtained on charcoal from the deposit, which was found within a slight hollow associated with a large number of pits and postholes likely to have formed a rectangular structure. The date, in common with that indicated by the Late Iron Age pottery (Quinnell, Chapter 3), suggests activity in the first century cal BC.

Structure 3

Two radiocarbon determinations were obtained from this structure. The dated samples came from a posthole and the infilling layer.

The determination from posthole [177], fill (176), 1816 ± 34 BP, cal AD 90–325 (SUERC-62686) was on charcoal. It is consistent with the anticipated date of the Structure 3, a hollow-set oval building which was associated with Roman period finds. The second date from layer (145), 1713 ± 34 BP, cal AD 245–399 (SUERC-62688), was from a deposit inside the structure. The date appears to be a little later than that from posthole [177] and this would be consistent with the stratigraphy.

Overall the dating and the general lack of intercutting features suggest that the structure was relatively short-lived and in use during the second to fourth centuries AD. The artefactual assemblage suggests that the structure may have been built in the late second to early third centuries and went out of use during the fourth century AD.

Structure A3, ditch [127]

The determination from fill (126), 1879 ± 34 BP, cal AD 61–228 (SUERC-62677) was a surprise. Ditch [127], which formed the eastern side of the oval Structure A3 contained Middle Iron Age **P7** and was therefore assigned to the later prehistoric period. The determination, however, places the ring-ditch in the Roman period, which means that the pottery is either residual or curated (Quinnell, Chapter 3 and Chapter 11). The pottery from Structure A3 features as a group would be appropriate for the first century BC to third century AD.

Structure A6, pit [456]

The determination from fill (455), 1842 ± 34 BP, cal AD 80–245 (SUERC-62678) is perhaps a little earlier than the earlier second century which the pottery suggests and is consistent with the finds assemblage overall if the Trethurgy bowl **S7** (Quinnell, Chapter 4) from an adjacent group of features is taken into account.

Table 8.1 Radiocarbon determinations from Newquay Strategic Road corridor.

Feature	Context	Material	Lab no	Age BP years	Calendrical years 95.4% probability
Ditch [127]	(126) fill of ditch in Structure A3.	Charcoal (twig)	SUERC-62677	1879 ± 34	AD 61 – 228
Pit [456]	(455) fill of pit in Structure A6.	*Ulex* charcoal	SUERC-62678	1842 ± 34	AD 80 – 245
Pit [346]	(345) fill of pit in Hollow 1.	*Quercus* charcoal	SUERC-62679	2028 ± 34	159 – 134 BC (4%) 116 BC – AD 55 (91.4%)
Pit [300]	(299) fill of pit in Structure 1.	*Ilex* charcoal	SUERC-62680	2995 ± 34	1382 – 1343 BC (6.7%) 1306 – 1117 BC (88.7%)
Layer (457)	(457), layer in Hollow 2.	*Prunus* charcoal	SUERC-62684	2065 ± 34	179 BC – AD 5
Pit [298]	(297) fill of pit within Structure 2.	*Ulex* charcoal	SUERC-62685	2100 ± 34	337 – 360 BC (0.6%) 204 – 40 BC (94.8%)
Posthole [177]	(166) of posthole within Structure 3.	*Rosa* charcoal	SUERC-62686	1816 ± 34	AD 90 – 100 (1.2%) AD 123 – 260 (85.7%) AD 280 – 325 (8.5%)
Posthole [233]	(232) fill of posthole within Structure A1.	*Ulex* charcoal	SUERC-62687	2114 ± 34	346 – 321 BC (4.1%) 206 – 45 BC (91.3%)
Layer (145)	(457), layer within Structure 3.	*Salix* charcoal	SUERC-62688	1713 ± 34	AD 245 – 399
Pit [300]	(299) fill of pit in Structure 1.	Ceramic residue	SUERC-62689	3081 ± 34	1427 – 1261 BC
Ditch [336]	(335) fill of ditch within Hollow 1.	Ceramic residue	SUERC-62690	1981 ± 34	52 BC – AD 85
Pit [346]	(345) fill of pit in Hollow 1.	Ceramic residue	SUERC-62694	2077 ± 34	189 – 20 BC (93.2%) 12 – 1 BC (2.2%)

Feature	Context	Material	Lab no	Age BP years	Calendrical years 95.4% probability
Gully [220]	(219) fill of gully within Structure A1.	Ceramic residue	SUERC-62695	2179 ± 34	365 – 161 BC (94%) 131 – 119 BC (1.4%)
Ditch [204]	(208) fill of ditch [204].	Charred hazelnut	SUERC-63278	4420 ± 28	3316 – 3273 BC (3.6%) 3266 – 3237 BC (6.6%) 3168 – 3165 BC (0.3%) 3112 – 2992 BC (85%)
Pit [309]	(308) fill of pit within Hollow 1.	Charred grain: hulled wheat	SUERC-63279	1984 ± 29	46 BC – AD 74
Pit [163]	(162) upper fill of pit.	Charred hazelnut	SUERC-64607	3635 ± 29	2131 – 2086 BC (11.7%) 2051 – 1912 BC (83.7%)

SECTION 4
INTERPRETATION AND CONCLUSIONS

Chapter 9

Introduction: Themes for discussion

Andy M Jones

Considering its relatively short length, the approximately 375m stretch of the Newquay Strategic Road corridor contained a remarkable density of archaeological features, which included structures, field boundaries, pits and hollows. The recorded sites spanned a period of more than a millennium and have greatly increased our knowledge of later prehistory and early Roman period settlement in the Newquay area.

It is, however, necessary to point out that, as with other linear investigations such as pipelines and road corridors, some frustration results from the only partial exposure of many settlement-related features (for example, Mudd and Joyce 2014, 102; Jones 2000–1). In many parts of the site it is impossible to disentangle the Iron Age and the Roman periods from one another. Some features, such as Hollow 1 were formed by pits and ring-gullies of both Late Iron Age and Roman period date, and there are many other features which do not have close dating at all. There is also a problem of redeposition of earlier artefacts into much later features. This is the result of recutting of ditches and repeated digging of pits in certain parts of the site.

In addition, and potentially more problematically, it is also the case that many of the gullies and ditches extended well beyond the confines of the road corridor, and consequently we do not know the full extent or form of the structures and field systems with which they were associated (Fig 9.1). There are also hints from the artefactual assemblage that occupation may have continued beyond the earlier Roman period but on present evidence it is not possible to determine the extent or character of the later activity.

Despite these limitations, several discrete features could be distinguished and disentangled from the background 'noise'. These included the Middle Bronze Age roundhouse, Structure 1, the Middle and Late Iron Age features Structure 2, Hollow 2 and Structure A1, and Structure 3 which dated to the Roman period. It is also possible to provide an outline phasing for many of the other excavated features. The following Chapter 10 is therefore organized chronologically, although obviously we do not suggest that activity or occupation in the area was divided into discrete temporal units which were entirely separate from one another.

Figure 9.1 Photograph of ring-gully [332] which is probably part of a structure of Roman period date which lies outside the road corridor. The size and form of the structure are unknown.

Figure 9.2 Photograph showing the quartz filled gully encircling Richard Lander Iron Age house 9, looking east.

The repeated engagement with a comparatively restricted locale over a considerable period is a significant finding, which invites interpretation. Indeed, it is the opportunity to consider the evidence for localized occupation from the perspective of the *longue durée* (Tilley 2017, 5–14), which makes the results from the project so interesting. This approach invites us to situate the recovered evidence in relation to performative practices. It also enables consideration of time from short-term cycles through to the longer-term influence of the past in the past (*cf* Bradley 2002). Oval structures and hollows defined by ring-gullies, for example, are found in all of the post Bronze Age phases, and, where entrances are identifiable, there is a preference for them to open towards the south or south east. This orientation occurs in all periods from the Middle Bronze Age onwards. Similarly, the deposition of artefacts and other materials into ditches and pits occurs in all periods and this is discussed further in Chapter 11. It is not suggested that such actions necessarily represent unbroken continuity of belief but they may reflect 'dispositions in means of inhabitation' which are passed down over time (for example, Jones 2013). Nonetheless, in some instances there may have been unbroken continuity in the occupation of the site, in particular during the Late Iron Age and Roman period. These are discussed below as one phase as there is no obvious interruption between them, and the use of the site area may have intensified and expanded over the period from *circa* 300 cal BC to AD 300.

In addition to the persistence in settlement activity, in each of the periods there are cross-cutting themes which run through the span of the site chronology. Chapter 10 therefore focuses on identifying the way that the area was inhabited and the types of structures which were in use over time, as well as the links between them. Again, we do not argue that values or associations were singular, remained constant or were so ingrained that they prohibited social change, but rather to explore the ways that certain regular practices, performative actions or social memory and stories of the place may have affected use of space over time (*cf*, for example, Connerton 1989; Bell 1992; Basso 1996). As Tim Ingold (2016, 80–81) has written, lives (and here extended to practices) over time can like lines become braided. The lives of children for example may diverge from those of their parents but they remember their grandparents' stories '… that in turn, will carry forward in life…'

The character of some of the deposits which were found within the investigated features is the main focus of discussion in the more broadly discursive Chapter 11. As will be discussed below, although there are difficulties with establishing formal continuity of religious practices from prehistory into the Roman and later periods, it is the case that the depositing of artefacts spans both periods and it is therefore an important element to consider in depth (for example, Hutton 2013, chapter 5).

Several commentators have drawn attention to evidence for 'structured' or 'special' deposits found in settlement-related contexts such as pits and boundaries as well as in domestic structures (Fig 9.2), which suggests that in the past the 'sacred' and the 'mundane' were frequently closely meshed within the settlement (for example, Hill 1995; Brück 1999a; Bradley 2005; Chadwick 2012; 2015; Baires and Baltus 2016). It is evident from the archaeological record and later mythological texts, that ritual and cosmology in Europe was frequently linked to the agricultural cycle, and this could have become a dominant metaphor in later prehistory, with symbolic connections being made between preparing the ground, growing crops and the harvest with the sequence of fertility, death and regeneration (Williams 2003; Graves 1999; Ovid 2004, 428; Leonard 2015b; Ten Harkel *et al* 2017). It is suggested below that although significant change is likely to have occurred, these underlying metaphors and associated practices also extended into the Roman period.

As will be seen, interpretation of 'special' deposits is not without difficulties, as some apparently 'special' or 'structured' deposits very possibly resulted (eventually) from day-to-day mundane activities in the formation of an archaeological record (*cf* Brudenell and Cooper 2008; Garrow 2012) and identifying truly 'special' deposits consequently requires very careful consideration (Chadwick 2015; Joy 2015). Part of Chapter 11 therefore examines the formation of particular deposits to determine the level of intentionality behind them, as well as, where possible, exploring the links between deposits found in different types of contemporary feature.

The second and concluding part of Chapter 11 reviews a related but distinct form of ritualized practice: the deliberate abandonment of houses. This has seen widespread discussion in the anthropological literature (Kis-Jovak *et al* 1988, 49; Waterson 1997, 137) and is well accepted in relation to Middle Bronze Age houses (Nowakowski 1991; Jones 2008; Ladle and Woodward 2009; Barnatt *et al* 2017, 120–121). However, potentially comparable practices in the later Iron Age and Roman periods have seen much less discussion (but see Sharples 2010, chapter 4 for Iron Age houses). Chapter 11 therefore takes the opportunity to review the post-Bronze Age evidence for ritualized abandonment from the south west peninsula and other parts of Britain.

Finally, Chapter 12 summarizes the outcomes and highlights from the project, as well as offering pointers for further research.

Chapter 10

Structures and boundaries: The wider later prehistoric and Roman period context

Andy M Jones

Aside from a single charred hazelnut shell assemblage which proved to be of Middle to Late Neolithic date, and a handful of flint artefacts, the archaeological intervention along the route of the Newquay Strategic Road corridor revealed four major episodes of activity, although as stated above, this does not indicate that these are discrete and necessarily disconnected from one another, or that during the periods before, between or after these chronologically identifiable 'phases' the site reverted to wilderness.

The remainder of this chapter discusses the results identified in these phases in more detail, to provide comparanda for the excavated sites and develop a picture of their wider context.

The Bronze Age (*circa* 2500 to 1100 cal BC)

Earlier Bronze Age (circa 25000-2000 cal BC)

The evidence for Early Bronze Age activity within the development area took the form of one or two Beaker associated pits and a number of lithic finds which for the most part were recovered from later contexts and are therefore residual.

Although pit [398] may have been of Early Bronze Age date, the only certain Early Bronze Age feature was pit [163], located towards the northern end of the stripped area. The deposits within the pit included charcoal, Beaker pottery, flint, cereal grains and fragments from charred hazel nutshells. A radiocarbon determination on the hazelnut dated to 3635 ± 29 BP, 2131–1912 cal BC (SUERC-64607). Although the radiocarbon determination is a little later than the majority of dated Beaker sites in the south west, the content of pit [163] is broadly comparable with several other Beaker-associated pits which have been recorded across Cornwall, including those at Treyarnon, Scarcewater, St Stephen-in-Brannel and Trebehor, near Porthcurno and Tregurra, near Truro (Jones and Taylor 2009–10; 2010, 5; Quinnell 2014c; Jones *et al* 2012; Taylor, forthcoming). The contents of these Beaker pits typically include flints and charcoal and often small quantities of charred foodstuffs. The deposits within several pits have been interpreted as representing the ritualized clearing up of debris or in some instances the more formalized burial of material culture (for example, Jones 2013). Although the evidence from the Newquay site is limited to just one pit, this interpretation is consistent with what was found there: the deposition of charcoal is likely to have been associated with the cooking of food, and the charred remnants of a meal (hazelnut shell and charred grains) may have been swept into the open pit along with sherds from a broken Beaker vessel and four discarded flints. Given the apparent absence of further Beaker associated pits in the immediate vicinity, it is possible that pit [163] was associated with a short-term occupation.

Middle Bronze Age (circa 1500-111 cal BC)

A later phase of Bronze Age activity was associated with Structure 1, a Middle Bronze Age hollow-set roundhouse, with a probable diameter of around 10m. Only the entrance area was located within the road corridor, and less half of the roundhouse could be examined. This means that any conclusions are partial and limited.

Structure 1 was clearly of hollow-set type and its probable size is comparable with the larger roundhouses of this type. These include Scarcewater house 1500 which was at least 12m in diameter and probably larger and Trethellan house 2222, which measured approximately 9.5m across (Jones and Taylor 2010, 16; Nowakowski 1991).

The radiocarbon determinations from pit [300], 2995 ± 34 BP, 1382–1117 cal BC (SUERC-62680) and 3081 ± 34 BP, 1427–1261 cal BC (SUERC-62689), place Structure 1 in the period *circa* 1400–1200 cal BC. This is consistent with the range of dates from other houses of this architectural type, which span the period 1500–1000 cal BC (Gossip and Jones 2008). However, given that only part of the site was investigated and only one feature dated, it is not possible to say how long the inhabitation of the roundhouse lasted, or whether the date was associated with the earliest or a later phase of occupation.

A number of internal features were uncovered. These included a post-ring which would have supported the roof of the structure and the remains of a floor layer. Although this represents a rare survival, the clay floor surface which was identified in patches within the house hollow is also paralleled elsewhere. A patchy clay floor was found preserved beneath the hill-wash deposit inside a roundhouse at Trevalga in north Cornwall (Jones and Quinnell 2014, 33) and floor surfaces were also found inside Trethellan houses 2001 and 2222 (Nowakowski 1991). In most cases, however, floor layers do not survive or are perhaps absent because they consisted of organic materials, such as rushes which have not been preserved in the archaeological record.

In common with other roundhouses of this type and period, the doorway was located on the south east side (Nowakowski 1991; Jones 2015). Two stone-lined pits or sockets were also located in this area and it is possible that they were associated with the entrance, possibly representing some kind of aggrandized doorway. Entrances into some lowland Cornish roundhouses during the Middle Bronze Age were clearly demarcated by architectural features. The roundhouse at Callestick, for example was entered via a long porch, the end of which was deliberately blocked by large quartz blocks when the house was abandoned (Jones 1998-9), and at Trevalga the doorway was framed by very neatly coursed drystone stone-walling (Jones and Quinnell 2014, 26-31). The entranceway into Trethellan house 2001 had flagged stone paving within it and was marked by a 1m wide holloway which was partly edged on one side by a low kerbed wall of quartz boulders that led directly towards the doorway (Nowakowski 1991). There is widespread anthropological and archaeological evidence for the marking of thresholds into buildings, which can be seen as being liminal or 'between and betwixt' places (for example, Parker Pearson and Richards 1994; Brück 1999b; Leonard 2015b, 275-278). Doorways into Middle Bronze Age roundhouses may have had a symbolic importance, as they could have delineated, for example, interior private space and the public exterior world or the clean and the polluted (*cf* Douglas 1966), and this division may have been marked at the roundhouse represented by Structure 1.

The large pit [300], which was located close to the entrance, held a substantial deposit of finely decorated Trevisker Ware pottery, which was in good condition and included parts of at least four vessels (**P1-4**). No other artefacts were present except for two flints and part of a saddle quern (**S1**). The flints may have been residual, but the quern is unlikely to have been. Querns were used for the transformation of agricultural produce into food and are likely to have become associated with symbolism associated with the agricultural cycle and potentially of life, death and fertility (Williams 2003; Robinson 2013). It is certainly the case that across the south west region saddle querns, or more commonly parts from them, were deposited into pits and within Middle Bronze Age roundhouses (see for example, Nowakowski 1991; Green 2009; Jones and Taylor 2010, 78-79), and that many of these objects were placed with a degree of formality (Watts 2014, 86-91).

In addition to the artefactual assemblage, pieces of quartz, some of which were burnt, were also recorded in the fill of pit [300]. Given the frequent association of quartz with ritualized contexts in the Middle Bronze Age (for example, Johns 2008; Jones 2015), these pieces may represent a deliberate inclusion of material which was believed to have symbolic or magical properties. However, quartz occurred naturally in the surrounding subsoil and it may have accidentally been incorporated into the fill. The matrix of the infilling deposit was, in spite of the large size of the pit, homogenous. It contained charcoal which had not been burnt *in situ* (Challinor, Chapter 7) but interestingly no charred cereal remains were recovered either from this feature or from any others inside the house (J Jones, Chapter 6). This might suggest that the fill of pit [300] was all derived from a single source and that it was backfilled into the pit along with the artefacts in one episode. As such, it is likely that the contents of the pit represent a deliberate or purposefully 'structured deposit', rather than a slow accumulation of rubbish or house-related waste into the pit. Indeed, given the slightly earlier radiocarbon determination from the ceramics, the pottery assemblage might represent a gathering together of a curated deposit of valued items or heirlooms which possessed particular associations and memories of past people and places (Gosden and Marshall 1999; Harris 2009).

The pottery within pit [300] had been covered by a stone and the pit itself appeared to be sealed by a lighter deposit which could have been a floor layer or an abandonment infilling deposit (Fig 10.1). This suggests that the artefacts had been carefully sealed and hidden. In this respect, the content and location of pit [300] has rather close similarities with a number of other deposits that have been found within hollow-set roundhouses (Jones 2015). At Scarcewater house 1500 a pit was excavated in the south-west quadrant of the post-ring. It was found to contain a collection of what may have been curated heirlooms which had been purposefully gathered together and buried inside it. The artefactual assemblage incorporated most of the ceramics from the roundhouse and included selected rim-sherds that may have been curated for some time prior to burial (*ibid*). At Trethellan house 2001, a large pit holding a saddle quern, rubbing stones and sherds of pottery was found in the south-west part of the house; within Trethellan house 2222 a pit close to the southern part of the post-ring was found to contain rubbing stones (Nowakowski 1991). Comparisons can also be made with the roundhouse at Callestick, where selected sherds from a ceramic vessel were placed

Figure 10.1 Photograph of Pit [300] within Middle Bronze Age Structure 1. Note the lighter colour of the upper part of the pit which may represent a floor layer or infilling deposit.

between the wall and the cut for the house hollow, just to the left of the doorway when looked at from outside (Jones 1998–9).

The phasing of pit [300] within the construction and use of the Structure 1 roundhouse cannot be determined. It is possible that it was, like the pottery behind the wall at Callestick and possibly the pit within Scarcewater roundhouse 1500, a foundation deposit. On the other hand, it is also possible that the deposit was made into the pit during the abandonment phase and represents an act undertaken as part of the closure of the roundhouse.

There were, nonetheless, differences from at least some of the other excavated hollow-set roundhouses known in Cornwall. The planned abandonment (Nowakowski 2001; Jones *et al* 2015, 183–189) which is a strong feature of many other lowland roundhouses in the county was not especially evident. The overlying infill deposit was not readily distinguishable from the overlying ploughsoil (Fig 10.2), and unlike other houses – for example, those at Trethellan and Boden (Nowakowski 1991; Gossip 2013) – it was devoid of finds. Likewise, artefacts discovered within the postholes were restricted to a small number of flints and pottery, which did not appear to have been deliberately placed within them. This scarcity of finds contrasts with other houses such as, Trevilson and Scarcewater houses 1250 and 1500, and especially with Tremough roundhouse 1. At these sites there is good evidence for the deliberate placing of artefacts, including worked stone, pottery and, at Tremough, metalwork into postholes (Jones and Taylor 2004, 27; Jones 2015; Jones *at al* 2015, 186–187). However, the paucity of artefactual evidence from abandonment layers within Structure 1 is not entirely without parallel. At Scarcewater, for example, in the large roundhouse 1500 the layer sealing the hollow produced only one sherd of pottery; the infill layer in the Middle Bronze Age structure at Harlyn Bay did not produce a single sherd of pottery and no artefacts were recovered from the postholes (Jones and Taylor 2010, 16; Whimster 1977; Jones 2008). Although in this instance the scale of the excavation was too small to draw any particular conclusions, it has been argued elsewhere that roundhouses varied from one another because they were linked to the biography of their occupants (Jones 2015; Jones *et al* 2015) and had effectively developed their own 'personhood'.

The Middle Iron Age period (*circa* 400 to 100 cal BC)

The Middle Iron Age period was represented by two buildings, Structure 2 and Structure A1. The appearance of structures dating to the Middle Iron Age is of interest as this period is marked by a much larger number of identified sites than are known from the preceding Late Bronze Age and Early Iron Age periods both in

Figure 10.2 Photograph of Middle Bronze Age Structure 1 taken from the east. Note the lighter colour of the lower part of the section, which is likely to be a Bronze Age infilling deposit.

Cornwall and the wider south west region generally (Nowakowski and Quinnell 2011, 352–353; Nowakowski 2011). Indeed, the area around Newquay, especially to the north, is particularly rich in later prehistoric settlements (Nowakowski *et al* 2009; Nowakowski and Quinnell 2011, 352–353). The main phase of the Trevelgue Head cliff castle or promontory fort, which lies less than three kilometres from the Newquay road corridor site, is dated to the Middle Iron Age (*ibid*) and at Atlantic Road, Newquay, traces of Middle Iron Age activity were found on a coastal site buried beneath wind-blown sand (Reynolds, in preparation).

Both of the structures were located in the south west part of the stripped area and the radiocarbon dating suggests that they were broadly contemporary with one another. Both were defined by ring-gullies, although aside from this they were rather different.

Some further comment can, however, be made about their architecture.

Structure 2

Structure 2 was oval and measured 4m by 4.5m. Unfortunately, it was not well-preserved and consequently contained few internal cut features or artefacts. A pit within the structure produced a radiocarbon determination of 2100 ± 34 BP, 337–40 cal BC (SUERC-62685). In part, the lack of internal features may have been the result of truncation, as the topsoil was much shallower in this part of the site. The gaps in the ring-gully might imply that the entrance to the building was located either on the north western or south eastern sides. The ring-gully could, as with the Middle Iron Age roundhouses at Penmayne, near Rock on the north Cornish coast, have held a wall (Gossip *et al* 2012) and this would have negated the need for an internal post-ring, although it is also possible that the gully simply enclosed a space within which a small structure stood (below).

Structure 2 is broadly similar to a range of simple ring-gullied structures of Middle Iron Age date which are found across Britain (for example, Crane and Murphy 2010; Sharples 2010, 215–220; Germany 2014) (Fig 10.3). In a Cornish context, a comparable gullied structure has been excavated nearby at Nansledan (Rainbird and Pears, forthcoming). There, two ring ditches formed an oval structure with an internal diameter of approximately 17m. The site is considerably larger than Structure 2, the ditches were deeper, and it is thought to have been a ceremonial monument of, on ceramic dating, Early Iron Age date. Nonetheless, there are morphological similarities, and the east – west orientation of the ditches also echoes that of Structure 2, which arguably suggests a link between ceremonial and domestic architecture (Chapter 11).

Another possible parallel lies with structure 4 at Penryn College, which was again sub-oval in plan, 7m by 6m, and defined by gullies (Gossip and Jones, forthcoming). The structure at Penryn College was, however, not

Figure 10.3 Middle Iron Age structures in Cornwall and Devon: (1) Twinyeo structure 3, (2) Twinyeo structure 1, (3) Penryn College structure 2, (4) Twinyeo structure 2, (5) Nansledan and (6) Newquay Structure 2.

closely dated, although it is thought to belong in the later part of the Iron Age, in which case it would post-date Structure 2. The structure at Penryn College was also associated with internal features, which included pits and postholes (*ibid*).

Other parallels for Structure 2 perhaps lie with three recently excavated sites at Twinyeo in mid Devon (Farnell 2015). There, three structures comprised of segmented ditches were uncovered (structures 1, 2 and 3). With diameters in excess of 10m, these were rather larger than Structure 2; however, the radiocarbon dating of Twinyeo structure 1, 2250 ± 42 BP, 397–204 cal BC (SUERC-50122), places it in broadly the same period (Fig 10.3).

In common with Structure 2 the Twinyeo sites appear to have been part of an unenclosed settlement. Two of the Twinyeo structures were associated with iron working (*ibid*). Unfortunately, the near absence of features and artefacts within Structure 2 makes comment on function difficult. It is, however, possible that it was a domestic dwelling.

Structure A1

Structure A1 was less truncated than Structure 2 but at least half of it lay outside the confines of the stripped corridor. If it was roughly circular it might have had a diameter in excess of 13m. On balance, it seems likely that structure A1 was a roofed building, as a line of deeply cut postholes may have supported a roof. However, as with Structure 2, little can be said about activities within the structure as no hearth was identified and there were no traces of floor surfaces.

The location of the entrance is also uncertain, although the ring-gully [220] terminated to the south and did not run under the baulk to the west. This might suggest that there was an entrance on the south east side of the structure. There was little evidence that the structure had been renewed, as the encircling ring-gully had not been recut and there was no evidence for the recutting of the postholes inside the enclosed space. The radiocarbon determinations from the ring-gully 2179 ± 34 BP, 365–119 cal BC (SUERC-62695) and posthole [233] and 2114 ± 34 BP, 346–45 cal BC (SUERC-62687) are also likely to be contemporary with one another (Chapters 2 and 8). It is therefore likely to have been a single phased building.

The most prominent feature associated with Structure A1 was the ring-gully which formed the perimeter. It has been thought that ring-gullies were for the drainage of rainwater away from the walls of buildings. However, experimental work on reconstructed roundhouses revealed that such gullies do not work particularly well as drains (Reynolds 1982, 197) and more recently it has been argued that some ring-gullies were in fact dug to hold the bases of vertically-set timbers forming the walls of roundhouses. Ring-groove roundhouses are widely distributed and have been recorded in southern England and Wales (Smith 1979, 29; Cunliffe 2010, 273; Crane and Murphy 2010). In the south west region examples have been identified at Berry Ball (Manning and Quinnell 2009) and Blackhorse in east Devon (Fitzpatrick *et al* 1999, 163–166) and Cannards Grave, Somerset (Birbeck 2002), and in Cornwall three large Middle Iron Age ring-groove roundhouses with diameters ranging from 14m to 18m were investigated at Penmayne (Gossip *et al* 2012).

However, while it is possible that the gully around Structure A1 held a wall, it is, given its wide and shallow profile, rather more probable that it did not mark the position of the house wall but instead enclosed a space around it. This arrangement has been found at two Late Iron Age settlements in Cornwall. A recently excavated roundhouse, structure 4, at Camelford was represented by a post-ring with a diameter of approximately 6m (Jones and Taylor 2015). Around this was a well-defined ring-gully with a diameter of 14.5m. Although it is possible that Camelford structure 4 was a very large roundhouse, it seems more likely that a smaller roundhouse sat within its own gully-defined enclosure. Evidence for roundhouses encircled by non-structural ring-ditches was even clearer at the Iron Age settlement at Higher Besore, near Truro (Gossip, forthcoming), where several of the structures were sited within their own enclosures. A particularly good example was house 4, where a shallow groove for the wall, with stakeholes, was set 1.5m inside the circuit of the main ring-gully (*ibid*) (Fig 10.4).

Given the character of the Structure A1 ring-gully, it is possible that it was intended to provide a clearly demarcated perimeter around a building which stood inside it. As noted above, this gully is not likely to have been for drainage and unlikely to have been structural, or indeed deep enough unless associated with a bank, to have formed a stock-proof barrier, which would have kept animals out of the building. The lack of obvious functionality is of interest as there is evidence for architectural associations between circular ceremonial monuments and roundhouses throughout the Bronze Age (Bradley 2012; Jones *et al* 2015, chapter 11) and there are a growing number of Iron Age ceremonial sites in Cornwall which are of circular form (Jones 2010; 2014; Rainbird and Pears, forthcoming). The link between circular domestic architecture and ceremonial monuments is discussed more fully below in relation to the later structures which were excavated; nonetheless, it is worth noting here that at Camelford School the link between 'secular' domestic spaces and 'sacred' ceremonial architecture was quite

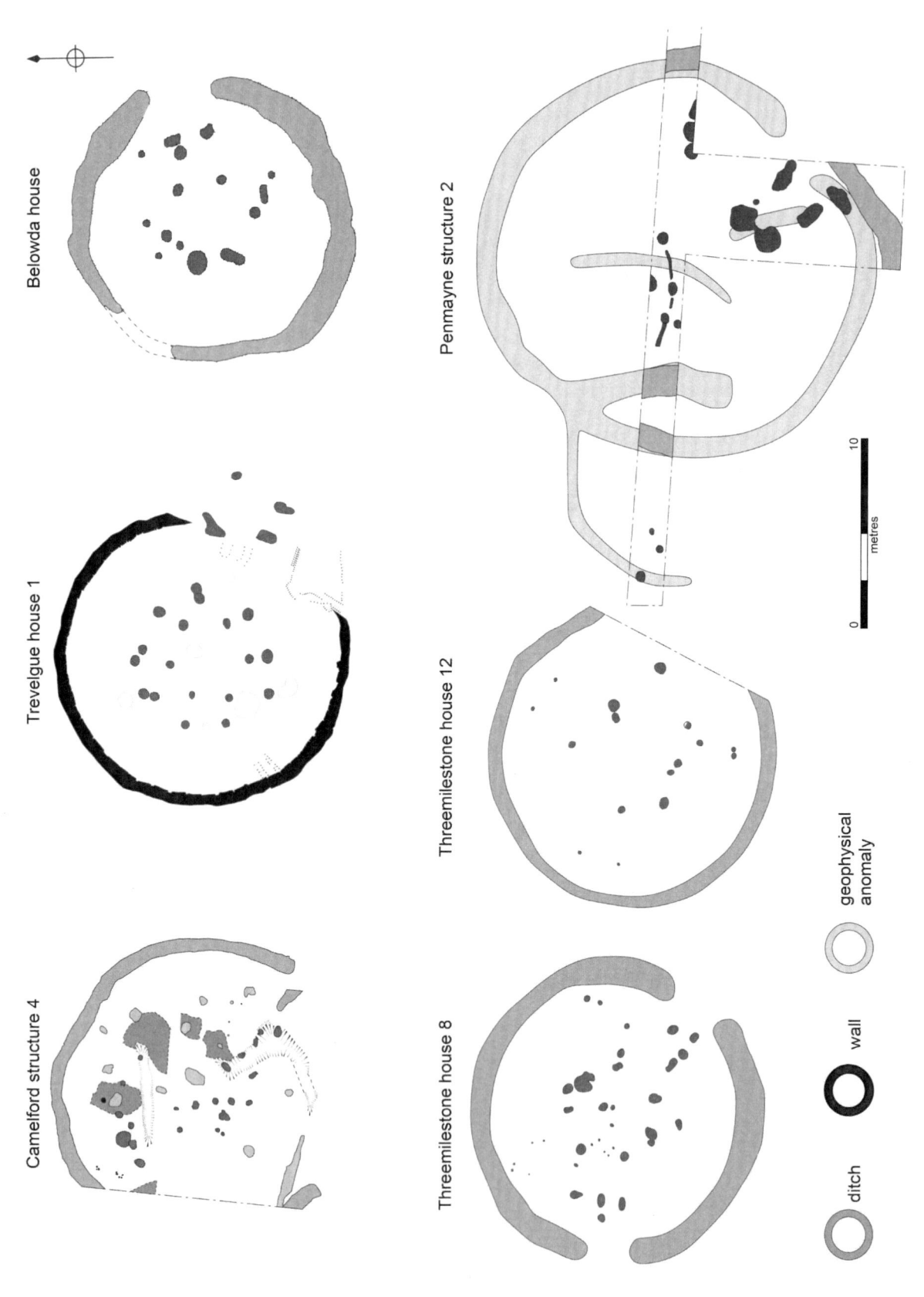

Figure 10.4 Iron Age roundhouses in Cornwall: Camelford School structure 4, Trevelgue Head house 1, Belowda, Threemilestone houses 8 and 12, and Penmayne structure 2.

explicitly made (Jones and Taylor 2015). At Camelford, two ceremonial sites dating to the Late Iron Age were uncovered, enclosures 1 and 2. These were encircled by ditches that were the focus for structured deposits, which included midden-rich material and artefacts. Nearby was the substantial post-built roundhouse structure 4 and encircling it was a gully which was not structural but which appeared to be intended to define a circular space. It is possible that there were metaphorical references between different kinds of enclosed space; that is to say, just as the ring-ditch and banks around enclosures 1 and 2 defined the community's ceremonial activities, so the ring-gully around structure 4 defined the living space around the community. The gullies around Structure 2 and Structure A1 at Newquay may therefore have been drawing on a wider shared symbolism. Again, this point will be returned to in relation to the Late Iron Age – Roman period below (Chapter 11).

The ring-gullies around Structure A1 and Structure 2, however, produced little evidence for formalized or structured deposition and there was little in the way of artefactual material in Structure 2, although a few artefacts were found in pits and postholes inside Structure A1. However, it is of interest that sherds from a Middle Iron Age vessel **P7** were retained and buried in the early Roman period ditch [127] which encircled Structure A3 (Chapter 11, below).

The immediate landscape around Structures 2 and 1A is poorly understood. Two ditches, [274] and [293] may also belong to the same period, although their phasing is based upon a handful of sherds of Middle Iron Age pottery which may very well be residual. It is therefore not possible to tell whether the structures stood within a contemporary field system or were located in open ground.

The nature of the surviving evidence limits what can be said about the character of the occupation of either of the structures. There was a complete absence of charred plant macrofossils (J Jones, Chapter 6), which means that it is not possible to establish the wider environmental background or determine what crop processing took place in the settlement.

Likewise, there was a dearth of evidence for industrial activity during this phase. A significant quantity of iron ore was found recovered from Roman period contexts (see R Taylor, Chapter 4) and some slag from Late Iron Age ditch [120]; however, none was recovered from the Middle Iron Age phase. This absence is of interest given the large-scale evidence for the working of iron ore during Middle Iron Age at Trevelgue Head (Nowakowski and Quinnell 2011, 342–344).

The Late Iron Age to Roman period (*circa* 100 cal BC to AD 200)

The evidence for Late Iron Age to Roman period activity comprised several elements: gully-defined structures, hollow-set activity areas and structures, and potentially a spatially separate area used for burial. The period also saw the first certain evidence for the bounding of space by a ditched enclosure and field boundaries, and traces of industrial activity.

Artefact finds suggest that a number of the Late Iron Age features continued in use into the early Roman period (Table 3.14). The radiocarbon dating also indicates a more-or-less continuous span of occupation from the Late Iron Age into the second century AD (Chapter 8), with Hollow 1 in particular appearing to having been used from the Late Iron Age into the Roman period. As with the Middle Iron Age, however, none of the structures can clearly be identified with domestic occupation and the character of much of the evidence is ambiguous.

Establishing the wider context for the Late Iron Age phase is also beset by the same problems as the Middle Iron Age, in that there are few excavated sites with close dating the immediate vicinity. However, a large number of enclosures have been identified in the surrounding area (Young 2012, 115). The largest and apparently most elaborate of these is that at Manuels, which is located on a ridge to the south east of the road corridor. It is one of the most complex enclosure sites in Cornwall.

In addition to enclosures, geophysical survey and aerial photographs also reveal a large number of field systems in the surrounding area (for example, Lawson-Jones 2011; Rainbird and Pears, forthcoming; and see below), which are also likely to date to before the medieval period. None, however, are securely dated and their contemporaneity with one another or the excavated features along the road corridor is unknown (see Fig 1.1).

The environmental record from this phase is not as sparse as for the Middle Iron Age, although it is the case that charred plant remains are largely restricted to a few key contexts (J Jones, Chapter 6). The evidence suggests increasing cultivation and consumption of cereals, with a marked rise in the Roman period. One caveat, however, is that the largest quantities of cereals were recovered from contexts which might be regarded as being 'special', and this is discussed below in Chapter 11.

Hollow 1

Hollow 1 was an oval space 14.5m by 7.5m defined by multiple ring-gullies. Even allowing for truncation, the majority of the gullies were not very deep and they were

Manuels enclosure: A landscape focus

The enclosure at Manuels is a multivallate site. It is however, difficult to categorize, as it is formed by an unusual arrangement of ditches and, although very large by 'round' standards, it is quite unlike a hillfort in layout, scale or arrangement of ditches. As noted above, the enclosure has not been excavated; however, the digging of a test pit within the enclosure led to the recovery of a copper-alloy brooch which is likely to date to the Roman period (Carl Thorpe, pers comm).

Aerial photographs reveal a multiple enclosure (Figs 10.5 and 10.6), comprising an inner roughly circular cropmark approximately 50m diameter, with up to five concentric ditches which take the overall diameter to around 250m. The space between the two inner enclosures and the next concentric ditch appears to be divided radially into a number of cells. This arrangement of concentric and radial earthworks is unique, although the site is unexcavated, so the character of the radial divisions and contemporaneity with the ditch circuits is unproven. The spacing between the ditch circuits does, however, have similarities with the multi-ditched hillslope enclosures in the south west, such as Tregeare Rounds (St Kew) and Clovelly Dykes in Devon, identified by Lady Aileen Fox (1952).

Multi-ditched hillslope enclosures were interpreted by Fox (1952) as being associated with the keeping of cattle and it is possible that the cells between the enclosing ditches, may be indicative of yards to hold cattle. Multiple circuited enclosures are found in the Lleyn peninsula in north-west Wales (RCHM Wales 1964, 72–73). Raimund Karl (2016) has made an interesting observation with regard to the enclosure site at Meillionydd, which he argues on linguistic grounds could have been a high-status site or court. He suggests that in Welsh the words for yard and court could have been derived from the same root. Some yards may have taken on special functions and become courts, the residences of community leaders and also places where animals could be exchanged, transactions undertaken and legal disputes settled. It is possible that the site at Manuels, in common with some multi-ditched enclosures, may not have been purely used for occupation and could also have fulfilled a ceremonial function. A multiple ditched enclosure at Bogee, St Issey, for example, has an Early Bronze Age round barrow outside it and there was also a possible mound inside it (Young 2012), which would suggest that the focus of the enclosure was not settlement. Likewise, the nearby hillfort at Castle-an-Dinas to the east contains two round barrows (Soutar 2013; Jones, forthcoming), which would have provided a visual link to the 'ancestral past' and, given the limited evidence for occupation, the hillfort may have been a place of gatherings, perhaps drawing people and animals together from a wider area. The Manuels enclosure may have been a seat of local political power and like some Irish enclosures of the later Bronze and Iron Age could also have had a ceremonial purpose (for example, Lynn 2003; O'Brien et al 2014–2015; Madgwick *et al* 2017).

Seen in this way, the Manuels enclosure could have been an important focus in the landscape, a place where animals could be corralled and exchanged and disputes between parties settled. Such a place may well have exerted a considerable influence over the inhabitants of the surrounding landscape in terms of where settlement occurred and what activities took place, including the working of iron which may itself have been linked with the maintenance of social power.

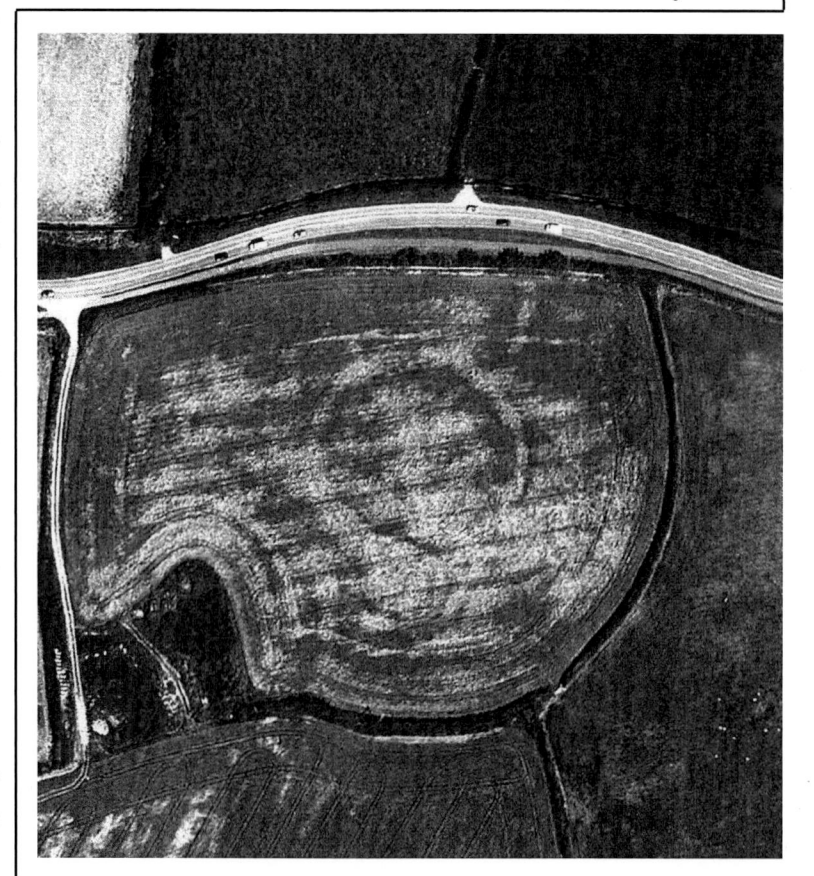

Figure 10.5 Aerial photograph of the Manuels enclosure, showing an inner roughly circular cropmark approximately 50m diameter; the site as a whole may have an overall diameter of around 250m. Part of the south-eastern side is preserved in the hedge bank (© Cornwall Council).

Structures and boundaries: The wider later prehistoric and Roman period context

Figure 10.6 The plotting of the cropmark enclosure at Manuels by the National Mapping Programme revealed that there are up to five concentric ditch circuits and that the space between the two inner enclosures and the next concentric ditch appears to have been divided radially into a number of cells.

not apparently structural. In an age of predominantly circular buildings, they are also hard to parallel. One possible comparable site of Late Iron Age date has been excavated less than 2 kilometres away at Nansledan (Rainbird and Pears, forthcoming). Like Hollow 1, Nansledan ring-gully [1022] was an oval site with an overall diameter of around 9m, which showed signs of recutting. It did not, however, contain any internal features.

The (re)defining of the central space within Hollow 1, however, does seem to have been important, as not all of the gullies are likely to have been contemporary with one another. It is possible, for example, that the original perimeter may have been the larger one, formed by gullies [360] and [400], with

Figure 10.7 Photograph of half excavated pit [309], which may have been associated with the preparation of food.

a smaller space being defined subsequently by [336], [411] and [408]. This interpretation of the sequence is by no means certain. Pits [309] (Fig 10.7) and [346] produced radiocarbon determinations of 2077 ± 34 BP, 189–1 cal BC (SUERC-62694), 1984 ± 29 BP, 46 cal BC – cal AD 74 (SUERC-63279) and 2028 ± 34 BP, 159 cal BC – cal AD 55 (SUERC-62679), all three of which fell in the Late Iron Age or the first century cal AD. Both pits were within the hypothetically larger enclosed space but were outside the potentially smaller one defined by ring-gully [336], which produced a slightly later radiocarbon determination 1981 ± 34 BP, 52 cal BC – cal AD 85 (SUERC-62690), spanning the Iron Age–Roman transition period.

Whatever the sequence of the ring-gullies, the central area of the hollow held a large number of cut features which clustered into two areas. The northern group appear to have held posts, although there is no clear evidence that they formed an arrangement which would have supported a roof, and hollow 1 is therefore interpreted as an unroofed space which was used for open-air activities. Several of the postholes were intercutting, which suggests that the space may have been in use for some time.

The second group of features was located in the middle of the hollow and all are interpreted as pits. Several were rectangular in shape and contained evidence for heating in the form of burnt stone and charcoal. Finds were few and largely limited to a few sherds of Late Iron Age pottery, but again evidence for recutting and the large number of features suggests that activities took place over a prolonged period. This is also supported by the stone bowl fragment S5 which dates to the Roman period.

Identifying what the hollow was used for is problematic. Open 'working areas' have been identified at a number of Late Iron Age and Roman period sites in Cornwall, including Little Quoit Farm, where several hollows up to 5m in diameter were found to be associated with industrial activity in the form of small-scale smithing of iron (Lawson-Jones and Kirkham 2009–10) (Fig 10.8). However, no industrial residues or iron objects

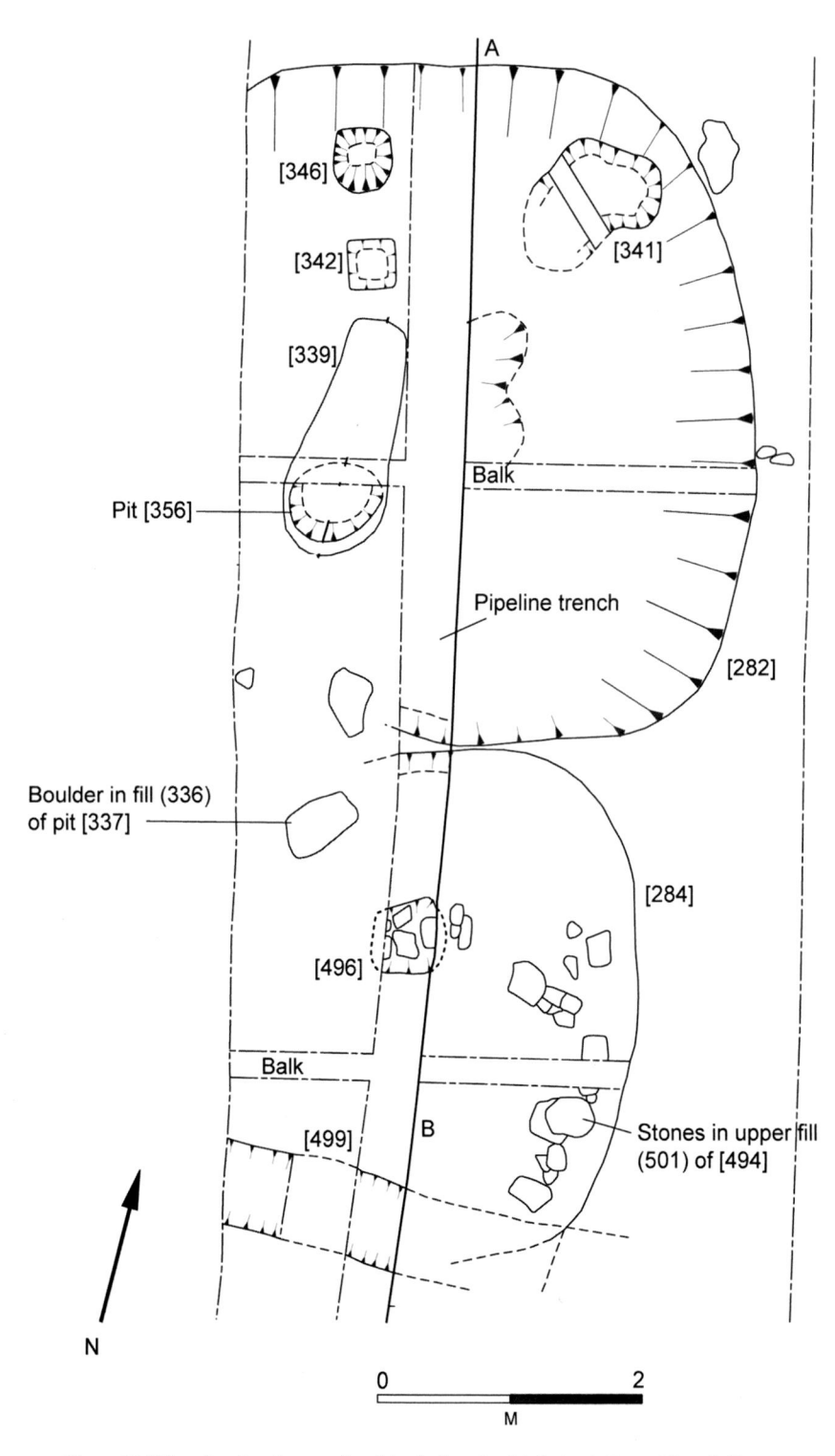

Figure 10.8 Plan showing the open 'working hollows' at Little Quoit Farm. These hollows were associated with small-scale smithing. (After Lawson-Jones and Kirkham 2009–10.)

were found in any of the pits in Hollow 1 or within the hollow itself. Pit [346] may have been used for cooking or heating as the natural subsoil around the edge of the pit had been scorched red. The heat reddening around pit [346] might imply some industrial use, which would be consistent with the charcoal assemblage (Chapter 7); however, no metalworking residues were found and a domestic use is perhaps more likely.

An alternative is that the pits containing burnt deposits were used for open-air food preparation and cooking: a fragment of a stone bowl **S5** which would have been used to prepare food (Quinnell 1993) was found in pit [334], and ceramics, possibly associated with the storage of food were recovered from pits [346] and [309]. Pit [346] contained 12 sherds from **P10**, a well-made storage jar, and pit [309] 13 sherds from **P9**, a Late Iron Age Cordoned Ware vessel. Burnt stones and a few charred cereal grains were found within pit [309], and a small quantity of charred grains was recovered from three of the features in the centre of Hollow 1 which might also support this interpretation; there was no animal bone but unless very charred this would be unlikely to have survived in the harsh acidic soil conditions.

Stone bowls were undoubtedly functional but they are, as Henrietta Quinnell (1993) has pointed out, also rather elegant and may have been displayed at the table. In common with bronze cauldrons, which span the Iron Age and Roman period (Joy 2014), they may have been associated with display and ritualized preparation of special foods for particular gatherings (for example, Baldwin and Joy 2017). Food production, processing, preparation and public consumption are frequently associated with social strategies involving feasting, which can provide the opportunities whereby individuals can obtain or maintain status (Weissner 1996; Dietler 1996). The evidence for feasting in later prehistoric Europe is well documented (for example, Dietler 1996) and in Britain there is evidence for such activity in the form of middens, cooking sites, deposits of animal bones and large storage vessels used for keeping quantities of food (Buckley 1990; McOmish *et al* 2010; Madgwick and Mulville 2015).

Two bronze cauldrons, now lost, were found in a streamworks at Broadwater in Luxulyan, in 1792 (Penhallurick 1986, 199–200). These may have been votive offerings but certainly reflect the growing importance of feasting in the Atlantic sea zone from the later prehistoric period onwards. Evidence for the symbolic role of food is also provided by the worked stone assemblages from later prehistoric and Roman period sites in Cornwall. Recent study of querns from later prehistoric sites across the south west (Watts 2014, 102–125; 2017) has revealed that ritualized practices associated with them found within Bronze Age settlements persisted, and even increased, during the Iron Age, with querns being deliberately broken and placed into pits and, as at Camelford enclosure 2, within ditches (for example, Jones and Taylor 2015; and see Chapter 11). The Camelford quern, like many others, had been deliberately broken, possibly as a means of ending its use-life. Given that it was of granite, this would have taken some force. It is of interest that fragments from three stone bowls were found at the Newquay Strategic Road site, as this implies a continuing tradition of deliberate destruction of worked stone objects associated with the preparation of food into the Roman period.

Within the hollow itself, posthole [351] is of interest in this context as it contained a tiny assemblage of charred plant macrofossils. This assemblage could be argued to have entered the posthole by chance; however, in this instance the posthole was capped by slates, which means that the post must have been deliberately removed with the infill deposit entering the posthole before the slates were placed across it. The fragment of Trethurgy type bowl **S5**, in pit [334] is significant because it indicates that activities within the hollow extended into the first century AD. It is one of three stone bowl fragments from the site, all of which, as noted above, had been deliberately smashed. As with the finds described above, these bowls are likely to have been associated with food preparation and may have had other social and symbolic functions too (Chapter 11). Taken together, although the evidence is very slight, there is a possibility that Hollow 1 may have been a defined open area associated with the preparation and cooking of food, and perhaps with its sharing too.

Hollow 2

Hollow 2 was the second oval space of Late Iron Age date. There was, however, no evidence to suggest that its use continued into the Roman period. It was smaller than Hollow 1, measuring 8m long by 7m wide, but unlike that hollow, it was not defined by ring-gullies, although there may have been a low bund of redeposited upcast around it that would have physically defined the perimeter.

The main difference between the two features, however, was the fact that Hollow 2 contained a rectangular post-built structure measuring approximately 4m by 4.5m. Square or rectangular buildings and 'four-post' structures of Late Iron Age date are rare in Cornwall (for example, Miles *et al* 1977), but are widely found elsewhere in England and Wales (Cunliffe 2010, 411–412; Lynch *et al* 2000, chapter 4), and Devon (for example, Hart and Sheldon 2017). Rectangular buildings, and especially 'four-post' structures have often been interpreted as utilitarian grain stores or animal barns, as at Little Woodbury and Gussage All Saints in Wiltshire, for example (Gent 1983; Fowler 1983, 183). However, as anthropological study has shown, storage buildings can carry their own symbolism and be used for the public display of produce (for example, Weiner 1987, 92–96). Adrian Chadwick (2012) has argued that display was important and that some 'four-post' structures were imbued with greater social significance. He suggests that charred grain recovered from the postholes of 'four-post structures' at Sutton Common in Yorkshire probably resulted from 'apotropaic foundation rituals' which were intended to 'maintain the fertility of crops, animals and people and the continued favour of gods, supernatural forces or ancestors' (*ibid*).

The rectangular building inside Hollow 2 may well have been used for storage, but no traces of the contents survived. It was, however, a substantial construction which is likely to have been very visible in the surrounding area. Its abandonment may also have been marked by a 'special deposit' (Chapter 11, below), which may again suggest that it was of some significance.

In addition to the building, there were a number of other features in and around Hollow 2, including a number of pits and postholes, and a remnant occupation surface which was radiocarbon dated to 2065 ± 34 BP, 179 cal BC – cal AD 5 (SUERC-62684). The majority of these contexts were devoid of artefacts or environmental material but a handful produced a few sherds of Late Iron Age pottery. Two of the pits, however, slate-lined hearth pit [435] and [491] are worth further comment and are discussed in Chapter 11.

Structure 3

Structure 3 was an oval building measuring approximately 5m by 4m and of second to fourth century AD date (Fig 10.9). It was located towards the northern part of the main excavation area and is likely to have been situated within an enclosure defined by slight ditches [125] and [129] and [201] and [204]. It was simply constructed and comprised a hollow around which was a circuit of postholes. None of the posts had been renewed, so it is probable that it was a single phased building. The entrance was not well-defined but is likely to have been on the south eastern side. The building could have been a domestic residence although the floor was uneven and there were no obvious occupation deposits or signs of a floor surface. Alternatively, the structure may have been an agricultural store, or used for industrial purposes or for the preparation of food. The recovery of charred wheat, oat and weeds (J Jones, Chapter 6) and fragments from two rotary querns (**S2** and **S3**) and a stone bowl **S6** could suggest that grain was processed or perhaps consumed in the building. Just outside the structure

Figure 10.9 Photograph of Roman period Structure 3 during excavation. Note standing section and material filling the hollow which includes quartz blocks.

were three pits which bore signs of scorching and one also contained small assemblage of charred cereal grains, which might suggest that they were associated with the preparation of food. However, the quantities of grain from within and outside Structure 3 are still quite small and, as will be discussed below, the quern and stone bowl fragments could have been deposited as part of a formalized deliberate act of abandonment (Chapter 11).

Structure 3 is, however, comparable with a number of oval buildings that date to the Roman period in Cornwall (Figs 10.10 and 10.11). Most buildings of this type and period excavated to date are, however, associated with 'rounds'; that is, settlements enclosed by deeply cut ditches (for example, Schwieso 1976; Appleton-Fox 1992; Quinnell 1986, figs 3 and 4; 2004; Nowakowski and Johns 2015, chapter 7). Oval-shaped buildings were, for example, found within Trethurgy Round (Quinnell 2004). Most of the structures within Trethurgy Round were, however, defined by stone walls and were much larger than Structure 3, with the biggest ranging from 12m to 17m long and 7m to 9m wide. House D at Trethurgy, however, was of a similar size and date to Structure 3 (*ibid*, 170).

Structure 338 at Tremough, Penryn (Fig 10.12) perhaps offers more in the way of a direct comparison with Structure 3. Radiocarbon dating and the ceramic assemblage placed the use of the building in the second and third centuries cal AD, from around *circa* AD 170 until after AD 300, which means that it was broadly contemporary.

Unlike the buildings discussed above, structure 338 was, like Structure 3, instead sited within a slight, open-sided enclosure at the western end of a field system which had its origins in the Late Iron Age (Gossip and Jones 2007, 23–24). It was defined by an arrangement of postholes, pits and gullies measuring 8m by 6.7m (Gossip and Jones 2007, 23–24). Unlike Structure 3, however, the building appeared to be long-lived as many of the features inside it showed signs of being renewed. In the centre of the structure was a hearth, which may have been used for small-scale industrial as well as for domestic purposes. The plant macrofossil assemblages from structure 338 also revealed evidence for the processing of grain and comprised emmer, spelt and bread-type wheat, hulled barley and oats. The pottery assemblage included sherds from several types of Cordoned ware pottery and there was a mensuration weight made of fine-grained porphyritic elvan, which had been placed with a whetstone into a posthole near to the entrance. In common with Structure 3, the infill deposits overlying the structure also contained worked stone, including a fragment of stone from a mortar that had perhaps subsequently been used as a smelt pot, a whetstone and a fragment of greisen rotary quern. The stone weight, the whetstones, and the possible reworked smelting crucible could all have been associated with small-scale metalworking. In common with Structure 3, however, the mensuration weight and much of the stonework may have been deliberately deposited as part of the abandonment of the building, and this will be discussed below.

There are obvious differences between the two structures; as structure 338 seems to have been used for a much longer period than Structure 3; there was, for example, good evidence for the renewal of the structural posts. It also seems to have been a domestic dwelling, as well as being used for small-scale metalworking (*ibid*, 48).

Structure 3, by contrast, appears to have had a shorter life-span and there is no evidence for either renewal or of domestic occupation. The floor appears to have been left rough and uneven, and the majority of artefacts were associated with its abandonment (Chapter 11). Structure 3 and structure 338 form part of a larger but currently poorly understood pattern of open or lightly enclosed Roman period settlements with buildings that are not very substantial. Structure 3 appears to have been built within an area enclosed by fields and although it is likely that other buildings stood nearby, it is possible that the principal settlement within the wider vicinity was the enclosure to the south east at Manuels (see insert, above).

Slighter buildings outside enclosures have been difficult to locate but a handful of scattered examples from across Cornwall demonstrate that oval as opposed to circular building in various forms also occurred in open or lightly enclosed settlements. A small Roman period structure was excavated at Carngoon Bank, Lizard, comprising pits and stakeholes surrounded by an outer gully and measuring 7m long and 6m wide (McAvoy 1980), while at another Roman period salt-making site at Trebarveth, on the Lizard, a symmetrical oval structure measuring 5.5m by 4m was set into a hollow and defined by stone walling (Peacock 1969). At Porth Godrevy, near Gwithian on the north west Cornish coast, was an irregular oval stone-walled structure 8m by 5m with some internal postholes (Fowler 1962). These examples are all in coastal locations and appear to have involved quite specialized tasks, such as salt making, rather than those connected with more commonplace farming activities.

Structure A3 and structure A6

The final two Roman period structures investigated on the Newquay road corridor are difficult to characterize. Structure A6 may, in fact, have been little more than a slot to hold some kind of screen as a shelter for outdoor

Figure 10.10 Selection of Roman period oval-shaped structures found across Cornwall: (1) Newquay Structure 3, (2) Tremough structure 338, (3) Trebarveth structure 3, (4) Grambla structure 1, (5) Chysauster structure 5, (6) Castle Gotha and (7) Porth Godrevy.

Figure 10.11 Selection of Roman period oval-shaped structures found across Cornwall: (1) Trethurgy A1, (2) Trethurgy T4, (3) Trethurgy T2 and (4) Trethurgy Z2.

activities, including those associated with adjacent pits. As such, it is probably best interpreted as serving an agricultural purpose, although a fragment from a stone bowl or Cornish mortar, **S7** was recovered from it, and the structure can probably be linked with the evidence for expansion of enclosure and cultivation in the early Roman period.

By contrast, Structure A3 was much more substantial. It was a ring-gullied building which enclosed a line of large postholes. Only one side of this structure was revealed but it seems likely that it was a rectangular-shaped building set within circular or oval ring-gully, which could have enclosed a space of around 10m. The break in the ring-gully might suggest that like the other excavated ring-gullies and hollows, the entrance was on the south eastern side. In form it was very similar to the Middle Iron Age Structure A1, which is likely to have been slightly larger; however, the radiocarbon determination of 1879 ± 34 BP, cal AD 61–228 (SUERC-62677) dates the structure to the Roman period. As discussed above, oval buildings are typical of the Roman period in Cornwall and a broadly comparable ring-gullied structure was uncovered outside Penhale Round in mid-Cornwall. Structure [5517] was sub-circular and measured approximately

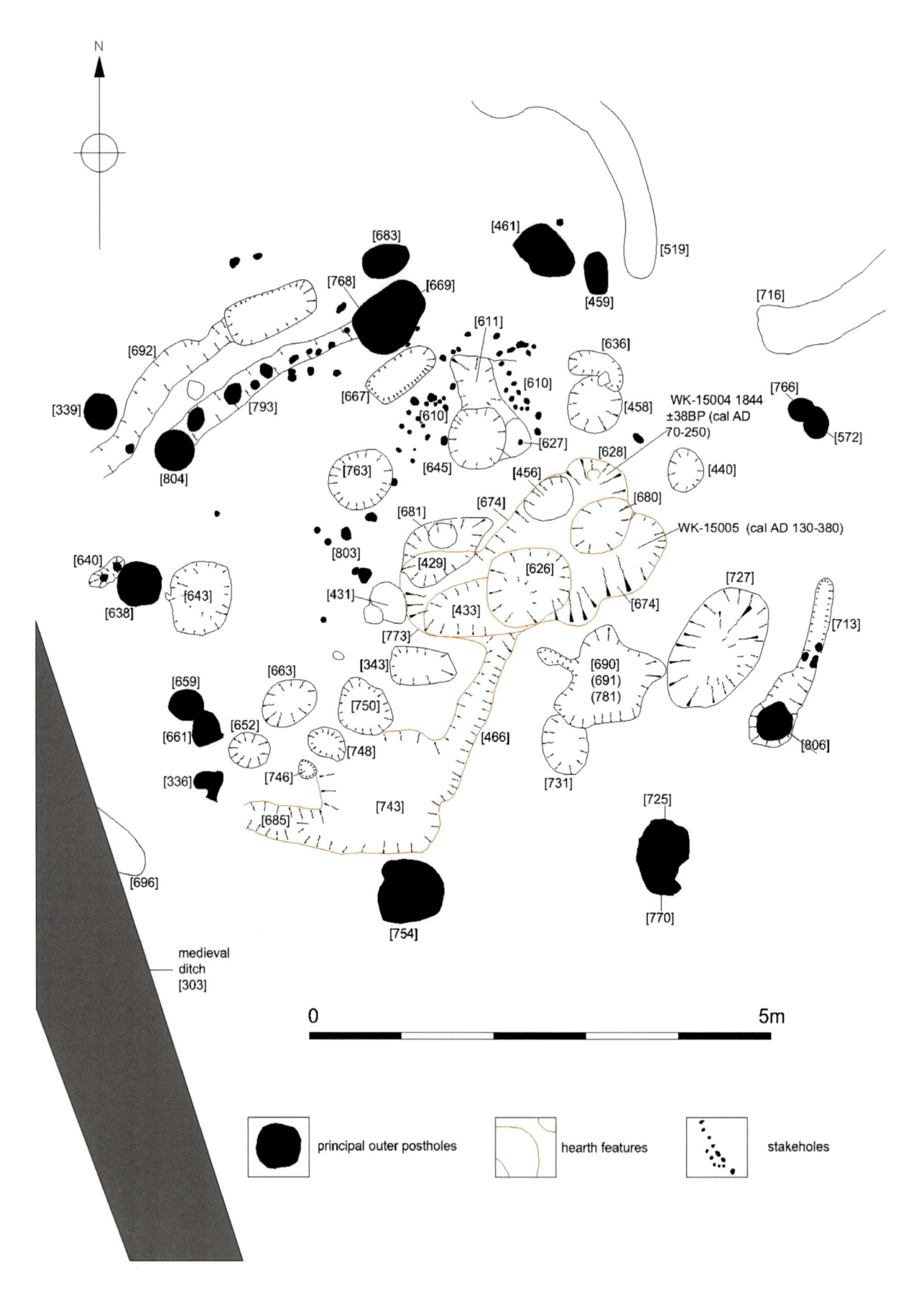

Figure 10.12 Plan showing Tremough structure 338. This oval shaped structure associated with small-scale metalworking and occupation. (After Gossip and Jones 2007.)

7.5m in diameter (Nowakowski and Johns 2015, 210). This building was occupied during the period AD 90 – 420 (although it may have had Late Iron Age origins) and appears to have been used as an ancillary crop-processing building (*ibid*, 211). The cereal assemblage from Structure A3 was small but is indicative of crop-processing and it is possible that it had been used as an agricultural building.

As with Structure A1, it is possible that the encircling gully was a structural device. However, as discussed in relation to A1, the profile of the ring-gully does not support that hypothesis and there was no trace of an associated bank. The gully may represent a continuing tradition of encircling buildings with well-defined ring-gullies. Another link with the past is indicated by the discovery of sherds of presumably curated Middle Iron Age pottery within the ring-gully and this is discussed below (Chapter 11).

Field system(s) and curvilinear enclosure

In addition to the structures and hollows, the Late Iron Age – Roman period also saw the first evidence from the road corridor site for the enclosure of land by ditched fields, although whether this took place before or after the Roman Conquest is not certain. The field system, like those at Trenowah, Penhale Round, Camelford School and Tremough, may have had its origins in the later Iron Age (Johns 2008; Nowakowski and Johns 2015, 295; Jones and Taylor 2015; Gossip and Jones 2007, 22–23). However, in common with the ditched boundaries at Scarcewater in central Cornwall and Gover Farm, near St Agnes (Jones and Taylor 2010, 49–55; Good 2015), the majority of the fields at Newquay probably post-date the Iron Age. Indeed on current limited evidence, the major phase of enclosure and indeed re-enclosure of the landscape in Cornwall seems to belong to the Roman period.

Numerous other ditches were recorded at Newquay but it is difficult, on the excavated evidence, to make sense of them in terms of establishing a coherent field pattern: they are in fact 'messy' and likely to be the product of different times and different people working the land (Mlekuž 2012). It is, however, possible to get some feel for the overall layout (if not phasing) by taking into consideration uninvestigated ditches identified by the geophysical survey in the surrounding area (Fig 1.1), some of which may also be of later prehistoric or Roman period date. Field boundary ditches were also located at Nansledan to the north east of the road corridor site, but pottery recovered from them ranged from the Middle Bronze Age to the Early and Late Iron Age and they are not closely dated (Rainbird and Pears, forthcoming). It is important to remember; however, that geophysics and crop-mark data cannot by itself provide an accurate indicator of time-depth or for subtle processes of modification to field systems (Chadwick 2013).

Unlike many of the later prehistoric and Roman period ditched field systems which have been investigated in Cornwall (for example, Gossip and Jones 2009–10), the identified ditches at Newquay do not appear to form the simple rectilinear or 'brick-shaped' field patterns which have been found in other parts of Cornwall and more widely in Britain and are often assigned to the period on typological grounds (Fowler 1983, 143; Peacock 1969; Riley 1980). Instead, the pattern formed by the ditches has an accreted look with both curvilinear and rectilinear elements to it, and it is probable that this reflects a complex pattern of continuing expansion and periodic reorganization over time.

The field system is difficult to disentangle because it was clearly of more than one phase, artefacts were quite limited, and the width of the road corridor meant that several key stratigraphical relationships between boundaries could not be investigated. The northern boundary of the field system may have been established by ditch [120] in the Late Iron Age. All the other boundaries and settlement-related features found within the road corridor lie to the south of this boundary and, given that the dating rests on a single sherd of Iron Age pottery, it is possible that ditch [120] continued to be a significant division in the landscape into the Roman period or in fact was of that date. Alternatively, it is possible that it was part of a curvilinear enclosure which might be suggested by the geophysical survey (Figs 1.2, 1.4 and 2.17. Unfortunately, there were no stratigraphic relationships with the enclosure formed by ditches [125], [129], [204] and [201] and given the number of linear features on the geophysical survey and gaps between them, other interpretations are possible.

Approximately 7m to the south of ditch [120] were two parallel ditches [125] and [129] which may have been associated with a bank, the stones from which had been pushed into ditch [129]. Approximately 30m to the south were two more large ditches [201] and [204]. Ditch [204] appeared to terminate just before the eastern baulk and the ditch end became the focus for a 'special' deposit, which included a significant quantity of iron ore, discussed below. A third ditch or pit [210] to the east and its recut [212] may have continued the alignment of [204] but it mostly lay beyond the edge of the road corridor. It was, however, filled with a deposit that was also rich in iron ore, which suggests that it was related to ditch [204] and that together these features formed an entrance into an enclosed space.

Ditches [125], [129], [201] and [204], and possibly [210] / [212] were in fact probably all components of a two-phased oval enclosure, measuring approximately 30m across, the outline of which is discernible on the geophysical survey (Figs 1.2 and 2.17). The component ditches were not deep enough to represent a 'round' type site but are rather more likely to have been associated with a stock-proofed enclosure. If this were the case, it would mean that Structure 3 was situated within an enclosed space. Comparable enclosures defined by slight ditches include the one around structure 338 at Tremough (Gossip and Jones 2007, 43; above) and at Penryn College, where two small enclosures were found to encircle structures 1, 3 and 4 (Gossip and Jones, forthcoming).

To the south of the curvilinear enclosure, there is evidence for long linear ditch boundaries, which may form a more rectilinear field pattern. The excavated ditch [230] is likely to be part of this field system, but direct dating and phasing is extremely limited and the relationship to the curvilinear element is unclear.

The same combination can be seen in the wider landscape around the road corridor (Fig 1.2). Comparable patterns of small enclosed spaces surrounded by larger fields have been identified elsewhere in Cornwall, as at Stencoose which lies approximately 13 kilometres to the south west and which was dated to the period *circa* 300 cal BC to AD 300 (Jones 2000-1). The smaller enclosed spaces are indicative of stock management, to pen animals overnight or for functions such as milking or shearing and exclude them from areas which were occupied by other structures or being used for other purposes such as cooking or storage (above), or for small-scale cultivation. Animals must have been kept, but unfortunately the prevailing acidic soil conditions meant that no animal bone was recovered from the site.

Other Cornish sites with better levels of preservation, however, have produced assemblages of animal bone. In particular, the Romano-British site at Atlantic Road produced cattle and other domesticated species, with sheep / goat forming the dominant part of the assemblage (Reynolds, in preparation). There, the animal bone assemblage may have changed from a predominantly young population in the earliest Roman phase, indicating animals butchered for meat, to an older population in the later phases, suggesting a greater use of wool and milk and animals kept partly for manuring. At Trevelgue, cattle bone was predominant in the Iron Age followed by sheep / goat, the majority of which were adult or sub-adult when slaughtered (Hammon 2011, 305). Both sites are, however, located in marginal coastal locales and in the case of Trevelgue the animals were probably brought to the site from elsewhere (*ibid*). Nonetheless, they do provide evidence for the utilization of animals for meat and other products in the Iron Age and Roman periods.

Increasingly open spaces are indicated by the charcoal assemblages, which are suggestive of a decline in mature woodland after the Middle Iron Age (Challinor, Chapter 7). A growing reliance on cereal crops is apparent from the increased presence of cereal grains in Roman period contexts, especially within features located within the Enclosure Area (J Jones, Chapter 6), and the suggested late date for many of the investigated boundaries might suggest that there was an expansion of farmed land or large-scale reorganization of it in the Roman period. It is certainly the case that new field systems of this period have been identified elsewhere in Cornwall, as at Scarcewater and at Gover Farm, near St Agnes (Jones and Taylor 2010, 85-87; Good 2015).

The A2 'cemetery' area

The last element of the Late Iron Age–Roman period phase was located in Field 2, beyond ditch [120], and away from all of the identified settlement-related structures, hollows and ditches. It comprised three rectangular pits with rounded corners that were up to 2m long and aligned east-west. One of them, pit [108], was also capped with slates and marked at the western end by three postholes (Figs 10.13 and 10.14).

It is suggested that these features may have been inhumation graves, although it should be stressed that that no human remains survived within them and very few artefacts were recovered. Direct dating is extremely tentative: a sherd of pottery from feature [108] (Quinnell, Chapter 3) is of Late Iron Age or Roman period date, although it was potentially residual. Interpretation as Iron Age or Roman period graves is therefore entirely based on morphological comparisons with other sites of this type in Cornwall. It is also worth re-emphasizing that local soil conditions do not allow the preservation of non-cremated bone and human remains seldom survive in the south west region.

Nationally, Iron Age burial traditions are quite diverse and with cremation being preferred in some regions and inhumation in others (Cunliffe 2010, 561; Davis 2017), with disarticulated and articulated human remains also being found in settlement-related and other ritualized contexts (Brück 1995; Thomas 2005, 256).

In Cornwall and Devon cists and graves have been recorded (Whimster 1981; 273-284), mostly in coastal locales (Fig 10.15). Documented sites include those at Trethellan Farm (Nowakowski 1991), Stamford Hill in Plymouth (Bate 1864), St Mary's, St Martins and Bryher on the Isles of Scilly (Ashbee 1974, 120-147; Dudley 1960-61; Johns 2002-3; Johns and Taylor, forthcoming), Trelan Bahow (Jope Rogers 1873; Hill 2002-3), Harlyn Bay (Bullen 1912; Whimster 1977) and Trevone (Dudley and Jope 1965). Possible Iron Age burials have also been found at Calartha and at Crantock (Cornish 1883; Russell 1971, 29; Olson 1981). It has been suggested that cists might have been associated with groups who were linked through maritime trade (Henderson 2007, 278);

Structures and boundaries: The wider later prehistoric and Roman period context

Figure 10.13 Photograph of stone-capped 'grave' [108] prior to excavation. Note the in situ stone capping covering the feature.

Figure 10.14 Photograph of 'grave' feature [109] after excavation.

LATER PREHISTORIC AND ROMAN SITES ALONG THE ROUTE OF THE NEWQUAY STRATEGIC ROAD CORRIDOR

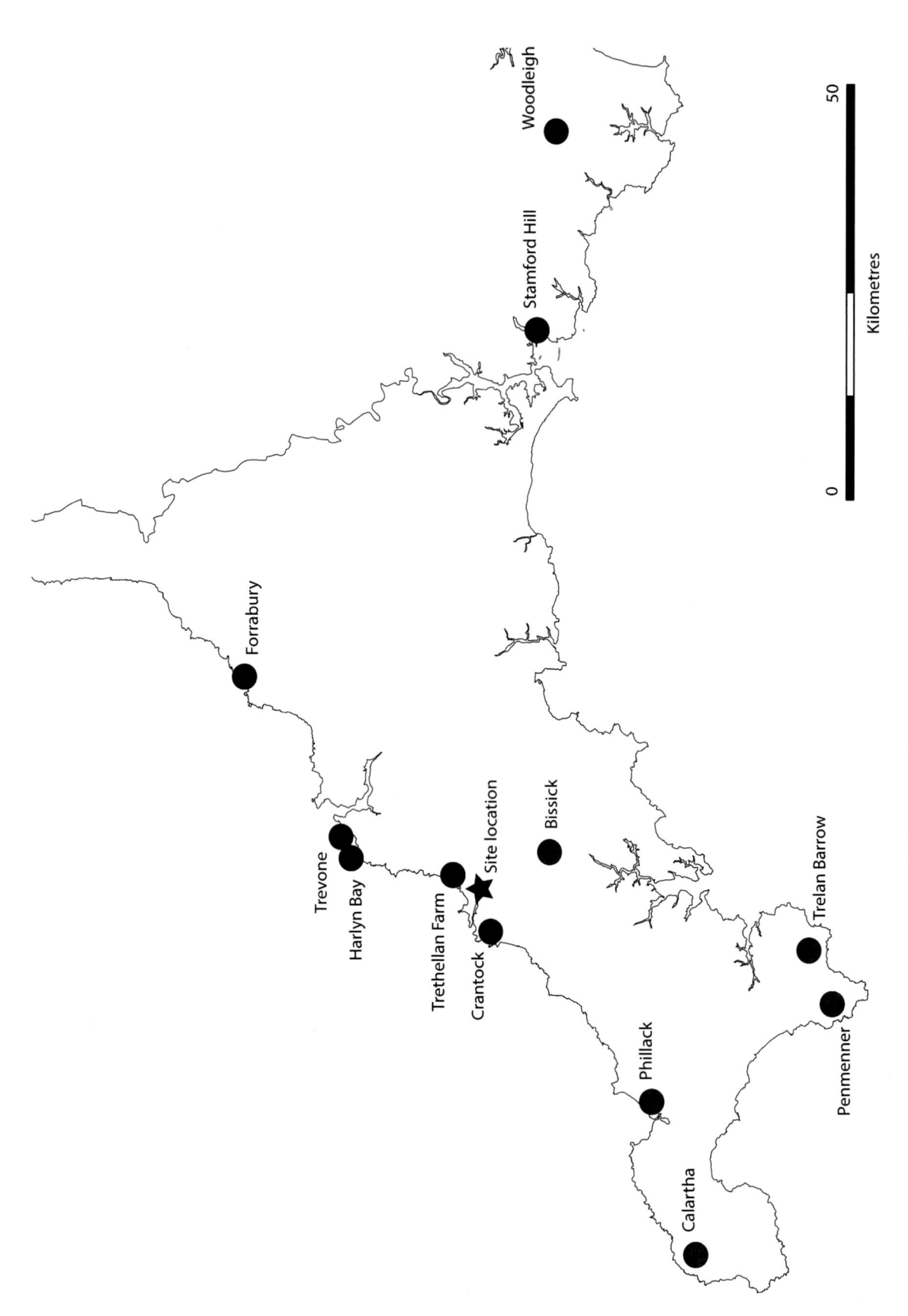

Figure 10.15 Map showing the distribution of Iron Age cist graves and pit graves in the south west peninsula.

Figure 10.16 Photograph of Forrabury stone-capped feature 13, which is of Iron Age date and similar to feature [108].

although as has been pointed out in relation to mirror-associated burials (Joy 2011), funerary activity needs to be understood in relation to the local context. In the case of the south west region the preference for cists and stone covered graves may reflect a continuation of later Bronze Age burial traditions, although there may well have been a resurgence of these traditions as a result of wider contacts (Jones and Quinnell 2014, 152; Wood 2015, 72).

The nearest known Iron Age cemetery to the Newquay Strategic Road corridor is at Trethellan Farm, where 21 oval, north-south aligned pits were found to represent an inhumation cemetery. These burials were dated to the Late Iron Age by the accompanying copper alloy brooches (Nowakowski 1991; 2011). The bone preservation was poor, but the size of the pits revealed that the burials must have been crouched.

Further away to the north east, along the north Cornish coast at Forrabury, near Boscastle, recent work identified an Iron Age cemetery comprising cists, graves and stone-capped features (Jones and Quinnell 2014, 38–50). Some were oriented east-west but others were on different alignments. Excavation was limited as the cemetery was for the most part preserved *in situ*. The radiocarbon and ceramic dating, however, placed its use from the Early to the Late Iron Age, with some activity continuing into the early Roman period. Six of the stone-capped features, especially feature 13, bore a resemblance to Newquay feature [108], which was of a very similar shape and size and also capped with flat slates (Fig 10.16).

None of the features at Newquay produced any surviving grave goods, although a water-rolled pebble was found in feature [108]. Pebbles were recovered from the cemetery at Forrabury (Jones and Quinnell 2014, 42–43). There, feature 4 contained a water-rolled quartz pebble (Fig 10.17) and feature 16 a large oval pebble. Pebbles have also been recorded with the fills of the Stamford Hill burials (Bate 1864), and within

Figure 10.17 Photograph of Forrabury cist 4, with in situ water rolled quartz pebble.

the cists at Poynter's Gardens on St Mary's in the Isles of Scilly (Dudley 1960-61). The majority of recorded pebbles are of quartz, which are one of the most commonly reported grave finds within the Harlyn Bay cist cemetery (Bullen 1912, 52).

Across Cornwall, where documented, cemeteries appear to have been separated from settlements. The Forrabury cemetery appears to have been located away from the nearest settlement and at Harlyn Bay, the cist graves were located at a discrete distance from the roundhouses (Jones and Quinnell 2014, 146–152). At Scarcewater, an extended inhumation in an east-west aligned grave, a second probable grave and a cist of Roman period date were found on the outer margins of a field system (Jones and Taylor 2010, 55–59) but the location of the settlement is unknown. Spatial separation of graves from settled areas at Forrabury and Harlyn Bay suggests that the dead were segregated from the living. The same may be true at Newquay, although a wider area would have to be investigated to confirm this.

Chapter 11

Inscribing the landscape and hiding in plain view

Andy M Jones and Graeme Kirkham

This chapter is intended as a synthetic extended essay which can almost be read in isolation from the rest of the monograph. It is in two parts. The first considers the evidence for 'structured' or 'special deposits'. As we shall see, neither of these terms are without their difficulties, not least because of the baggage that they have acquired and the lack of precision with which they are often used. Nonetheless, it is argued here that with proper deliberation these deposits provide a useful way for examining patterns of practice over time. Because of this, the locales where these deposits occur, whether at places such as ancient monuments or field boundaries, are considered, as are the commonalities and contrasts between Iron Age and Roman deposits.

The second area for discussion is a particular form of 'special' practice, namely that of deliberate or ritualized abandonment. The evidence for this in the Middle Bronze Age has seen wide discussion in the archaeological literature (Brück 1999a; 1999b; Ladle and Woodward 2009) but until recently far less has been said of the Iron Age and Roman periods. The second part of the chapter is therefore an initial attempt to rectify this.

Structured deposition, 'special deposits' and marking the spatial limits in the later Iron Age and Roman period

Waste or ritual deposition?

Structured deposition in Iron Age contexts has been widely accepted for the last few decades, particularly since the publication of J D Hill's monograph in 1995. By contrast, the study of ritualized deposits in Roman Britain has until recently developed along rather different lines to those of the preceding Bronze and Iron Age periods. As Richard Bradley (2017, chapter 2) has noted, the Roman Conquest marks one of the fault lines in the way that the archaeological record is studied and interpreted. Formalized ritual associated with shrines and temples (for example, Wheeler and Wheeler 1932; Rahtz 1951; Woodward and Leach 1993) has long been recognized, but 'odd' deposits dating to the Roman period, especially those found in 'uninteresting', 'marginal' areas of Britain (Chadwick 2004), have generally had rather less discussion than their prehistoric counterparts. It is only comparatively recently that hoards and deposits from Roman and later periods have been considered in a non-functional way (for example, Bland 2015).

However, following the work of scholars such as Manning (1972), Hill (1995), Clarke (1997), Chadwick (2004) and Hingley (2006), structured deposition or the placing of 'special' deposits within both late prehistoric and Romano-British settlement contexts, such as ditches, pits, wells and postholes is increasingly being recognized by both academic and field archaeologists across Britain (Maltby 1994; Hingley 2006; Chadwick 2012; 2015; Cool and Richardson 2013; Humphreys 2017). For example, at Rothwell Haigh, Leeds, a fourth century AD well within an enclosure was found to contain a huge number of artefacts (Cool and Richardson 2013). The assemblage included a rotary quern roughout, articulated animal bones (probably originally whole carcases, including at least 34 sheep / goats) and a decapitated human skull, probably curated, plus pieces of leather, shoes and complete ceramic vessels. As the authors of the paper note, the finds from the well contain all the 'usual markers of structured deposition' and, as they state 'Over the past quarter of a century there has been a growing realisation that items previously categorised as simple rubbish had frequently been placed, often in rites of termination and with some form of votive or placatory intent' (*ibid*, 191).

As noted above, identifying this type of activity is not without its difficulties and it is not always clear what criteria have been used to decide how a deposit is determined as being 'special'. As Adrian Chadwick (2015) has cogently argued, many sites are not adequately sampled to sort out the 'magic' from the 'mundane', and by their nature it is often difficult to ascertain which 'mundane' objects were deposited for 'magical' purposes (Beck 2016). In Cornwall, there is an additional problem in that most sites lack the faunal assemblages which can, for example, provide evidence for the deliberate deposition of articulated animal bone (for example, Morris 2007; 2011; Chadwick *et al* 2013).

It is also likely that much that ended up in archaeological 'sites' was, after cycles of use and reuse (*cf* McOmish *et al* 2010), disposed of without much thought as refuse, and that the majority of actions involving discard were of a quotidian nature, undertaken routinely with very little deliberation. Some pits, for example, may have been dug to hold 'special deposits', others may have been deliberately infilled with deposits in a deliberately ritualized way, but the majority are likely to have been filled without much premeditated thought. Nonetheless, as Henrietta Moore's (1986) classic anthropological study of the Endo people of Kenya revealed, the ritualized deposition of everyday artefacts can, regardless of overt intention, be filled with symbolism. Indeed, it is well-known from sociological studies that such 'everyday' routine actions help structure human experience of the world (for example, Bourdieu 1977; Giddens 1984).

The deposition of apparent 'waste' may, for example, have metaphorical links to agriculture and the production of food, and to other activities such as metalworking (for example, Moore 1986, 111–115; Williams 2003). These links may have structured routines and dispositions and consequently, individuals are likely, at least at a subconscious level, to be guided by a set of unquestioned and enmeshed functional and symbolic requirements, 'providing a mnemonic for day to day action within ordered space' (Moore 1982, 79), which could operate at a 'day to day' activity routine level, although at other times they could inform deliberate action.

It is also certainly the case in pre-modern and / or non-industrialized societies, or among the disenfranchised, that frequent, usually small-scale, apotropaic and healing rituals were undertaken as a matter of routine (Thomas 1971, chapter 8; Merrifield 1987; Harte 2018), as part of everyday life. These were undoubtedly considered to be effective and carried out with pragmatic intent to achieve practical, desired outcomes (Brück 1999a).

However, because such actions are part of a continuum of practice (Thomas 2012), distinguishing which deposits are 'special' from those which are not is difficult, although arguably those found in certain liminal parts of the settlement where boundaries or thresholds were crossed, such as doorways, enclosure entrances and ditch terminals (Brück 2001; Chadwick 2015), may have been undertaken with more formalized intent. With this in mind we will return to Newquay and highlight a number of deposits in key locations on the site which credibly have the potential to represent signs of greater deliberation or to have been carried out with 'knowledgeable intent' (*cf* Leonard 2015a).

Special deposits in later prehistoric and Roman period Cornwall: bridging the gap

Despite legitimate reservations (for example, Joy 2015), the deliberate selection and placement of artefacts is accepted as relatively commonplace in Iron Age contexts, and increasingly so in those of the Roman period, with the persistence into these eras of long-established ritualized patterns of practice (or elements of such practices) (for example, Richardson 1997, 88; Ten Harkel et al 2017). An obvious instance of this can be seen in the continuing deposition of metalwork into wet places, which spans the Bronze Age, Iron Age, Roman and post-Roman periods, and which occurs across many areas of Britain and widely across northern and western Europe (Bradley 1990; 2017; Bradley *et al* 2015; Haselgrove 2015; Naylor 2015).

In Cornwall there are numerous examples of metal objects of both Iron Age and Roman date found in or close to wet or 'watery' areas during the exploitation of streamworks (Penhallurick 1986; 1997) (Fig 11.1), which were worked for tin and probably gold (Timberlake and Hartgroves, forthcoming) from the Early Bronze Age into the medieval period. Finds from streamworks commence from the Early Bronze Age and are usually recorded as being found 'on the tin ground' (Penhallurick 1986, 173–174), and it is possible that they were deliberately deposited into the streamworks, as offerings during the time that they were being worked. It is also worth noting that more documented artefacts have been recovered from streamworks in Cornwall, than in rivers, which are frequently places of deposition in other parts of Britain (for example, Bradley 1990).

In addition to the Broadwater cauldrons mentioned above, Iron Age artefacts recovered include a La Tène brooch from Red Moor, Lanlivery, and a neck collar or torc from a peat bog near Bodmin (Penhallurick 1986, 197–198). Roman period finds include a tin bowl with a lid and a brooch from Treloy, near St Columb Minor, and around 1000 coins in a pot in marshland near Marazion (Gilbert 1817, 193), which appear to have been deposited without the intention of later recovery. At Pennance Point on the Lizard a hoard of approximately 1000 Roman coins was found during ploughing in 1865; these may have been within a bag that had been placed on a 'rude stone floor', approximately 0.6m below the surface (Penhallurick 2009, 177). The site, which may have been a structure of some sort, was on a hillside above Sunny Cove.

Comparable coin hoard deposits from creek-side locations are known from a significant number of locations in Cornwall, including St Michael Caerhays, Malpas, Condurrow (on the Helford), a creek in Constantine, Tywardreath, Turnaware and Lerryn (Penhallurick 2009, 192–209, 141, 36, 37, 247–251, 251, 109–115). In the case of one creek-side location at Hayle Causeway the coin hoard was particularly unusual in that 'probably some thousands' of coins were buried in a copper vessel; many of the surviving coins seem to be copies and could be considered to be 'mock money' made for ceremonial purposes (*ibid*, 50–51). Additional finds have also been made by metal detectorists in

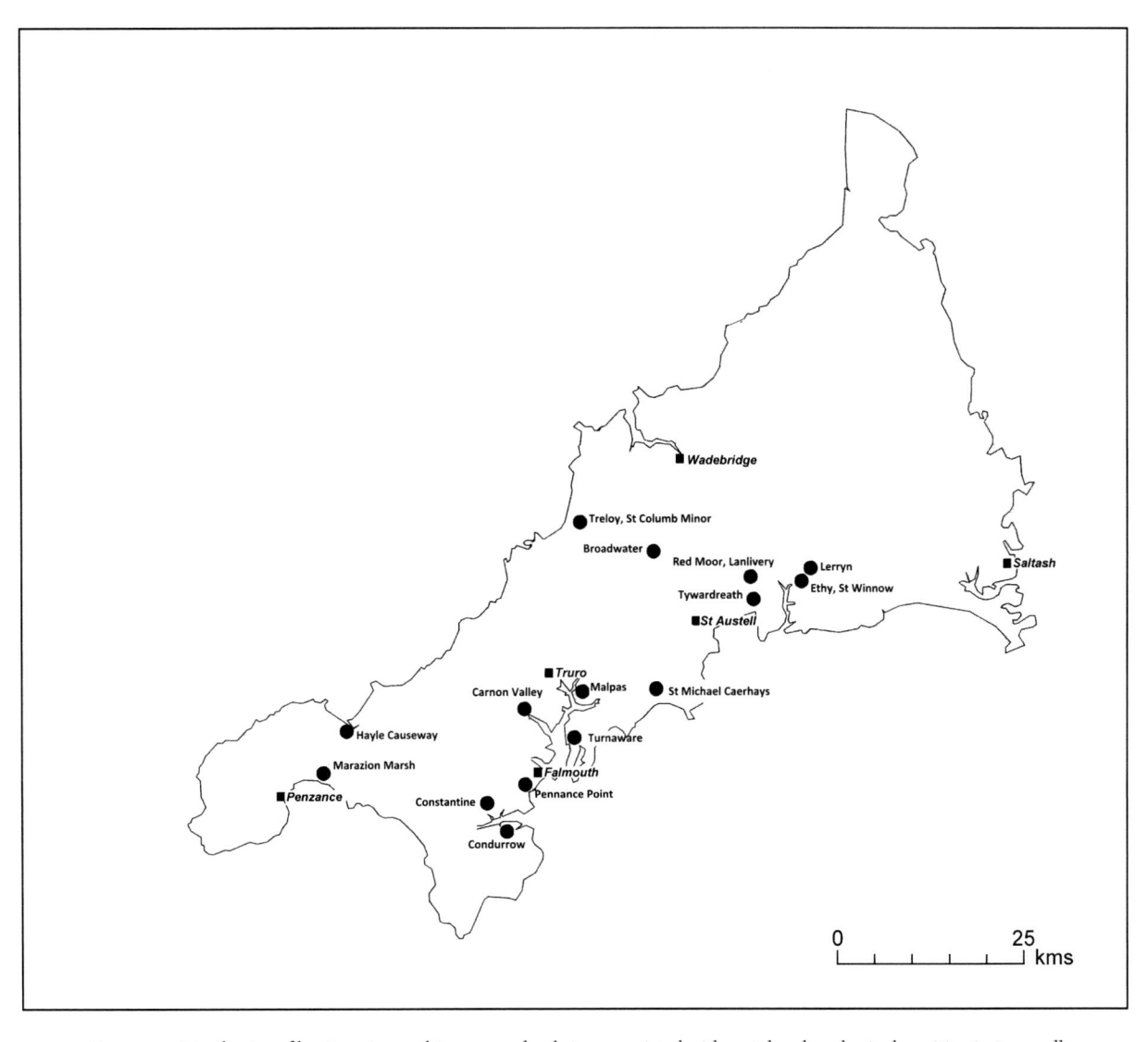

Figure 11.1 Distribution of key Iron Age and Roman wetland sites associated with metalwork and coin deposition in Cornwall referred to in Chapter 11.

recent years; for example, 1091 radiates found in a pot beside a creek at Ethy, St Winnow (Penhallurick 2009, 42).

The Fal Valley and especially the Carnon Valley appear to have been important foci for deposition, with finds from the Fal Valley including the Trenowth collar and a pewter bowl, and the Carnon Valley an Early Bronze Age flat axe and a (now lost) coin hoard of third century AD date (Penhallurick 1986, chapter 25).

Arguably, the tradition of depositing metal artefacts may have continued long after the Roman period. Early-medieval brooches have been recovered from streamworks in St Ewe and Lanivet and the recovery of the spectacular Trewhiddle hoard from beneath a heap of stones in a hole within a streamwork at a depth of 5m below surface suggests deliberation, although this has usually been interpreted as concealment with the intention of later recovery (Penhallurick 1986, 181–183, 187, 200; Wilson and Blunt 1961). Given the long-established tradition of depositing metalwork into streamworks and the recognition of comparable early medieval activity elsewhere (Thomas 2008; Naylor 2015), it is possible that ritualized depositional practices in Cornwall extended into the later ninth century AD. Traces of the practice may even have continued beyond that: medieval coins have been recovered from streamworks near St Austell, in St Stephen-in-Brannel and at Treloy (St Columb Minor), and part of a medieval crucifix came from a depth of 9m in the Carnon River (Penhallurick 1986, 182, 187, 190, 194, 203).

Nonetheless, as Humphreys (2017) has demonstrated in relation to metalwork hoards, there were changes to ritualized practices in the Roman period, some of which are paralleled on the Continent, and there is likely to have been a *bricolage* comprising continuity of tradition and changes to and selective borrowing of beliefs after the Conquest, if not before during the Late Iron Age (Cool and Richardson 2013; Garland 2013). It is therefore probable that many aspects of life during this period in Cornwall showed a 'distinctive mix of indigenous Iron Age traditions with adapted Roman ideas' (Quinnell 2004, 236).

In addition to deposits in 'wet places', most frequently streamworks, it is certainly the case that across Cornwall, excavation of rounds and other forms of enclosure have provided good evidence for both 'mundane discard' and the presence of 'special deposits' in the Iron Age and beyond. For example, at the Roman period round or enclosed settlement at Trethurgy, in addition to 'mundane discard' of an artefactual assemblage which included samian, South Devon Ware and BB1 ceramics, part of a Trethurgy-type stone bowl and a rotary quern had been buried during the construction of possible shrine structure G (Quinnell 2004, 236–237). On the same site, pit [78] had been infilled with a saddle quern, waterworn stones, sherds of pottery and an iron ring. The pit is of particular interest because it was situated close to structure E, a probable granary (*ibid*), and there is an obvious potential symbolic association between the quern and a place where grain was stored.

The interplay of continuity and change between the Iron Age and Roman period may be indicated by the deposit found within one of three sub-rectangular enclosures at Bosence, near St Erth. William Borlase (1769, 316) recorded that a shaft was found in the north-west corner of the easternmost enclosure in the group. This was approximately 11m deep and 0.8m in diameter. At the bottom were found a pewter *patera* (libation bowl) dedicated to Mars, a lead jug, two stone weights, a 'small millstone' (probably a rotary quern), a second *patera* with two handles, fragments of horns, bones, half-burnt sticks and pieces of leather, shreds of worn-out shoes (Fig 11.2), and a 'dish or bowl'. Borlase described the pit as a well and, while this functional interpretation may be correct, shafts and wells were frequently used for ritual deposition in the Late Iron Age (Ross 1974, 46–59; Green 1986, 150–157), although the majority have been argued to be of Roman date (Webster 1997). Overall, the datable items suggest that the artefacts from the Bosence shaft belong to the third or fourth centuries AD (Wilkes *et al* 2012). The date of the Bosence enclosure(s) is uncertain, as square enclosures can be Late Iron Age or Roman in date (for example, Gossip and Jones 2009-10; Gossip 2013). It is, however, very possibly of significance that the site is overlooked by Castle Pencaire, a major prehistoric earthwork enclosure on Tregonning Hill which lies to the east (Cornish 1906, 472). Numerous find-spots of Late Bronze Age metalwork have been recorded in the immediate area of the Bosence enclosures in recent years, including one gold and 44 bronze pieces from three locations in the same field at Gulyn, approximately 300m to the west (Cornwall HER MCO41903), and a socketed chisel from outside Bosence round (Cornwall HER MCO45411). In addition, large numbers of Roman coins have long been known in the wider vicinity of Bosence, suggesting perhaps that the area continued to be the focal point for deposition over a very extended period (Hencken 1932, 198–199; Penhallurick 2009, 23).

Although the Bosence enclosures may belong to either the Iron Age or Roman period, the character of the deposit within the shaft, which included animal bone and a quern stone, arguably has affinities with deposits known from Late Iron Age sites, including, for example, those placed into the ditch which encircled enclosure 1 on a site at Camelford (Fig 11.3). There a substantial pit was cut into the enclosure ditch terminal with deposits which included a large number of Late Iron Age Cordoned Ware sherds, a hand-forged nail, a water-worn pebble, notched slates, quantities of burnt stone, a large amount of burnt mammal bone fragments and a smaller amount of unburnt bone (Jones and Taylor 2015). The placing of structured deposits within the enclosure at Bosence could therefore be argued to represent continuity of tradition from the preceding Iron Age. The choice of some of the materials at Bosence, such as the pewter *patera* with its dedication to the god Mars, must indicate interactions with the Roman world and a desire to formally mark them through their inclusion within a structured deposit.

Figure 11.2 Photograph showing the Roman patera and jug recovered from the shaft / well at Bosence. (AN1836 p.126.146 and AN1836 p.127.179. Image © Ashmolean Museum, University of Oxford.)

for repeated structured deposits; at, for example, a 'fortified enclosure' at Chygwidden in Sancreed, a deposit recorded behind the rampart in the nineteenth century was said to have included coins with 'pottery, ashes and grinding stones' (Penhallurick 2009, 36). At Treryn Dinas, there are reports of 'a brass pot of coins' and later reports of coins and glass being found (Russell 1971; Penhallurick 2009, 225). Similarly, at Maen Castle there are 'odd' finds in the form of a Roman steelyard weight from the surface (Herring 1994) as well as pebbles, a glass bead and sherds from many vessels within the enclosure, and Roman coins from a deposit in a field boundary in the immediate vicinity (Crofts 1954–55; Russell 1971; Nowakowski and Quinnell 2011, 382). Both these latter sites are located in spectacular liminal locations (Sharpe 1992) and are likely to have been revered places in both the Iron Age and Roman periods.

The recovery of Roman coins at enclosures could be argued to have antecedents in the local Iron Age, given the discoveries of two coin hoards dating to the first century BC on Carn Brea, near Redruth (Borlase 1769, 242–247; Penhallurick 2009, 29).

Figure 11.3 Photograph of Camelford enclosure 1, showing the pit cut into the southern ditch terminal.

A comparable discovery was made within the Iron Age hillfort at Cadbury Castle in east Devon (Wilkes *et al* 2012), where a deep shaft within the enclosed area was found to contain a very large artefact assemblage of late Roman date which included many bracelets, glass beads, a copper-alloy finger ring and ear-rings, pottery and animal bone. As the authors note, most shaft deposits of this type are now dated to the Roman period and pre-Roman evidence is limited, but religious practices in the south west region are significantly different (for example, in the lack of temples and formal shrines) from those found elsewhere in Roman Britain. Further away in Dorset, Somerset and Gloucestershire it is certainly the case that hills with earlier earthworks became the locations for shrines and temples in the Roman period (Wheeler 1943; Pearce 1978, 86; Woodward 1992, chapter 2; Woodward and Leach 1993; Casey and Hoffmann 1999). The lack of comparanda from other hillforts in Cornwall and Devon probably reflects the dearth of excavation or buildings that can readily be assigned as being non-domestic (for example, Romankiewicz 2018).

There is, however, evidence that some enclosed settlements in the region may also have been the focus

It is interesting to note that excavation of one of the Iron Age roundhouses on Carn Brea also produced a Roman brooch and a coin (Peter 1896; Mercer 1981). In light of the discovery of a Late Bronze Age hoard and a socketed axe on Carn Brea (Pearce 1976; Cornwall HER MCO360), deposition on the hill may have even earlier origins. Taken together these finds suggest that Carn Brea may also have been a locale which became a focus for repeated deposition over a period of a millennium and more.

Later Roman finds described as votive or 'special 'deposits' are exemplified by those found at Nornour in the Isles of Scilly (Dudley 1967; Butcher 1978; 2000–1; 2014). Here, buildings of Bronze Age construction with later Iron Age occupation were again reused in the Roman period. The Roman period was, however, not marked by domestic occupation; instead, a former house became the focus for the deposition of a remarkable number of artefacts. These included over 300 brooches of later first to later third century AD date (Butcher 2014). In addition, there were clay figurines, including two goddesses, coins, finger rings, glass beads, bracelets and 30 miniature vessels which may have been used to hold small votive offerings (Butcher 2000-1). The miniature vessels are odd because they are made of gabbroic clay from the mainland and have cord impressions, reflecting much older Bronze Age ceramic practices (Henrietta Quinnell, pers comm). The site has been interpreted as a shrine, perhaps to the goddess Sulis, with the suggestion that the artefacts were placed as offerings by sailors journeying between Britain and the Continent (Thomas 1985, 163-165; Butcher 2014). This may well be the case, but what is striking is the apparent length of time over which the shrine was used and the fact that a disused settlement was selected as the place for the deposits to be made.

Such activities are not confined to the south west peninsula. For example, in Wessex, beside the Roman road at Cold Kitchen Hill (Brixton Deverell), 'a remarkable collection of artefacts' stretching from the earliest Iron Age into the Roman period suggest that the site was used as a shrine for votive offerings (Cunliffe 1973, 216), and it is also possible that a temple may have been located there in the Roman period. Tan Hill, in Wiltshire, on the southern edge of the Marlborough Downs, is marked by a complex of linear earthworks of probable later prehistoric date (Kirkham 2005). The hill was the focus for deposition of a variety of metalwork through the Bronze Age (Barber 2005), but a small Roman coin hoard and a Roman period brooch are also known from the site (Wiltshire HER MWI 17812; 18531). As with Bosence and Cadbury Castle, the ancient or ancestral connection may have made such places particularly suitable as locales for deposition during the Roman period.

Revisiting monuments

In addition to the reuse of ancient enclosures, recent study has revealed that comparable Late Iron Age and Roman period interventions at earlier prehistoric monuments were widespread across Europe (Williams 1998; 2004; Bradley 2002, 116-119). Across Britain and Ireland, there are many instances of burial and coin deposition within round and long barrows and at megalithic tombs, henges and stone circles, including at Stonehenge, where a substantial number of Roman finds and a burial have been found (Dark 1993, 136-139; Darvill and Wainwright 2009; Bowden *et al* 2015, 79-81).

Silbury Hill, near Avebury in Wiltshire, was evidently a focus in the landscape in both the Iron Age and Roman periods. A Late Bronze Age / Iron Age copper-alloy bracelet was recovered from the ditch around the bottom of the hill and a possible Iron Age temple has been identified by geophysical survey to the east of it (Leary *et al* 2013, 300-301). Roman artefacts have also been recovered from the ditch around the Hill, to the south of which was a Roman settlement, from which they may have been derived. Roman coins have been recovered from the top of Silbury Hill and a significant number were also recovered from a well to the south of it which was excavated in the nineteenth century, and it is possible that they were votive deposits (Crosby *et al* 2013, 265, 280-281). Other wells around the bottom of the hill were filled with more 'mundane' deposits, but arguably they show the continuing importance of an ancient monument and could have been linked with Romano-British religious activity (Wheatley 2015). Recently a comparable pattern of deposition has been found at Urchfont Hill in the Vale of Pewsey, where 15 Late Iron Age and 398 Roman coins were found near to a Bronze Age round barrow (Roberts *et al* 2017). Subsequent survey and excavation revealed that the barrow was itself located within an enclosure of prehistoric date.

Beyond Wessex, the deposition of Roman coins and other gold objects, brooches and beads at the Middle Neolithic passage tomb at Newgrange, Co Meath, in Ireland is well known (O' Kelly 1982, 36-37, 74) but deposits of organic items – possibly food offerings – and bone artefacts dating to this period have also been recorded from other passage tombs and megalithic structures (Waddell 1998, 369; O'Brien 1999, 137-318).

Cornwall, too, offers several instances of later prehistoric and particularly Roman period activity of an apparently ceremonial nature at earlier prehistoric monuments. At Eathorne near Constantine, a standing stone of expected prehistoric date gave a radiocarbon determination which fell well outside the anticipated Late Neolithic – Early Bronze Age horizon assumed for standing stones in Britain (for example, Williams 1988) and instead returned a Roman period date (Hartgroves *et al* 2006). This strongly suggested that the stone had been re-erected, thereby indicating continuing interest in an ancient site. Although this date was initially a surprise, a review of the literature has revealed a number of earlier prehistoric sites in Cornwall which appear to have become the focus for activity in the Roman period.

Excavation of the Try menhir, Gulval, uncovered a Beaker-associated cist burial immediately adjacent to the east of the stone but also found that the western side of the cut in which the stone stood had been disturbed and a deposit of horse bones and a coin of Gallienus (AD 259-268) inserted (Russell and Pool 1963, 15). Although undated it seems most probable that the deposit was made within a relatively short time after the currency of the coin; the excavators proposed that the deposits probably occurred 'during Roman times' (*ibid*, 24). A hoard of approximately 200 Roman coins was found in 'clearing round a large stone' in a field at Lower Bodinnar in Sancreed parish in 1829 (Penhallurick 2009, 116), although in this case the 'stone' may have been a natural boulder, rather than a standing stone.

An urn containing Roman coins was said to have been recovered from the foot of a 'very long and large stone' near Carn, in Morvah (Hitchins 1803, 226-227; Borlase 1872, 183). Borlase (1769, 300, 307-308) also reported the discovery of Roman coins – almost certainly votive deposits – within large cists containing urned cremations at Golvadnek Barrow, Wendron, in 1700, and at the Giant's Rock, Towednack, in 1702. W C Borlase (1872, 247-252) found later Roman coins within a cist notionally sealed in a cairn on Morvah Hill in Penwith, a circumstance which unfortunately was to convince him of the post-Roman origins of Cornish cairns and barrows (ibid, 263-264). Finally, two Roman coins were recovered during rescue recording of a barrow at Trewrickle Beacon, Sheviock, in 1982 (Penhallurick 2009, 246), which is again indicative of engagement with an 'ancient' place.

From this rapid review it is clear that during a broad chronological period ranging from the later Iron Age into the Roman period there are instances of prehistoric standing stones and other earlier monuments becoming the focus for renewed ceremonial and votive activities. However, given the spans of time involved much of this activity may represent attempts to 'remember' or reinvent the past and create social memory, or, given the length of time between some episodes of reuse, to actively create a fictive 'continuity' (Bradley 1993, 116-117; Golosetti 2017; Jones, forthcoming b).

Enclosing: exits and entrances

As well as being found at 'ancient' monuments, 'special' deposits have also been identified in Cornwall in association with both Iron Age and Roman period pits, field boundaries, and settlement-related structures (for example, Jones 2000-1; Gossip and Jones 2007, 49; Johns 2008; Borlase and Wright 2014). It is undoubtedly the case that bounding spaces both large and small became of paramount importance, with enclosed spaces ranging from hillforts to rounds and compounds down to ring-gullies around individual structures and activity areas (Quinnell 2004; Gossip and Jones 2007; Edwards and Kirkham 2008; Borlase and Wright 2014). At Gear, on the Lizard, for example, not only was the hilltop enclosed by ditches and banks, but the space inside it was further sub-divided by small enclosures, within which were gullies around houses and perhaps a ditched field system (Edwards and Kirkham 2008). At the same time, there is evidence that particular activities, such as larger-scale metalworking, were undertaken within enclosed and bounded spaces. Enclosures including those at Little Quoit Farm, Killigrew and Hay Close (Lawson-Jones and Kirkham 2009-10, 220; Cole and Nowakowski, forthcoming; Jones 2014) may have been constructed to contain 'magical', ritualized tasks involving the production of iron (Hingley 1997; and see below).

Contemporary with this, as discussed above, the Iron Age and Roman period in Cornwall also witnessed the expansion of the ditch-defined boundary, as opposed to, for example, fields demarcated solely by banks or stone walls which are found in West Penwith (Young 2012, 91-94). The digging of ditched field systems could have been linked with an intensification of agricultural practices in the Roman period, which is also indicated by the very substantial increase in the number of enclosed farming settlements or rounds during the early Roman period (cf Quinnell 2004, chapter 12). This expansion must also, however, have been associated with changes to ownership or rights of access to land, which required the ground to be re-inscribed (Chadwick 2013). It is also the case that the creation, maintenance and reworking of field systems would have been important for the reproduction of personal and community identity (Chadwick 2004). Either way, this re-inscribing marked the land and the breaking of the ground provided places or junctions for deposits to be made.

Patterns of boundedness and deposition, found throughout the Iron Age and Roman period across Cornwall and elsewhere, were apparent along the route of the road corridor at Newquay, where there was evidence for the formalized marking of space, the deliberate infilling of certain pits and ditches and the deliberate closure of at least some structures.

A scattering of pits

One of the most commonly encountered contexts for 'structured' deposits are pits, which, as noted above, form a frequent repository for artefacts and other deposits. However, as previously noted, sorting out 'rubbish' from 'special' deposits can be difficult. Nonetheless, given the fact that 'waste' from settlements could, as in later periods, easily have been added to household or farm middens and then spread over the fields as part of a manuring regime, the excavation of pits for rubbish disposal in a rural context would not have been necessary. Pit digging can therefore be interpreted as a particular tradition or disposition.

At the Newquay Strategic Road corridor there were certainly several pits which could be argued to have 'special' or 'odd' contents. For example, pit [435] located just beyond the south east corner of Hollow 2. This was partially lined with slates, but where these stones were not present, the natural clay had become scorched and it is thought that the feature was a hearth pit. The fill of the pit, however, was not burnt but did contain one of the larger assemblages of Late Iron Age pottery from the site. This implies that the pit may have been deliberately cleaned out before the pottery was placed within it. Likewise, nearby pit [491] was filled by a quartz-rich deposit which contained **S4**, a decorated stone spindle whorl of Middle to Late Iron Age date (Chapter 4). On the north side of Hollow 1 were pits [309] and [346]. Pit [346] contained sherds from **P10**, a well-made storage jar, and prior to infilling may have been used for cooking or heating as the natural subsoil around the edge of the pit had been scorched red. Pit [309] contained sherds from **P9**, a Late Iron Age Cordoned Ware vessel and a small assemblage of charred cereal grains. Burnt stones were identified in the fill of the pit, which might have been linked to its use. The artefactual and environmental assemblages from these pits stand out from the majority of other features within the hollow, which were largely devoid of artefacts or charred macrofossil assemblages; the charcoal assemblage from these two pits was also far richer than any other from the area of the hollow (Chapter 7). This might imply that some activity associated with the hollow was perhaps marked by a careful (ritualized?) clearing away of items associated with it. Similarly, pit [334] in Hollow 1 had a fragment from a stone bowl of Trethurgy type **S5** and trimmed slates placed into it. This was the latest and only Roman period find from the hollow and arguably could have been associated with its closure (below).

By contrast, Roman period pit [367] to the west of Hollow 1 was found to contain charred cereal grains together with a large amount of burnt stone which had been dumped into it (Fig 11.4). This deposit is of an ambiguous nature and underlines the interpretative problems posed by certain types of features and their contents. It could be argued either that it represents a deliberate deposit of culturally charged material or simply the clearing away of stones and burnt material.

Other sites across Cornwall have revealed instances of what were apparently 'special' deposits, extending over a considerable span of time. Good examples include a Late Bronze Age pit [5027] at Higher Besore, which was found to contain eight cobble mullers that had apparently been stacked together; fragments of saddle quern and eight sherds of pottery were also recovered from the pit fill (Gossip, forthcoming) (Fig 11.5). This deposit was similar to examples at Trenowah, near St Austell, where pit [345] of Early Iron Age date was found to contain a structured deposit (Johns 2008). Pit [345] had been filled with a deposit which included pottery, saddle querns, rubbing stones and waterworn pebbles (*ibid*) (Fig 11.6).

Moving forward in time, an isolated pit [030] at Penhale Round had been filled by five layers which included clay, charcoal and iron slag from metal smithing, as well as sherds of Roman period pottery (Johnston *et al* 1998–9). As noted above, a good example of a structured deposit is provided by the contents of the Roman period pit [78] at Trethurgy, the finds from which included a saddle quern, waterworn stones and sherds

Figure 11.4 Post excavation photograph of pit [367].

INSCRIBING THE LANDSCAPE AND HIDING IN PLAIN VIEW

Figure 11.5 Photograph of worked stone objects found within Higher Besore pit [5027].

Figure 11.6 Photograph of the cache of worked stone artefacts found within Tremowah pit [345].

of pottery (Quinnell 2004, 236–237). To the south of the Roman period enclosure at Tremough, was pit [337] which contained a broken ceramic cooking vessel and a hammerstone; this showed abrasive wear consistent with repeated use for breaking up stone, perhaps as part of a metalworking process. The pottery was, however, of most interest as it accounted for between 80 and 90 per cent of the vessel and had been deliberately smashed, perhaps by the hammerstone (Fig 11.7). The 70 sherds from the vessel had clearly been carefully arranged, all with their outer faces uppermost, before the pit was backfilled (Gossip and Jones 2007, 49).

By contrast, at Middle Amble, a pit [2-05] filled with grain had been set into the floor of a Late Iron Age roundhouse (Borlase and Wright 2014) (Fig 11.8). Here, the nature of the deposit is more ambiguous and could either be interpreted as, given the potential symbolic association of grain with fertility (Leonard 2015b), a 'ritual' offering or alternatively as evidence for the mundane disposal of inedible charred waste. Although in the latter case it would still require explanation as to why a pit beneath a house floor was selected for 'rubbish' disposal.

Taken together though, the pits at Trenowah, Tremough and Middle Amble are all suggestive of long-held traditions associated with a wide spectrum of depositional activity, concerned on the one hand

Figure 11.7 Photograph of the pottery deposit placed the bottom of pit [337] at Tremough.

Figure 11.8 Photograph showing charred grain deposit in section within pit [2-05], Middle Amble. (Photograph Mark Borlase.)

with the burying of ceramics and worked stones associated with the processing of cereal-derived food, as well as food residues themselves, and on the other at Penhale with metallurgy which, as we shall see, is also a recurring feature.

The contents of most pits are by themselves, however, equivocal in nature. Arguably a better way of establishing the significance of deposits is to consider them in relation to their site geography and settings, and their spatial relationships with other features, such as field boundaries and gullies around structures which, as discussed above, are themselves often repositories for special deposits. The next section will therefore consider the marking of space and the placing of 'special deposits' in relation to one another.

Setting boundaries

The excavations along the Newquay Strategic Road corridor revealed two interesting patterns with regard to features demarcating spaces which also provided locales for 'structured' deposits.

The first form of demarcation was represented by gullies and ditches associated with structures and hollows. As suggested above, for the Newquay site this type of physical demarcation of space can be argued to have its roots in the Middle Iron Age, with Structure 2 and Structure A1 as the earliest examples. As also argued above, it is unlikely that these gullies either served as structural features or were eaves drip rings. It is possible that, if originally associated with banks, they may have kept animals away from the thatched roofs, from rubbing against daub walls or trying to get inside the buildings or working areas. However, there were no surviving traces of banks, and in some cases the gap between the internal features and the gullies was narrow, which would not have left much space for a substantial bank. Instead, by bounding space, they may have acted to reinforce the appropriate bodily movement by guiding people to the correct point of entry into the structure or hollow, as well as giving a sense of orientation. The latter point is of interest, as where entrances into the excavated structures were identifiable they tended to face towards the south east; postholes in this part of the structures were often marked by a greater number of artefacts. This doorway orientation would have faced towards the rising sun and has been argued in relation to later prehistoric roundhouses to have carried cosmological importance (for example, Parker Pearson 1996; Fitzpatrick 1994; 1997).

However, there is likely to have been a good deal of regional variation (for example, Webley 2007) and more generally in Cornwall during the Iron Age and Roman period there does not seem to have been a particularly strong directional association with the south east; the entrance into the roundhouse structure 4 at Camelford School, for example, faced south and both of the ceremonial enclosures were oriented to the east (Jones and Taylor 2015). Furthermore, analysis of enclosures in the hinterland of the Camel estuary has revealed that most enclosure entrances are located in the western quadrant, with a few in the east and north east (Young 2012). In fact, structures within rounds tend to have had entrances facing in towards the middle of the enclosed space, rather than in one direction, as for example, can be seen at Trethurgy and Shortlanesend rounds (Quinnell 2004, 7; Schwieso 1976).

The symbolic importance of ring-gullies has already been touched on above in relation to the ceremonial and domestic structures at Camelford (Jones and Taylor 2015). This significance is also suggested by the non-structural ring-gullies up to 20m in diameter which encircled roundhouses at Middle Amble Farm, St Kew. One of these gullies was nearly 1m deep (Borlase and Wright 2014). This is clearly much deeper than would be needed either as a drip gully or as a wall slot, and it is obviously not defensive. It would, however, have placed the roundhouse within in its own clearly delimited space. It is also worth noting that much older sites such as round barrows were often encircled by non-functional ditches which delimited the barrow site and were, in the south west peninsula, often the focus for structured deposits (Taylor 1951; Jones and Quinnell 2006b; Nowakowski 2007; Lewis 2007). While Early Bronze Age round barrows and Iron Age roundhouses are separated by a considerable period of time, ditched barrows would still have been landscape features and it possible that some social memory of past practices related to the bounding of space may have persisted (Jones, forthcoming b).

The symbolism of boundaries around Iron Age houses is even more unambiguously demonstrated at Higher Besore, Truro, where both house 3 and house 4 were enclosed by non-structural ring-gullies which had been filled with quartz (Gossip, forthcoming) (Figs 9.2 and 11.9). Quartz, as noted above, occurs frequently in ritualized contexts during the Bronze Age and this continued into the Iron Age, both in Cornwall and elsewhere in Britain (Jones and Taylor 2015; Burl 1976, 171–172; Bradley and Nimura 2016). The use of quartz at Higher Besore is therefore very unlikely to have been fortuitous and its deployment is likely to have been a deliberate act. The houses would have been surrounded by white rings, which may have been intended to be symbolic 'magical' barriers.

Beyond Cornwall, the 'special' marking of boundaries around houses has recently been very clearly demonstrated on a site at Glenfield Park, Leicestershire. As at Higher Besore and Camelford,

Figure 11.9 Photograph of the quartz filled gully encircling Richard Lander Iron Age house 9, looking north west.

the Iron Age roundhouses were set within their own small enclosures. When excavated, large numbers of cauldrons and other metalwork objects were found to been placed into the non-structural ditches which enclosed the roundhouses (Thomas 2017). In other words, the significance of the perimeter was either maintained or marked on abandonment through the deposition of valued items.

None of the ring-gullies around the excavated sites at Newquay had been infilled with quartz and archaeologically visible special deposits were comparatively few. However, these gullies were not structural and even allowing for subsequent truncation they were unlikely to be deep or wide enough to stop an individual or a determined large animal from crossing them, and the amount of upcast from their digging is unlikely to have created a very substantial barrier. Nor was there enough stone in the fills to suggest that there had been a wall or substantial stone face. It is possible that they could have provided enough of a barrier to function in a way which could have excluded children, fowl and small dogs from a particular space, however, this would not prevent them from carrying other symbolic meanings (*cf* Bradley 2005) associated with individual tenure of a particular space by a household, the separation of mutually incompatible activities, such as grain storage and keeping domestic fowl or 'special' activities such as metalworking or grain processing, or areas delimited by age or gender-derived functions.

The desire to maintain a defined space is certainly demonstrated at Hollow 1, where the edges of the hollow were re-inscribed by gullies on more than one occasion; it is, of course, possible that the gullies were regularly cleaned out, although unless carried out robustly enough to appear as a recut, this will not have left a trace in the archaeological record. It seems quite likely, therefore that their primary role was to demarcate the edge of the hollow, thereby spatially separating and defining the activities which took place inside it. Given the large number of intercutting pits in Hollow 1, the majority of which were found in the centre of the hollow and were associated with charcoal and burnt stone, it may be the case, as suggested above, that this part of the site was associated with food processing or preparation. The gullies around this hollow may therefore reflect a desire to separate and 'bound off' the preparation of food from other activities taking place in the surrounding area, and perhaps keep malign 'supernatural' or 'polluting' elements, as well as dogs and other animals at bay.

Similarly, the ring-gully around Structure A3 was, like that around the roundhouse at Middle Amble Farm, deeply cut (up to 0.5m deep within the natural and, of course, even deeper when the topsoil was present) and would have therefore formed a clearly defined boundary between the inside space of the structure and the outside world. The significance of the boundary around Structure A3 may also be reflected in the associated artefactual assemblage. Although Structure A3 was dated to early in the Roman period, the encircling ditch [127] was found to contain a substantial deposit of Middle Iron Age pottery (Quinnell, Chapter 3). This assemblage is much older than the structure and its good condition suggested that it had been curated prior to burial in the ditch (Chapter 3). As such, the pottery may well have been an heirloom which was placed into the bottom of the ring-gully. It is also interesting that, although separated by several centuries, Middle Iron Age Structure A1 and Structure A3 both had similar floor plans, and it is tempting to make a connection between them. Although this connection may not relate to the buildings' functions it may reflect a continuing desire to demarcate structural space in a traditional way.

The second form of spatial demarcation takes the form of depositions made at major ditched boundaries. As discussed above, many of these boundaries are likely to have been associated with the expansion of the field system from the Late Iron Age onwards. However, four of the ditches ([125], [129], [204] and [201]), and possibly [210] and [212], are likely to have been components of a slight two-phased oval enclosure, within which sat Structure 3. All the component ditches produced artefacts. However, the southern ditches ([204] and [201], and [210] / [212]), including what is likely to have been an entrance into the enclosure during one phase, became a focus for what can be interpreted as 'special deposits' which stand out from the background patterning of artefacts found across the site.

The terminal of ditch [204] was marked by deposits which included the largest quantity of charred plant macrofossils found on the site, a large amount of iron ore, sherds of Roman pottery and, rather remarkably, 472 charred hazelnut shell fragments (Fig 11.10). The latter represented the largest concentration of nutshells from the site, yet when radiocarbon dated they were found be of later Neolithic date. It could be argued that they are, like much of the flint from the excavations, entirely residual. However, this would not explain the concentration of the deposit, and another possibility is that when the hazelnut shells were found in the Roman period they were recognized as being food residues from an ancient time or even food belonging to the earth or deities, and because of this were reburied with care in the ditch terminal. As such, they could be argued to demonstrate the continuing biography of objects, or in this case food residue, well beyond the original intent of their users (Joy 2015).

This interpretation is given extra weight by the fact that several kilos of iron ore were also found in the excavated portion of the ditch. This would have been an important commodity, which is likely to have been obtained from the Perran Lode, located approximately 8 kilometres away on the coast to the west (Roger Taylor, pers comm). A second, similar deposit of iron ore was also found in the adjacent pit or ditch terminal [212], which was cut into the earlier ditch [210] (Fig 11.11). The deposition of ore into both of these ditch terminals implies that the identified entrance into the enclosure was a place to be marked by deposits of a valued material. Given that metalworking is likely to have been seen as both a highly dangerous, specialized activity and a magical process (for example, Eliade 1962; Budd and Taylor 1995; Hingley 1997; Giles 2007; Kuijpers 2013), the deposit could have been a propitiatory offering, returned to the ground from whence it came. Such an action may have even been means of ensuring a future supply of metal (Eliade 1962, chapter 3).

In fact, across Iron Age Britain, iron was frequently deposited into liminal places such as the entrances of enclosures or roundhouse doorways (Hingley 1990; 2006), and it is also the case that both metalworking and the production of artefacts were often shrouded in secrecy and undertaken away from 'inhabited areas' (Hingley 1997; Giles 2007; Dolan 2016). The smiths who worked the ores and made artefacts are likely to have been honoured or feared in Iron Age society and in Scandinavia were sometimes associated with death (Hutton 1993, 224–225; Goldhahn and Oestigaard 2008). In European folklore they were often considered to be able to wield supernatural powers through their metalworking (Lönnrot 2008, 88–119). Likewise, in early medieval northern European literature the people who worked iron were respected or often considered to be different from ordinary persons. For example, in *Egil's Saga* Skalligrim's status is reinforced by the fact that he was a great blacksmith and a 'wielder of iron' (Scudder 2004, 53). In the *Poetic Edda* (Larrington 1999, 102), magical weapons are made by the part-divine smith Volund or Wayland, who in *Beowulf* fashions the mail shirt worn by the hero before his combat with Grendel (Heaney 1999, 16).

In part, this significance may have derived from the inherent dangers of working with ores at high temperatures, but it is also likely that the production of iron, beginning with the collection of ore from the ground, through its preparation, and especially smelting, was rich in metaphorical associations. Melanie Giles (2007), following anthropological studies in Africa, has suggested that iron working may have been linked with fertility and the agricultural cycle and death (for example, Eliade 1962, chapter 9; Muller 1999, 268–271). As such, it may have been appropriate to return some of its constituents back to the earth as a deposit within a ditch (Bradley 2017, 119).

The magical properties attached to the iron ore could have been associated with warding off unwanted supernatural presences. Therefore, the iron ore in the ditch terminals at Newquay may also have been

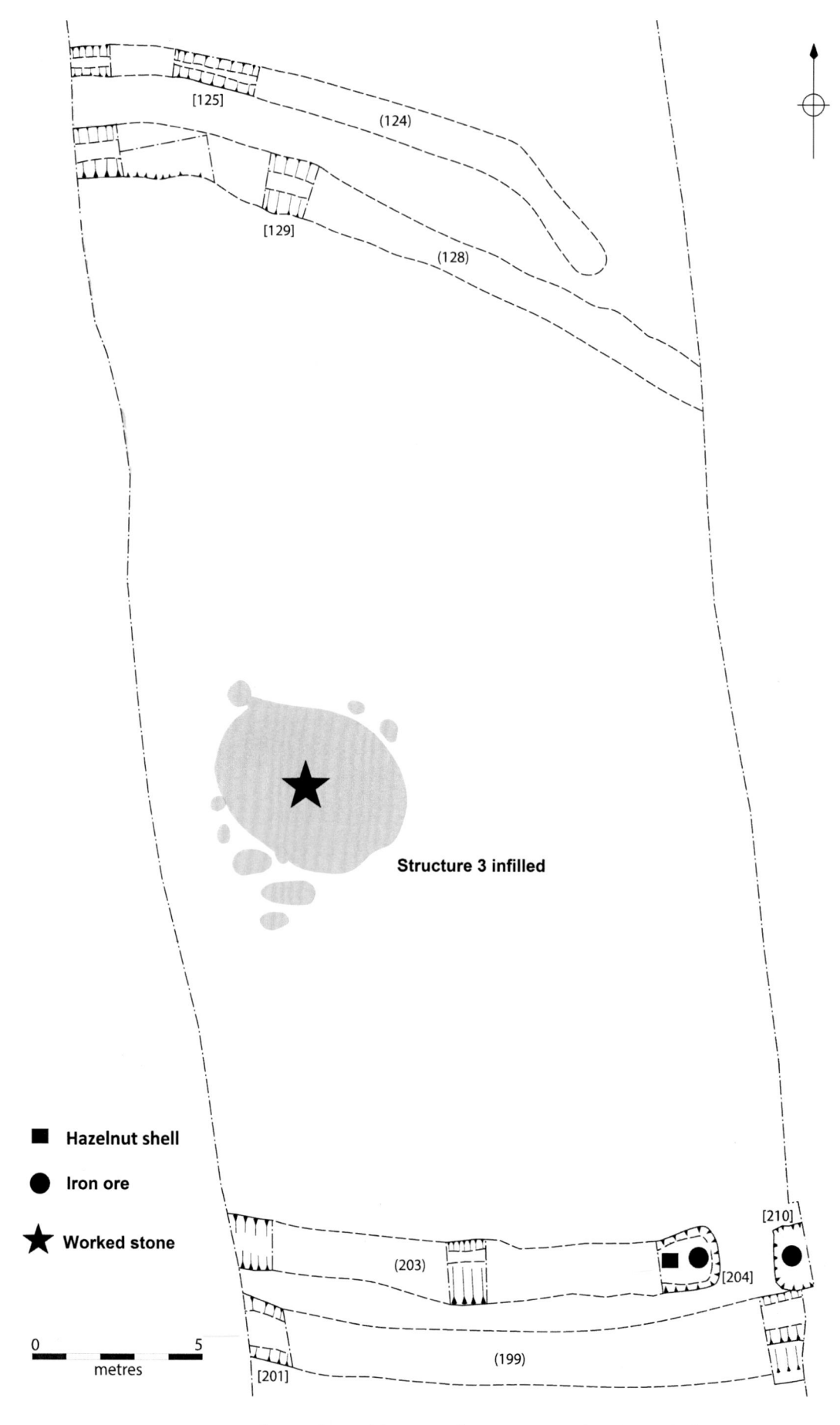

Figure 11.10 Distribution of 'special deposits' within Structure 3 and in adjacent ditches.

Figure 11.11 Photograph showing the deposit of iron ore in section within [210] / [212].

considered to have apotropaic properties, intended to keep malign influences out of the enclosure (Budd and Taylor 1995; Hingley 1997; Aldhouse-Green 2002; Beck 2016), and, in common with querns, they are also likely to have been linked with fertility and the agricultural cycle (below).

The marking of entrances into Iron Age and Roman period enclosures with a variety of deposits has been found elsewhere in Britain (Hill 1995; 1996; Tabor 2008; Chadwick 2015; Bradley 2017, chapter 10; Palmer 2017) and in Cornwall. At Nansledan, not far from the Newquay Strategic Road corridor, a deposit of Early Iron Age pottery has recently been recovered in the terminal of what has been identified as a possible ceremonial enclosure of Early Iron Age date (Rainbird and Pears, forthcoming). Within the enclosure itself, there was a deposit of later Iron Age date which sealed the earlier features; this is discussed below.

Another good example is provided by a slight enclosure of Roman date at Tremough (Gossip and Jones 2007). Here an oval building, structure 338 (above), was surrounded by a ditched enclosure which had two distinct phases. During both of these fresh sherds of pottery were deposited around the circuit of the ditch. The phase 1 ditch [306] contained sherds of pottery which had been fairly evenly spread along its length, the majority of which were freshly broken (Fig 11.12).

In the phase 2 ditch [565], most of the pottery was deposited in the northern arc, increasing in frequency towards its north eastern terminal and the closest point to structure 338: a second concentration occurred close to the south western ditch terminal (Fig 11.13). Almost all the sherds, except for one vessel which showed evidence of curation, were freshly broken and had been quickly covered after deposition (Gossip and Jones 2007, 49–50). They included a group of conjoining sherds which represented one-third of a single ceramic vessel. The very rapid covering suggests a certain degree of overt ritualization of this act: that it was undertaken with 'knowledgeable intent'.

Elsewhere in Cornwall, at a Roman period enclosure at Pollamounter, near St Newlyn East, a pit [242] close to the enclosure ditch was found to contain pottery belonging to two vessels together with burnt animal bone (Jones and Taylor 2004, 39). The pit was interpreted as representing the ritualized clearing away of food residues from feasting and, given its proximity to the ditch, with the symbolic marking of the settlement boundary (*ibid*, 115).

The structured deposition of artefacts within and near to enclosure ditches is paralleled by deposits found in or near to field boundaries, as at Stencoose (Jones 2000–1). There the terminal of a Roman period field ditch [6] at the uphill edge of the field system was the focus for

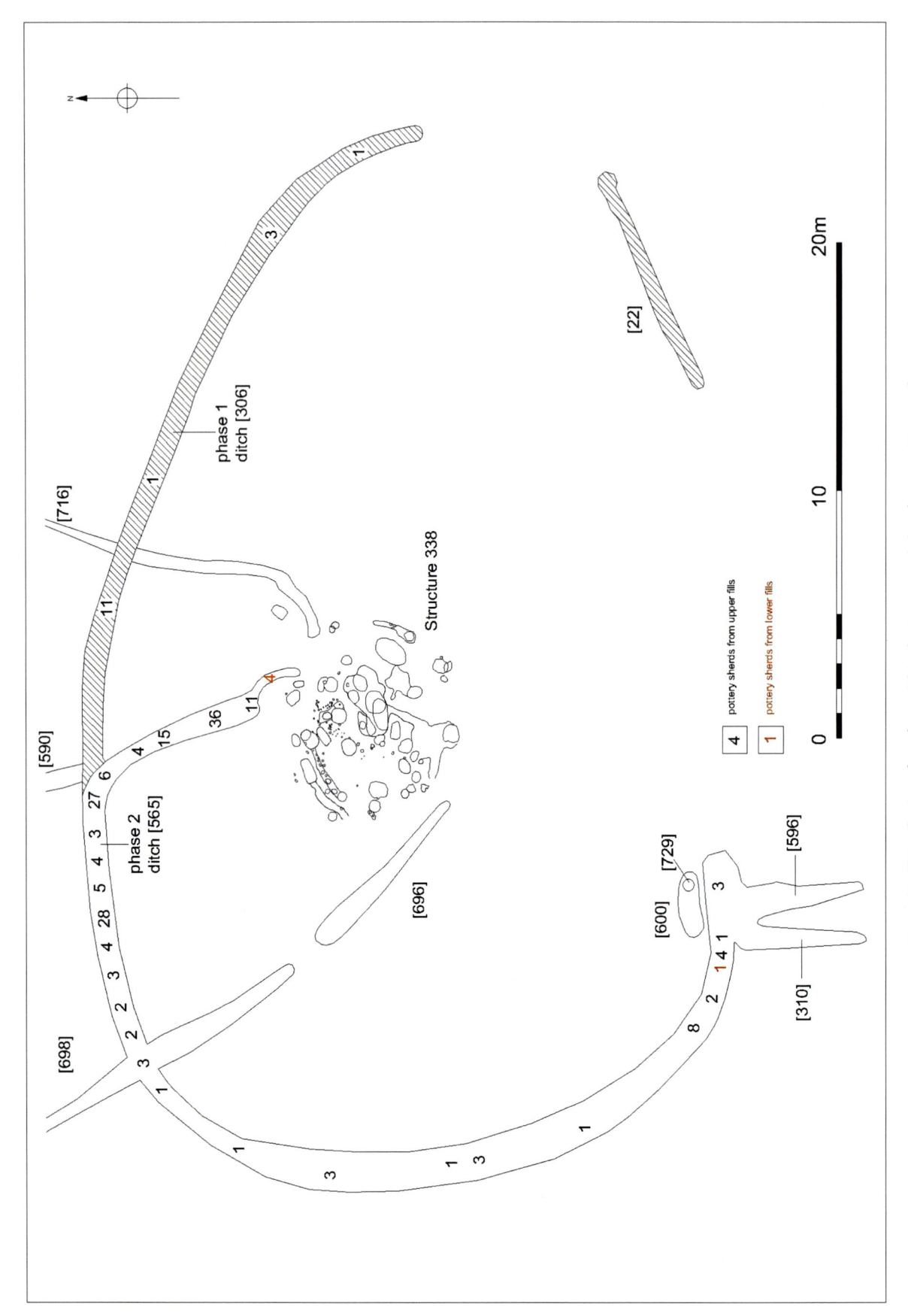

LATER PREHISTORIC AND ROMAN SITES ALONG THE ROUTE OF THE NEWQUAY STRATEGIC ROAD CORRIDOR

Figure 11.12 Distribution of artefacts within the Roman period enclosure at Tremough.

Figure 11.13 Photograph of the pottery deposit placed within the Roman period enclosure at Tremough.

Human remains may also have been placed on the margins of settled areas. As briefly described above, at Scarcewater the upper margin of the Roman period field system was marked by burials (Jones and Taylor 2010, 55–59) (Fig 11.14), and, although this may have been associated with a fear of the dead and a desire to spatially separate the living from the deceased, the depositing of human remains would also have personified the edge of the enclosed space, so that it became associated with past family or community members. Seen in this way, human remains, like other objects, may also have been used in a strategic way to reinforce the boundary of the settlement zone.

The examples from Newquay, Pollamounter, Tremough, Stencoose and Botallack Head all highlight the marking of field boundary edges and enclosure entrances with special deposits. It could be argued that this represented a symbolic marking of ownership or the protecting of weak transitional points between enclosed and open space, or perhaps invoking protection for the area enclosed by making offerings to particular entities thought to have appropriate powers. The materials selected – metal, pottery, and worked stone – are also likely to have been charged with metaphorical associations linked to their inherent properties, the places they were derived from, and the activities and people that they were associated with.

deliberate deposition of sherds of pottery, perhaps marking the boundary to the enclosed land. Two pits, [21] and [24], thought to mark the same alignment as the field system ditches, were also found to contain artefacts. Pit [21], in particular, had been filled with a large number of pottery sherds, an iron object, iron slag and a broken rubbing stone, suggesting special, ritualized emphasis of these alignments and boundaries (*ibid*).

In Penwith, at Botallack Head, near St Just, boundary ditch [5] was found to have been deliberately infilled with a large quantity of tin slag, which was radiocarbon dated to the third to fourth centuries AD, late in the Roman period (Lawson-Jones 2013). The ditch was located near to an oval structure and other pits and ditches, and the apparent deliberate infilling of ditch [5] with debris associated with metalworking was interpreted as representing the marking of a significant boundary with a selected, 'meaningful' deposit (*ibid*). This infilling event, as has been argued above in relation to the iron ore at Newquay, may have represented a partial return to the earth of a material taken from it.

The range of items selected for deposition at Newquay is likely to reflect the main activities which took places within the enclosure. Unfortunately, no evidence for ironworking was found in association with Structure 3, which was the only building within the enclosed space, so it is not possible to make a direct connection. Elsewhere, however, there are indications that there was a relationship between artefacts selected for deposition with activities which had taken place inside the enclosed space. For example, at Tremough (Gossip and Jones 2007, 49) the finds in the enclosure ditch mostly comprised sherds of broken pottery, which had probably been used for cooking and then buried soon after breakage. As such they may have been closely associated with the occupants of structure 338 and with some of the activities which were undertaken inside the enclosure.

Closing structures: saying goodbye and erasing the past

Another distinct aspect of ritualized activity which was identified at Newquay involved the deliberate closure of structures. Three instances of formalized

Figure 11.14 Photograph of the Roman period burial (note body stain in the bottom of grave) located at the upper margin of the field system at Scarcewater.

an accumulation of midden material spanning both Late Iron Age and Roman occupation, closure of the ring-ditch may not have led to total abandonment.

By contrast, the rectangular structure within Hollow 2 appears to have been fully decommissioned. Several of the posts within this structure seem to have been quite forcefully removed and / or obliterated. The post within posthole [418], for example, appears to have been wrenched out of its socket and pit [478] had been cut through two postholes. This must have occurred after the posts had been removed and may represent a deliberate act of obliteration of the sockets, rendering them unusable.

Pit [478] produced only a couple of sherds of Late Iron Age pottery and does not seem to have been the focus for deliberate deposition. This contrasts with pit [491], which was located on the south east corner of Hollow 2. It was very large, measuring 2m long and over 1m wide and 0.47m deep. Again, it appears to have been dug after the rectangular building within Hollow 2 had gone out of use, as two postholes associated with the structure were found at either end of the pit, and all were filled by the same deposit, which strongly suggests

abandonment were identified, at Hollow 1, Hollow 2 and Structure 3, spanning both the Late Iron Age and the Roman period.

The earliest instance of formalized closure was associated with Late Iron Age Hollow 1, where ring-gully [336] which defined the northern side of the structure was filled by a layer that contained a large number of sherds of Late Iron Age pottery (including parts of vessel **P11**) and a 'pot lid', **S13**. The fill deposit was unusual in that it was, by comparison with most of the other archaeological features on the site, artefact-rich. It had also been deposited in such a way that it extended beyond the confines of the ditch cut and also covered pit [346]. There is no indication that the layer had been deposited with any care but it would certainly have buried the ring-ditch and ensured that it was no longer a visible defining boundary around the hollow. The hollow did, however, appear to have been remembered or had some use after the defining gully had been infilled, as a fragment from a stone bowl of a Roman period Trethurgy bowl type **S5** was found inside one of the internal pits. In other words, unless the closure deposit was made using

that the posts had already been removed. The fill was notable in that it contained large pieces of quartz, a sherd of Late Iron Age pottery and a decorated stone spindle whorl **S4** (Fig 11.15). The decorated spindle

Figure 11.15 Photograph of the decorated stone spindle whorl found within pit [491].

whorl was a very fine example and is likely to have been a valued personal belonging. As such, it could fall into the category 'non-purpose made offering', that is to say an artefact made for a functional purpose which was then deposited as an offering (Hughes 2017). Again, it could have carried metaphorical associations with the keeping of sheep, the production of valued woollen garments and thereby the agricultural cycle. As such, it is unlikely to have been a casual loss and was more probably deliberately placed into the pit. As we have seen, quartz was used to demarcate the perimeters of Iron Age structures at Higher Besore (Gossip 2003). Quartz pieces are frequently found in pits and structured deposits throughout the prehistoric period in Cornwall and beyond (Jones 2015; Jones and Smith 2015; Darvill 2012), and it is likely to have been a symbolically charged material. The inclusion of quartz within pit [491] is therefore unlikely to be accidental. Whatever function the rectangular building in Hollow 2 had, considerable effort seems to have been made to remove it and to make a formalized closing deposit.

The deliberate destruction of buildings in Iron Age Cornwall is far less well-documented than in the preceding Bronze Age, nor is it as clearly evident as in the Roman period literature, as will be argued below. Nonetheless, it does seem likely that ritualized abandonment activity occurred at other Iron Age sites but has not been highlighted. In the single roundhouse at Penhale cliff castle, Perranzabuloe, the central hearth had apparently been cleaned out and a group of small, rounded white quartz pebbles of similar size placed on the floor opposite the entrance; a whetstone and a burnisher were also recovered from the layer over the floor. A pit close to the wall opposite the door contained 72 part-rounded slate pebbles and a single sherd of pottery and unabraded sherds from a single vessel had been spread in and outside the doorway (the fact that they were unweathered in this context suggests that they had been protected by another layer after deposition); a spindle whorl was recovered from the top of the roundhouse wall adjacent to the entrance (Smith 1984; 1988).

At Camelford School the ditches encircling both enclosure 1 and enclosure 2 were formally abandoned. Both were infilled with material which contained sherds of Cordoned ware pottery and worked stone, including a fragment from a rotary quern (Figs 11.3, 11.16 and 11.17). This suggests that the activity was broadly contemporary with the Late Iron Age phase at Newquay and occurred at the end of the Iron Age / start of the Roman period (Jones and Taylor 2015). The deliberate infilling of the Camelford ditches, like ring-gully [336], would have levelled the very feature which defined the enclosed space, and this act may have represented a deliberate attempt to prevent further use of the enclosures and erase them from memory (Jones, forthcoming b).

Investigations at Nansledan, Newquay, to the north east of the project area, included a 'hengiform' enclosure which excavation subsequently revealed to be of earliest Iron Age date. As noted above, the terminal of one of the ditches contained an interesting deposit, but the interior witnessed a complex history which extended into the Late Iron Age (Rainbird and Pears, forthcoming). Many of the postholes and pits were covered by a deposit which included 52 sherds of South West Decorated Ware and another 22 sherds of undiagnostic pottery of Late Iron Age date, four pieces of slag, a stone bead, a rubbing stone, a perforated slate weight and a worked slate. This infilling deposit may have been intentionally spread across the interior of the site: it effectively sealed it and prevented further use of the features within it.

Moving forward into the Roman period, Structure 3 on the Newquay road corridor appears to have been a single-phase building. There is for example, little evidence for renewal of structural posts. Most of the finds came from an infill deposit which covered the building after it went out of use. Interestingly, the

Figure 11.16 Photograph of Camelford enclosure 2, showing infill deposits within the northern ditch terminal.

Figure 11.17 Photograph of the quern fragment found in Camelford enclosure 2 ditch.

artefactual assemblage included fragments from two rotary querns (**S2** and **S3**) and a stone bowl **S6** (Fig 4.1). These objects highlight the long-lived (Watts 2014, 45–58) significance of querns and other worked stone in such closure rituals and the connection between the symbolism of the stone objects' association with nourishment and thus continuing life, and their breakage when the continuation of the domestic 'nurturing space' ceased or was given up.

There is every likelihood that local Iron Age ritualized practices associated with querns continued into the Roman period and it seems probable that these associations and practices were augmented by the deliberate fragmentation of other objects associated with the production and transformation of food, such as stone bowls. Broken stone mortars and stone bowls have been found at a number of sites across Cornwall (Quinnell 1993) and although their exact context is not always well-documented, several are from houses and / or associated with post-occupation layers (for example, Quinnell 1992a, 106). Surprisingly, little attention has been paid to how these objects became broken, despite the fact that it would have taken considerable force to break either a mortar or a stone bowl, and even more effort to fragment a quern. This suggests that breakage of these objects was intentional. It is possible that certain items, such as those used to process foods, had become so closely associated with the biographies of their buildings, that when the structure was abandoned, the artefacts were decommissioned and abandoned too.

The lower infill deposit within the Structure 3 hollow was not artefact-rich; however, it did include large granite blocks, which, as noted above, are likely to have been brought to the site from some distance, and blocks of locally occurring vein quartz. Given the frequent association of quartz blocks with ceremonial and ritualized contexts at later prehistoric sites in Cornwall (for example, Jones and Taylor 2015; and below), the selection and inclusion of the quartz blocks as infill deposits within Structure 3 may well have been deliberate.

The abandonment of Structure 3 followed a pattern which has been found, although not often discussed, at other Roman period sites in Cornwall and elsewhere. By contrast with the Neolithic period and especially the Middle Bronze Age, for which the planned or ritualized abandonment of houses across Britain and Europe is accepted and has seen widespread discussion (for example, Midgley 2005, 128–129; Smythe 2006; Russell *et al* 2014; Nowakowski 1991; 2001; Jones *et al* 2015, 177–183; Ladle and Woodward 2009, 72), the ritualized leaving of Roman period structures has not generated much consideration. This is perhaps surprising, given the growing literature on structured deposition in pits and field boundaries (see above).

In fact, comparable evidence for the ritualized abandonment process identified in Structure 3 has been found at a number of other Roman period sites in Cornwall (Fig 11.18). However, given that all the published examples where deliberate abandonment has been identified have been discovered or at least re-interpreted in recent years, it is very likely that the practice was much more widespread but has gone unrecognized. Hugh O'Neill Hencken (1933, 238) did observe, after excavating several courtyard houses at Chysauster in Penwith, that there was patterning in the distribution of artefacts: the 'bulk of finds from the house are to be expected to be found near the entrance to this room' (the large oval room). This distribution might reflect an act of deliberate placement of domestic material prior to abandonment. The interiors of the houses themselves had been infilled, although the excavator did not attribute this to an act of deliberate closure.

By contrast, the excavation of two courtyard houses at Porthmeor (Hirst 1937) revealed 'round rooms' which contained a significantly large number of artefacts. The 'round room' in courtyard house 2 was badly robbed but within courtyard house 1 there were two deposits in the 'round room' which were interpreted as 'occupation' layers. The primary layer was described as 3 inches (0.08m) thick and the secondary 12 inches (0.3m).

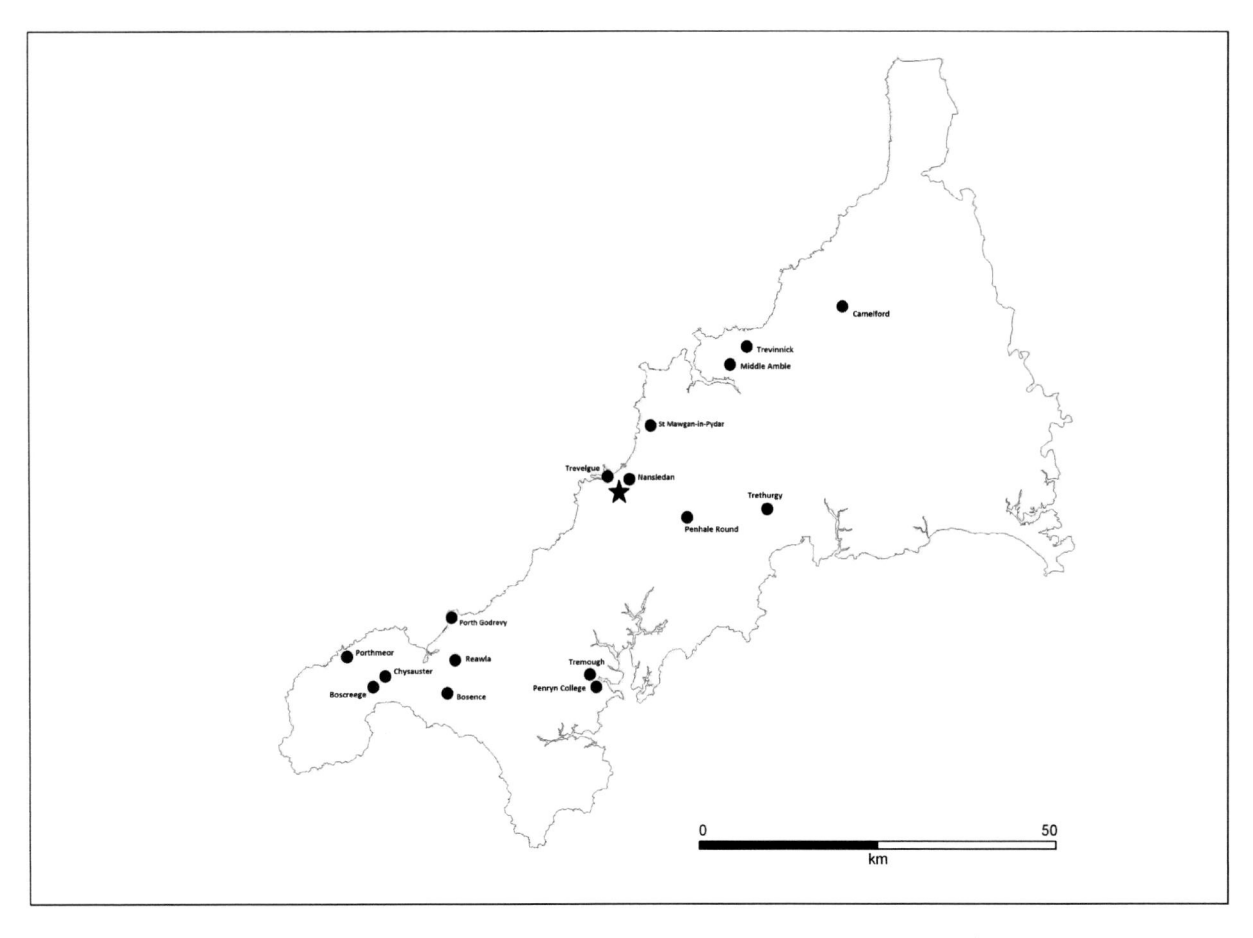

Figure 11.18 Distribution of key Iron Age and Roman sites with possible evidence for ritualized abandonment / special deposits in Cornwall referred to in Chapter 11 (star = Newquay Strategic Road corridor).

These layers contained charcoal and 'burnt matter' and produced a considerable number of finds including two Romans coins, one of which was of Marcus Aurelius (AD 174–175), six spindle whorls, worked stone objects and a large quantity of pottery (*ibid*, 30–31). At least some of this material sealed a hearth but it is not possible to establish how much of the finds assemblage came from within the later 'occupation layer'. There is no section drawing, but the published photograph (opposite page 30) appears to show that beneath the turf-line there was a thick deposit which also contained stones. The main entrance into the round room had been deliberately blocked and it possible to interpret this and the upper 'occupation' layer as being evidence for an episode of structured abandonment. Interestingly, Hirst (1937, 30) did note the 'round room' may have served 'some special purpose' but also commented there was 'no evidence to show what that purpose was'.

Likewise, the excavators of a Roman period structure at Boscreege recorded apparently unstratified finds in a layer above the floor, including a granite muller, a grit or siltstone hone and many water-worn pebbles; at Castle Gotha the interior of a substantial structure referred to as the 'oval hut' was found to have been covered by an artefact-rich layer which sealed all the features associated with the use of the building (Russell and Pool 1963; Saunders and Harris 1982). The finds at Castle Gotha were of mixed date and comprised Iron Age and Roman period pottery as well as worked stone, including a quern (Saunders and Harris 1982, 125). An artefact-rich layer was also recorded at Goldherring, where the infill layer within the interior of hut F was described as being 'unusually rich in sherds, in far greater numbers than in the occupation layers below' (Guthrie 1969, 17).

At Trevinnick, St Kew, trial excavation of an early Roman period rectilinear enclosure was undertaken to determine whether the site was a Roman fort. These investigations revealed that it contained two oval ring-ditches (Fox and Ravenhill 1969). Excavation of the central ring-ditch produced just a few sherds of pottery and three 'sling-shots'. Given the lack of internal features the feature was interpreted as a stock-pen. Partial excavation of the second ring-ditch to the south-west, however, revealed that the ditch had been deliberately infilled with large stones and an 'occupation soil' which included '...much charcoal, tiny scraps of bone and pottery as well as 39 small white pebbles which must have been brought to the site from a stream bed or the beach. The gully was sealed over by a 3 inch layer of small stones with a firm trodden surface beyond the 10ft by 13ft area cleaned.' (*ibid*, 94). These deposits were associated with a suggested episode of levelling prior to the enlargement of the 'stock-pen'. However, as we have seen in relation to later Iron Age and Roman period structures, the infilling of the ditch with quartz pebbles and occupation material could have been part of a ritualized abandonment process.

At Carloggas, St Mawgan-in-Pydar, occupation within a small enclosure appears to have extended from the first century cal BC to about the middle of the second century AD (Quinnell 2004, 216). Excavations in 1948–49 by Threipland (1956) identified 'occupation layers' in several roundhouses. In hut W this layer filled postholes as well as covering the floor surface, suggesting that it certainly post-dated abandonment and demolition of the structure. In this instance the layer incorporated two decorated spindle whorls, three iron brooches and two of copper alloy, a copper-alloy ring, a glass bead and possible iron bead, together with three 'loom weights', copper-alloy droplets and tin slag. Finds in an earlier occupation deposit in hut A included three spindle whorls, one of which was decorated, a copper-alloy brooch and a brooch pin, a schist 'counter' and two whetstones, with copper-alloy droplets, tin slag and crucible fragments. The structure was remodelled and the occupation layer from a second phase included two more spindle whorls, an iron key, two copper-alloy brooches and six whetstones. In hut Y finds from the occupation layer included 10 undecorated spindle whorls, an arrowhead, a penannular copper-alloy brooch, a copper-alloy ring, a clay 'counter', four 'loom weights', a hammerstone and a broken toothed saw-like object of schist [*sic* – almost certainly Trevose slate], possibly used in decorating pottery. From hut V came two decorated and three other spindle whorls, a copper-alloy brooch, four whetstones and a 'loom weight'; hut Z provided four spindle whorls, an iron ring, two copper-alloy brooches, a stone 'counter' and a bone bead. Roughly-trimmed sub-circular pieces of slate pierced by small holes had been placed over postholes in huts A, Y and W, after the posts had been removed.

Unfortunately, the excavation report does not provide enough stratigraphic detail to determine whether some of these finds derived from deposits likely to represent occupation of the roundhouses. However, the sheer quantity of distinctive and 'personal' objects, together with the deliberate placing of holed slates over postholes, does suggest that the 'occupation layers' may at least in part represent a process of purposeful deposition into the interiors of roundhouses at the time of abandonment. At the nearby site of Trevisker, St Eval, the Roman period reoccupation of an Iron Age house was sealed by a layer of rubble and soil. The provenance of finds within or beneath this is unclear but the excavators recorded a surprising total of a 'dozen spindle whorls ... in Iron Age or later layers' on the site, together with a number of perforated pieces of slate and shillet (ApSimon and Greenfield 1972).

Identification of these layers in the sites commented on above as providing possible evidence for deliberate abandonment deposits can for the most part only be inferred from old excavation accounts. However, more recently excavated sites have provided less equivocal evidence. At Penryn College it is probable that the Late Iron Age and Roman period buildings within the settlement had been formally abandoned (Gossip and Jones, forthcoming). This is especially evident in the Roman period structure 2, where one posthole was found to contain fragments of skull from a sheep-sized mammal and a second held the complete upper part of a rotary quern (Fig 11.19). These artefacts could only have been deposited into the sockets after the posts had been removed. The gully around the same house also produced a rare example of a copper-alloy toilet set or chatelaine, which is likely to have been a highly valued personal possession and, again, unlikely to have been a casual loss (Fig 11.20). All three deposits are therefore likely to have been associated with the closure of the building (*ibid*).

As LaMotta and Schiffer (1999) have noted, ethnographic evidence suggests that there does not need to be any straightforward correlation between what is found within the abandoned house site and the way it was inhabited, and most objects on the floor of an abandoned structure are likely to be related to its abandonment. Ethnographic study has also shown that buildings can have their own 'biographies' or 'lives' which can become deeply entangled with the lives and memories of their inhabitants (Waterson 1997; Carsten 2018), and as such houses can become repositories for heirlooms of their communities and inhabitants.

Seen in this way, the personal associations of objects such as spindle whorls and chatelaines are relatively easily understood, but other deposits may have had a symbolic connection with other aspects of domestic activity such as food preparation or storage. At Trethurgy Round the small structure G, interpreted as a shrine, was infilled with an artefact assemblage, which included a fragment from a rotary quern and part of a stone bowl (Quinnell 2004, 237). Another of the Trethurgy buildings, house A1b, was also found to contain deliberately selected and buried material, which included pottery and a stone mensuration weight, which was in good condition. The deposit was interpreted as a probable closing deposit for the house (*ibid*). Likewise, at Penhale Round structure 2045/5054 was found to be sealed beneath a midden deposit which contained a large assemblage of Roman pottery, a copper-alloy bell and, very notably, fragments from 11 elvan stone bowls (Nowakowski and Johns 2015, 265).

Figure 11.19 Photograph of in situ rotary quern found within a posthole inside structure 2 at Penryn College.

Figure 11.20 Photograph of a copper-alloy toiletry set found within a gully associated within structure 2 at Penryn College.

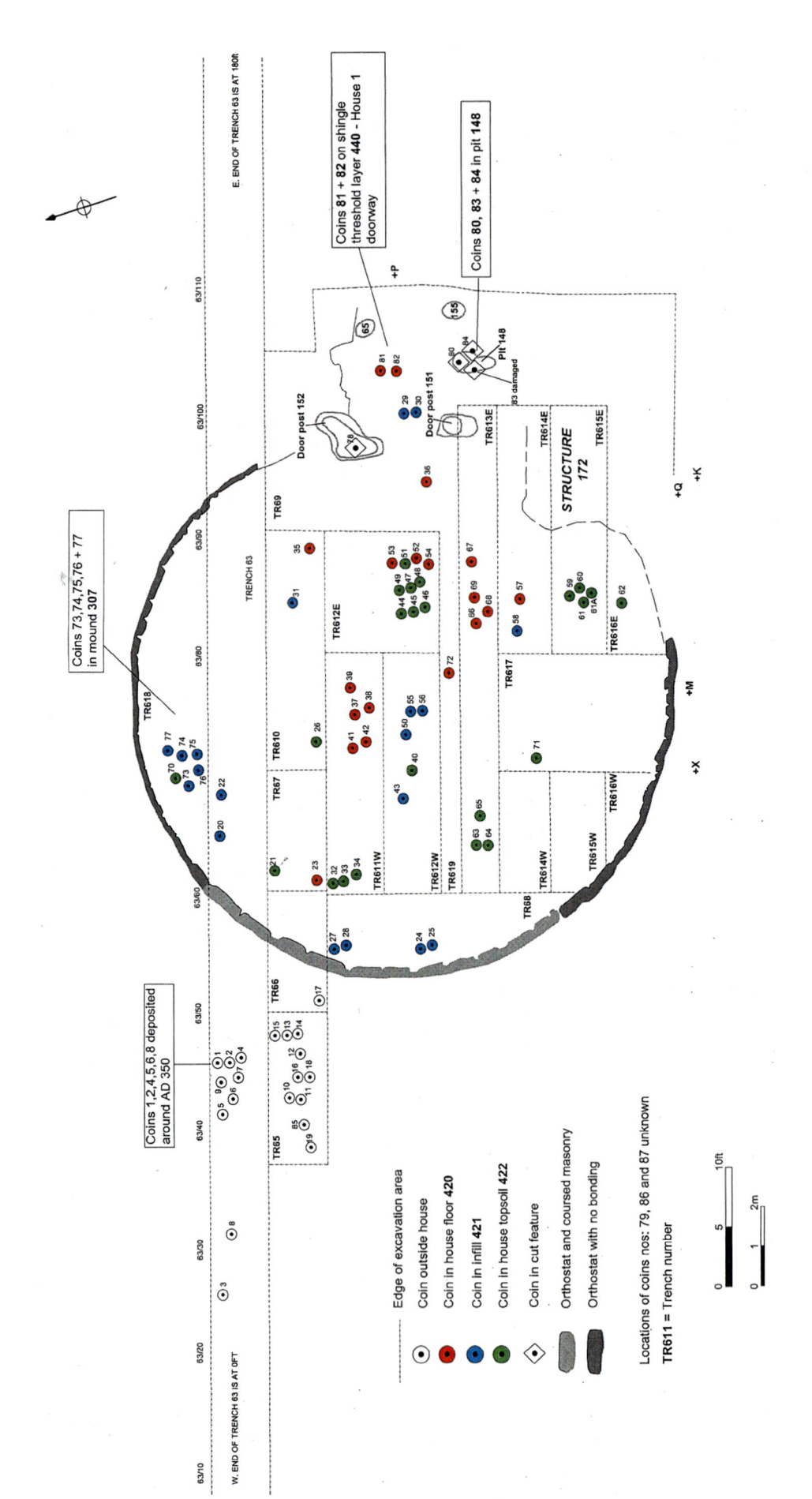

LATER PREHISTORIC AND ROMAN SITES ALONG THE ROUTE OF THE NEWQUAY STRATEGIC ROAD CORRIDOR

Figure 11.21 Plan of Trevelgue Head, house 1 showing the distribution of Roman coins within and outside the structure (after Nowakowski and Quinnell 2011).

At the cliff castle at Trevelgue, Newquay, just over 2 kilometres north of the Newquay Strategic Road, site, a very large roundhouse of Iron Age date, which had been disused for a long period, was reused in the Roman period and then formally abandoned (Fig 11.21). Around AD 320 the house was reused as an unroofed ceremonial focus (Nowakowski and Quinnell 2011, 55). Roman coins were deposited within a doorway posthole and within a pit outside the former entrance to the structure. At the end of this renewed phase of use in the fifth century AD, there was an elaborate pattern of abandonment (Nowakowski and Quinnell 2011, 360–361). Late Roman coins found in the infill deposit on the floor of the building were a little later than those in the layer above, and they may have been stored elsewhere on site prior to deposition. The infill layers also contained a lot of ceramic and other finds and it is likely that they derived from a midden. There can, however, be little doubt as to the intentionality of the other deposits. Large slabs from the wall were thrown onto the floor and a mound of quartz blocks constructed inside it. The remainder of the house hollow was then infilled with soil layers, perhaps from a number of different middens, containing Roman, Middle and Late Iron Age pottery, all of which may have been associated with the 'life history' of the building (*ibid*). The infill would have completely buried the house site from view and, as the authors noted, the intention may have been to obliterate it, or perhaps by contrast monumentalise its 'history'.

Comparison has already been made between Newquay Structure 3 and Tremough structure 338. At the latter site there was also good evidence for structured deposition of artefacts into abandonment contexts (Gossip and Jones 2007, 49–50). The slight hollow in which structure 338 was set had been covered by layers that included a stone mortar fragment, a whetstone and a fragment from a rotary quern, the burial of which shows clear parallels with Structure 3. The abandonment layers also included a large assemblage of sherds of fresh unabraded pottery (*ibid*). However, selection of objects for deliberate deposition as part of the abandonment process was most clearly demonstrated by the placing of a complete mensuration weight within a posthole close to the entrance to the building (Fig 11.22). The weight was found in the same feature as a stone bearing for a spindle and a whetstone; these appeared to have been sealed in place by covering with stone, and the artefacts can therefore be interpreted as a deliberately placed assemblage. The outer postholes of the structure also contained significant pottery deposits, sherds from a large storage vessel, in several postholes, as well as a whetstone. The fresh condition of the sherds indicated deposition and covering soon after the vessel had been broken. Indeed, the unabraded state of many of the artefacts, and their placement within empty postholes suggests that this activity took place during abandonment of structure 338. It is clear that abandonment included infilling layers having been deliberately deposited to cover the abandoned house and also the burial of carefully selected artefacts in cut features.

Comparable finds have been found in what appear to be abandonment contexts at other sites in Cornwall, although the details of their discovery are often less well-documented or were not identified by their excavators as being of a ritualized nature. At Porth Godrevy, Gwithian, for example, the excavated house was interpreted a 'native dwelling' which the author suggested could have been deliberately abandoned (Fowler 1962). Little comment, however, was made on features and deposits which may have been associated with ritualized abandonment. These included a boulder mortar set in a floor surface but obtruding upwards, which was found with a much worn granite bowl set in the mortar hollow, covered by an oval

Figure 11.22 Photograph of the stone mensuration weight within a posthole close the entrance into structure 338 at Tremough.

slate. Utilized stones had been placed into some of the postholes and eight sherds of samian ware from the site, three of which were found to join with two larger ones, were all apparently recovered from layers over the Roman period archaeology. There is also possible 'closure' of the key phase II feature, which Fowler interpreted as a central posthole (a hearth was subsequently constructed over it), by the insertion of an inverted upper stone from a rotary quern. The quern was unused and undamaged; the lower broken stone was also found on the site. A 'drain' in the central area was packed with carefully selected quartz pebbles, 'remarkable for their uniformity' (Fowler 1962, 28–29). Another 'drain' was a groove cut in bedrock containing quartz pebbles (ibid, 30). Taken together, these features hint that abandonment of the building amounted to rather more than the suggested removal of iron tools from the site.

More recently, at Gerrans, on the Roseland peninsula, an infilled hollow measuring approximately 9m by 8m was uncovered (Jones and Shepherd 2009–10). The infilling layer produced sherds of Iron Age or Roman period pottery and a radiocarbon date of 4420 ± 30 BP, 70–230 cal AD (SUERC-29740) was obtained on residue from one of the sherds. After discovery and limited investigation the site was preserved *in situ*, which means that the character of any underlying structure sealed beneath this material remains unknown. Likewise, hollow [309] at Gover Farm, St Agnes, was found to be filled by layers which produced Roman pottery, a complete rotary quern and what was described as stone 'rubble', which was possibly from 'a collapsed structure' (Good 2015). This site was only evaluated so its full extent is unknown; nonetheless, the rubble infill and the deposition of a complete quern are reminiscent of practices which have been discussed in connection with other Roman period buildings, including Structure 3 at Newquay and Penryn College.

At the Roman period enclosed settlement at Reawla, near Hayle, there were several instances of houses, as well as an industrial area, being sealed by midden deposits (Appleton-Fox 1992). Excavation of house A revealed that the hollow in which the structure had been set was infilled with an accumulated deposit of 'rubbish', which included pottery forms ranging in date from the second to the fourth century AD. This process was interpreted as having been gradual (*ibid*, 81), but given the evidence from elsewhere for the use of 'historic' midden material in covering abandoned structures this may not have been the case. Reawla house B had similarly been infilled by what appears to have been a substantial midden deposit, the finds from which included pottery, sherds of glass and a fragment from a stone mortar. A third house, C, also appears to have been deliberately infilled with artefact-rich midden material.

A non-domestic part of the site at Reawla, labelled the 'industrial area', also appears to have been formally abandoned. The unused top stone of a rotary quern had been placed in midden material beside a small platform of quartz stones described as a 'stone pad' (Appleton-Fox 1992, fig 7). This midden deposit was rich in ceramics, which the ceramic report noted for the size of the sherds and the freshness of most of the breaks (Quinnell 1992b). The formation of the deposit in which the quern was found was not discussed in the excavation report and neither was the significance of the quern and the 'stone pad' or platform. However, as the midden layer sealed an area which had been used for industrial activity, it is possible that both the quern and the quartz platform were associated with the formalized closing down of the area. The lack of interpretative comment on the sealing of various structures at Reawla with midden material was probably due to an underlying assumption that Roman period agricultural settlements operated solely as 'practical' farmsteads, and other forms of activity were not considered. However, while the Reawla enclosure undoubtedly did function as a working farmstead, the inhabitants clearly undertook some actions which were outside the purely 'practical'.

Sites with similar indications of ritualized abandonment have been found elsewhere in the south west (Fig 11.23). For example, at Pomeroy Wood, in east Devon, roundhouses 3415 and 4642 were found sealed beneath a thick overlying layer described as 'akin to a midden deposit' containing pottery and worked stone objects (Fitzpatrick *et al* 1999, 243). The authors noted that many Roman period sites were associated with such layers (*ibid*, 401). Likewise, excavations at Cannards Grave, in Somerset, led to the discovery of a late Roman structure, possibly of masonry and timber, with 'relatively large quantities of animal bone . . . recovered from the deposits which appear to represent the demolition or decay of this possible structure . . .' (Birbeck 2002, 57–58). The adjacent well had also been deliberately infilled (*ibid*), which implies that an attempt may have been made to decommission the settlement.

Further afield, the site of a Roman building at Cottington Hill, Ebbsfleet, Kent, was identified by evaluation trenching (Perkins 1990). A layer over the footprint of the structure incorporated charcoal, calcined chalk and pottery, some sherds of which appeared to have been broken *in situ*, together with masses of oyster shells and bones. The excavator concluded that the layer represented 'debris from fire-damage to the building, topped-off with midden material after abandonment'.

At another site in Thanet, at Tothill Street, Minster, significant deposits occurred in some of a row of

INSCRIBING THE LANDSCAPE AND HIDING IN PLAIN VIEW

substantial vertical-sided pits within a Roman period settlement enclosure. The secondary fill of one pit contained a 'small group of complete and semi-complete pottery vessels connected with the storage and consumption of drink', with a complete pot deposited upside down in the upper fill. 'The inversion of the vessel would appear to represent a deliberate act of termination' (Cotton nd, 33). A shallow pit nearby on the same alignment contained a bone-handled iron clasp knife in the form of a gladiator, the quality of which suggests that it was probably a treasured personal possession, together with a fragment of copper-alloy bar (ibid, 33, 63). The excavator suggested that the various objects appeared to have been deliberately buried, 'perhaps as part of customary observances associated with the commissioning or closure of activity' (ibid, 33).

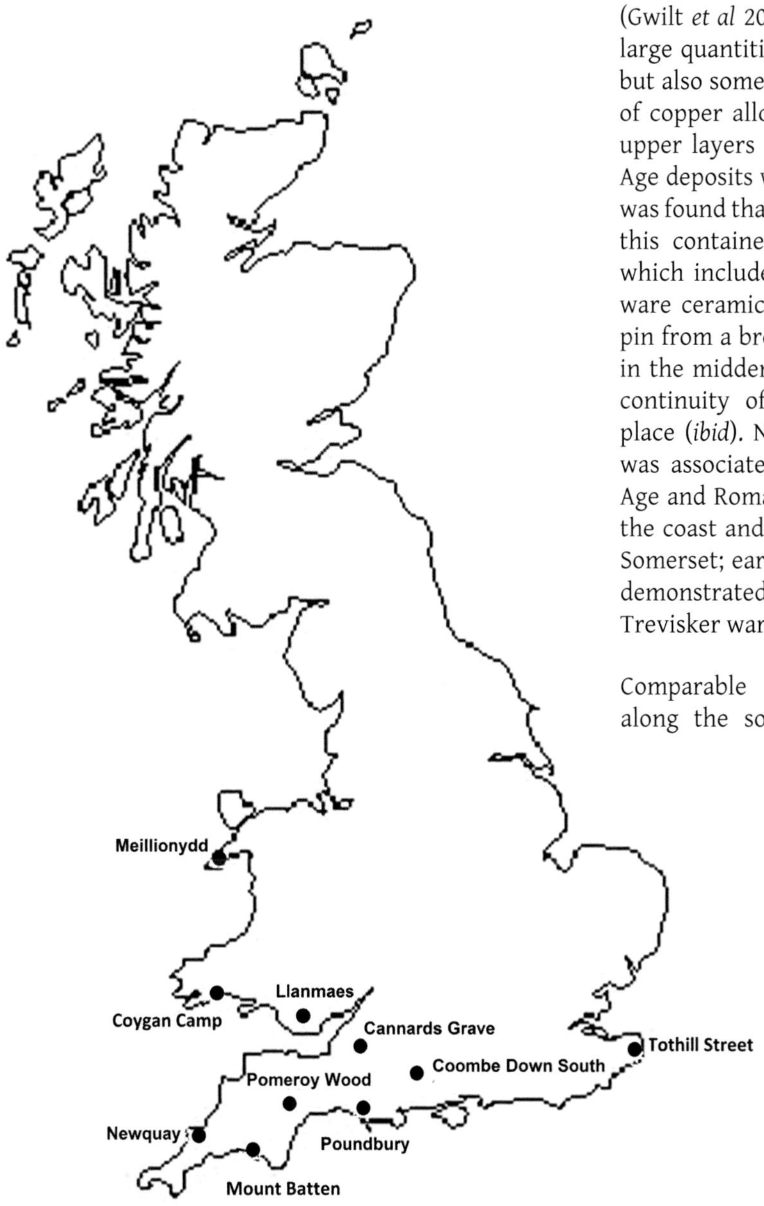

Building 1 on this site, a sunken featured structure dating from a late phase in the life of the settlement, had an unusual number of distinctive iron objects within its occupation and disuse deposits, together with a collection of pestle-shaped beach pebbles and a fossil echinoid. It was suggested that these may have been deposited as part of a 'termination rite' (ibid, 50–51, 64). After abandonment, the building was backfilled with dumped deposits incorporating a substantial quantity of pottery, with larger sherds and more complete profiles to the vessels than were found elsewhere on the site (ibid, 51).

Abandonment sequences have also been recorded at sites in coastal parts of Wales. At Llanmaes, in the Vale of Glamorgan, an extensive midden of Early Iron Age date was found to cover roundhouses belonging to the Late Bronze Age to Earliest Iron Age period (Gwilt et al 2016). The midden deposit contained very large quantities of bone, mostly derived from animals but also some human, over 300 metal artefacts, mostly of copper alloy and over 1000 sherds of pottery. The upper layers had been ploughed away and later Iron Age deposits will have been lost, but significantly a pit was found that had been cut into the top of the midden; this contained a structured deposit of Roman date which included a complete, crushed Black Burnished ware ceramic vessel, sherds of samian pottery and a pin from a brooch. The pit had been deliberately sited in the midden and, as the authors note, this suggests continuity of practice as well as remembrance of place (ibid). Nearby, there is a large enclosure which was associated with features and finds of later Iron Age and Roman date. Interestingly, the site is close to the coast and overlooks the north coast of Devon and Somerset; earlier connections with the south west are demonstrated by the discovery of Middle Bronze Age Trevisker ware pottery in an earlier phase on the site.

Comparable activity may have occurred further along the southern Welsh coast at Coygan Camp, in Carmarthenshire (Wainwright 1967). Here an Iron Age promontory enclosure located in a topographically dramatic locale was reoccupied in the Roman period when a rectangular building and other structures were constructed inside it. Selective deposition of metalwork at this time is implied by the deposition of a patera, a 'strainer' and other items within a narrow cave located on the eastern part of the hill (Allen 1901). These finds have similarities to the discovery of the metalwork within the shaft at Bosence. Indeed, most of the artefacts were associated with the later Roman period occupation

Figure 11.23 Key sites beyond Cornwall referred to in Chapter 11.

and there was evidence for a midden covering the site, although its full extent was not defined. The site was, however, extremely complex, and significant 'odd deposits' included the skull of a *bos longifrons* in the base of a Roman period structural posthole within the enclosure. This could have been a foundation deposit, as suggested in the report, but it is also possible that it was associated with the closure of the building. Large numbers of artefacts including pottery, animal bone and iron objects were also found. The metalwork assemblage included a dagger and three spearheads found together. It was suggested that the large quantity of well-preserved iron finds might have been related to a hurried abandonment (Wainwright 1967, 59); however, it is also possible that exactly the reverse may have been the case and that they represent intentional deposits. The same may also be true of two La Tène bracelets and a carved serpentine ring recovered from within the Roman period deposits, near to hut 3. These artefacts are clearly much older than the layers in which they were found and may have been curated prior to burial. However, given that many finds were recovered after bulldozing of part of the site it is not possible to be certain as to how many of them were 'special deposits'. Ninety-four Roman coins were certainly recovered from along the north and west perimeter of the camp (mainly around hut 1), and what was referred to as a 'counterfeiters' hoard' comprising 315 coins was found in a pit cut into the floor of the same hut, covered by smashed stones. The coin hoard was interpreted as the concealment of incriminating material (*ibid*, 60) but an alternative view would be to interpret it, like the Hayle Causeway hoard noted above, as 'mock money', made for ceremonial burial and possibly associated with the closure of the structure.

A third Welsh site is located at Meillionydd on the Lleyn peninsula in north-west Wales (Karl 2016). This provides closer comparison with the abandonment of buildings which we have seen in the south west. The site at Meillionydd is a double ringwork enclosure. Recent excavation revealed that the enclosure overlies a settlement of Late Bronze Age to Early Iron Age date and that new stone-built houses were constructed inside it during the Middle Iron Age. Pits dug into the floors of the houses produced glass beads, spindle whorls, a saddle quern and a mortar, and these features accounted for most of the finds from the site (*ibid*). These have been suggested to be possible burial pits, although, as at Newquay, they may have been structured collections of artefacts. During the Late Iron Age the enclosure and the roundhouses were formally abandoned and all upstanding remains were slighted and the entrances into the enclosure badly damaged. In particular, all the roundhouses were deliberately infilled with large quantities of stone, much of which was heat affected. Interestingly, Castell Odo, another Iron Age enclosure on the Lleyn Peninsula also showed evidence for the slighting of its banks (Alcock 1960). Given the limited number of excavated enclosure sites on the Lleyn Peninsula these examples may suggest that formal closure of settlement sites was quite widespread in the area during the Iron Age. Given the suggested links in settlement form and patterning between west Wales and Cornwall and other parts of south-west Britain during the later prehistoric and Roman periods (Johnson 1981; Nowakowski 2016, 191), it is also conceivable that there was a common tradition relating to settlement abandonment.

Turning now to Wessex in southern England, what have been referred to as destruction or demolition layers have also been identified on a number of sites of both Iron Age and Roman date. Wessex is, of course, associated with a long tradition of creating large mounded middens, as at All Cannings Cross where the mound covers three hectares and is in excess of 3m deep (Field and McOmish 2017, 103). This practice commenced during the Late Bronze Age and Early Iron Age when immense spreads of midden material, which incorporated pottery, vast quantities of animal and some human bone, worked stone and items of metalwork were heaped up (Cunnington 1923; McOmish *et al* 2010; Tullett 2008; Sharples 2010, 52–53). These activities may have been grand visual statements which memorialized people, events and places.

Two of the three sites of this type in the Vale of Pewsey, Potterne and East Chisenbury (Lawson 2000, 35–37; McOmish *et al* 2010; Barrett and McOmish 2009), also produced Roman finds, although direct association and the form of the activity represented is not necessarily clear; as noted above, however, a further site at Cold Kitchen Hill became the focus for votive offerings and possibly a temple in the Roman period (Cunliffe 1993, 233). The midden mound at East Chisenbury appears to have been situated within a massive enclosure, the upper fills of the encircling ditch producing sherds of Roman pottery (Wessex Archaeology 2017).

The midden sites in Wessex comprised huge amounts of material and may have been linked with social display and the standing of the communities who generated them. Social memories of these associations may have persisted down through the generations and into the Roman period, although it is also possible that these places may then have been subsequently 'rediscovered'.

Midden or feasting-generated material may have taken on a different symbolic role in the Roman period, being seen as suitable for covering earlier settlement activity. At Poundbury in Dorset, for example, the excavator reported that in structure R16 'The destruction levels were notable for producing quantities of butchered pig bones and large unabraded sherds of an amphora of East Mediterranean type' (Sparey Green 1987, 62).

Another building, structure R19, was partially filled by a deposit which 'contained a large quantity of fitting, unabraded sherds both of first century and fourth century AD vessels, and the fill over structure R20 produced quantities of unabraded late Roman pottery (*ibid*, 63).

On Salisbury Plain, in the settlement site at Coombe Down South, a late Roman 'working' hollow and an adjacent earlier Iron Age enclosure ditch was covered by a substantial dark loam midden deposit, which contained over 3 kg of Roman pottery sherds, a large quantity of animal bone and a complete late Roman bronze bowl associated with a coin; a cow skull was recovered from the surface of the deposit (Fulford *et al* 2006, 39, 76, 80–82). in the same report Seager Smith (2006, 120) notes that similar deposits have been found at other Roman sites in Wessex and suggests that discrete piles of midden material had been spread over areas after settlements were abandoned. Comparable midden material was, for example, noted in the vicinity of the Roman period settlement at Butterfield Down, near Amesbury, and a large number of Roman period finds were recovered during the preliminary field walking (Rawlings and Fitzpatrick 1996), although the relationship between them and the underlying buried archaeology is not explicitly discussed.

It may be that in some instances the spreading of midden material occurred as part of agricultural practices in prehistory or the Roman period or, as documented in a number of examples from the post-medieval period, in more recent times (*cf* Kirkham 2012, 14–15, 16). Many of these settlements were located within field systems; once abandoned they might have been middened over in order to bring the site back into cultivation, possibly to deepen the soil, rather than leaving a 'dead' area within the agricultural land. However, this would not explain 'special deposits' in cut features and arguably the midden material would have been more economically deployed on fields, rather than over old settlements. The spreading of midden material over a formerly occupied area could in itself have formed part of a deliberate and ritualized abandonment process aimed at returning an otherwise 'dead' place to productive life and fertility. Only widespread hand-dug sections, however, across sites which possess midden deposits overlying archaeological features would help resolve these relationships.

With the exception of the promontory site at Mount Batten, in Plymouth harbour, there is less evidence in the south-west for large-scale midden deposits. It is notable that excavations at Mount Batten have produced not only finds of Bronze Age and Iron Age date, but also a considerable number of Roman finds. These included pottery, brooches, finger rings, bracelets, pins and coins (Cunliffe 1988, 100–103). In addition, significant quantities of animal bone were found in the Middle to Late Iron Age midden (*ibid*, 28–35), a high proportion of which was skulls and mandibles, which may, as has been found at Llanmaes, reflect the selection of specific body parts. The overall scale and extent of Mount Batten is unknown, although the recovery of metalwork suggests that it is likely that a significant, possibly non-domestic Roman phase of activity occurred on the headland (Gardiner 2000). Its character as a prominent topographical feature and its coastal location suggests parallels with Llanmaes.

The use of midden material on Roman period sites in Wessex is likely to have evolved out of different regional traditions (Sharples 2010, chapter 6) from those in the south west, where, with the exception of Mount Batten, it was generally deployed on a much smaller scale to cover individual structures. However, midden material was clearly an important resource in both regions and in both it could be used to hide earlier structures, seal them off from later activity and ultimately erase them from memory.

Retrospect: an outline of a theory of practice

The sites discussed in this chapter provide an outline of abandonment practices associated with structures in the Late Iron Age and Roman period in Cornwall and elsewhere. Clearly, however, much more consideration (with detailed re-examination of site records) needs to be given to abandonment practices found on Iron Age and Roman sites before there is an understanding of these comparable with that which has been acquired of those associated with Middle Bronze Age roundhouses (above).

Some further points can, however, be made in relation to the abandonment processes found at Newquay. Firstly, many of the items recovered from abandonment contexts in Structure 3, as well as many of those recorded in abandonment layers on sites elsewhere in Cornwall, show use prior to breakage and discard; these are items that were perhaps linked to specific individuals or functions, with related memories and biographies. The need to reinforce a sense of belonging and continuity may have been at the root of the manner of their deposition.

Secondly, it has been argued that the ritualized deposition of everyday artefacts such as querns and stone bowls could have reflected metaphorical links to the agricultural cycle and the production, processing and consumption of food. Likewise, the deposition of metal ore may have made a link to the extraction and working of iron and a cycle of transformation and renewal which required the returning of some of the ore to the earth for regeneration. At times these activities may have been carried out as an informal, albeit deeply embedded behaviour, rooted in tradition, such as the

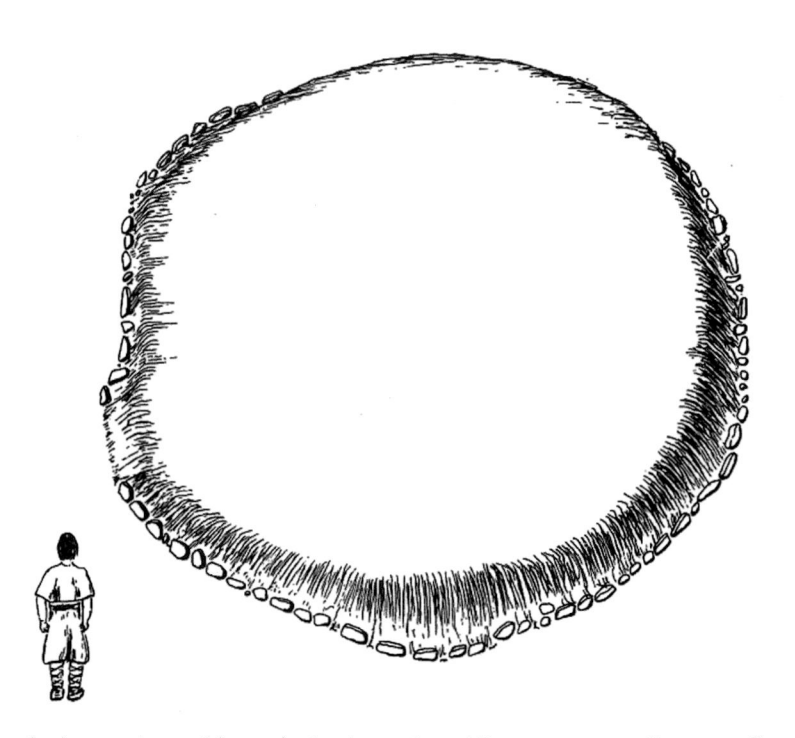

Figure 11.24 From roundhouse (top) to round mound (bottom). Abandoning the Middle Bronze Age roundhouse at Callestick. (Drawing Nigel Thomas.)

routine dumping of certain domestic rubbish into a ditch. At others, the deposition of artefacts and other materials may have been part of a more complex ritual of overtly ceremonial nature, which may have occurred, for example, during the 'closure' of Structure 3.

The selection of domestic artefacts for deposition into pits and ditches could be taken to imply a 'mundane' world view, but this should not necessarily be assumed to be so. It should also be remembered, as Julian Thomas (2012) has pointed out, that obvious 'special deposits' can be seen as the tip of an iceberg, which greys into the routine deposition of artefacts. Symbolic associations may also have made even the most 'mundane' objects 'special' and appropriate for deposition.

It is implicit in the material in this chapter that the end of the Iron Age did not mark a shift towards a significantly different world view from that of the preceding period, certainly not the end of a mentality in which ritualized behaviours were fundamental components. As was the case in prehistory, the world of the Romano-British farmer was one where even everyday actions could be imbued with a symbolism, where ritual need not be distinct from the profane in terms of either the content or location of deposits (Hill 1995, chapter 10). 'Practical' apotropaic actions were still needed to ward off harm and it is certainly the case that even in the medieval and post-medieval periods, thresholds into houses were sometimes marked by protective signs or had devices such as witch bottles buried under them to ward off evil (for example, Merrifield 1987, 116–121; Pitts 2009; Gordon 2015). Similar concerns are almost certain to have been prevalent in the later Iron Age and Roman periods. It has been argued here that such actions were undertaken to ensure the success of the agricultural cycle. In this context it is notable that depositional practices previously associated with saddle querns were extended in the Roman period to include rotary querns and stone bowls. In short, the range of materials increased, but underlying dispositions affected what was chosen for deposit as well as where the deposition should be made.

Lastly, but perhaps most significantly, the ritualized levelling of buildings, especially in the later Iron Age and Roman period, has been argued to be a much more widely found phenomenon than has been suggested before. However, this practice may itself have had long antecedents. In the Middle Bronze Age houses were infilled and covered by low mounds and may have become barrow-like memorials to their former occupants (Jones 2015) (Fig 11.24). In the later Iron Age and Roman period, by contrast, there seems to have been a retreat from monumental abandonment to levelling activities, to prevent further access to sites (for example, Bradley and Nimura 2016, 121). This type of activity was possibly linked with a desire not to perpetuate memory but rather to erase it, to hide the past in plain view (Jones, forthcoming b).

Chapter 12

Review and overview

Andy M Jones

The excavations along the Newquay Strategic Road corridor were of particular interest because they provided a linear slice through settlement-related activity spanning the Middle Bronze Age and Middle Iron Age through to the earlier part of the Roman period.

The main period of settlement-related activity was bracketed within the period from *circa* 400 cal BC to AD 200, with the most intense phase occurring after *circa* 100 cal BC. Features dating to this period included field ditches, oval structures and hollows defined by gullies, open working areas and a square building set within a hollow. Some of these structures may have been used as dwellings, others for storage or as ancillary structures. The presence of iron ore also suggests the probability of small-scale industrial activity in the vicinity.

However, there was no clear focus for the type of domestic occupation that has been found at other recently excavated Iron Age open settlements, such as at Penmayne, where there were up to four roundhouses, or Higher Besore where 12 houses were recorded (Gossip *et al* 2012; Gossip, forthcoming), or Camelford where houses and ceremonial structures were found in close proximity (Jones and Taylor 2015). Nonetheless, there are indications that one of the Roman period buildings, Structure 3, may have been situated within a slight enclosure encircled by ditched, stock-proof boundaries. Additional curvilinear, and linear anomalies were also detected by the geophysical survey but these lay outside the development area and were not investigated.

The available evidence, although limited, suggests that there were several phases of field system, that the enclosure of the surrounding area increased from the Late Iron Age onwards and that the fields became more rectilinear in layout away from the settlement. This model of an expanding and increasingly open agricultural landscape is also supported by the charcoal assemblages, from one dominated by woodland taxa in the Bronze Age and Middle Iron Age to heathland taxa in the Late Iron Age and Roman period (Challinor, Chapter 7). This pattern of expansion during the Late Iron Age and Roman periods is one, albeit with distinct local variations, which has long been noted by scholars in other parts of Britain (for example, Williamson 1987; 1998; Tabor 2008; Straker *et al* 2008b; Rippon *et al* 2015, 309–315; Ten Harkel *et al* 2017). Analysis of the charred plant macrofossils from the excavations could be interpreted as suggesting that settlement activity in the area may have been associated with the control of livestock, and increasingly with the cultivation of cereals, which become more apparent in Roman period contexts. The decorated stone spindle whorl is, in addition to being a personal item, also indicative of the processing of sheep wool, and thereby acts a proxy for the presence of animals. As at the nearby Atlantic Road site (where a faunal assemblage was preserved and a carding comb recovered), sheep may have played an important role in the local later prehistoric and Roman period economy (Figs 12.1 and 12.2).

Figure 12.1 Photograph of the iron carding comb from Atlantic Road, Newquay. In a region lacking in good organic preservation this artefact acts as a proxy for the importance of wool in the local economy.

REVIEW AND OVERVIEW

systems, and it is interesting to note the recovery of the copper-alloy Roman period brooch from the Manuels enclosure. However, as Ten Harkel *et al* (2017) have argued, enclosure may not just have been related to economic intensification but may also have been linked with more complex concepts involving both control of the land and ritualized practices associated with its use, which were deeply embedded in beliefs about the agricultural cycle.

Tantalizingly, the presence of iron ore in Roman contexts strongly suggests that iron working was taking place in the near vicinity, although actual evidence for iron production was limited to a piece of ferrous slag from the Late Iron Age ditch [120]. It is nonetheless tempting to link the expansion of the field system and the iron ore with the nearby multivallate enclosure at Manuels to the south east (see Fig 12.3 and inset Chapter 10, above). If it is accepted that control over metal working and the supply of ore were socially important, it is possible that the inhabitants of Manuels could have overseen these processes. It is interesting to note that at Hay Close, St Newlyn East evidence for Late Iron Age / Roman period iron smelting was found to have taken place near to a large henge-like enclosure of Early Iron Age origin (Jones 2014).

Figure 12.2 Photograph showing Roman period plough marks (foreground) at Atlantic Road, Newquay. Despite being in a marginal location ploughing had taken place, before being covered by windblown sand.

As has been argued by others (for example, Trow *et al* 2009, 64–71), it is possible that Romanization led to changes in the way that local 'elites' defined themselves. In a Cornish context there was certainly a proliferation in the construction of enclosed settlements (Quinnell 2004, 215–217) and in the expansion of ditched field

Likewise, there are indications that there were ritualized activities within domestic or settlement-related contexts (*cf* Brück 1999a; Williams 2003; Bradley 2005; Ten Harkel *et al* 2017). The most commonly encountered example of this type of activity was associated with deposits found in pits, and on the Newquay site this tradition can be traced from the Beaker-associated pit [163] through to one of the latest features, the Roman period pit [367]. Structure-associated deposits are apparent in the Middle Bronze Age roundhouse, Structure 1, where a large pit containing curated artefacts was placed in the

Figure 12.3 Reconstruction of the Manuels enclosure. (Painting Freya Lawson-Jones.)

Figure 12.4 Photograph of late fourth century AD Roman coins buried in a pit outside the entrance to Trevelgue Head, house 1. (Photograph Anna Tyacke.)

entrance. During the Late Iron Age and Roman period the gullies around Structure A3 and Hollow 1 were marked by special deposits. The terminals of two ditches defining the southern entrance into the enclosure in which Structure 3 lay were also marked with significant deposits.

There is also evidence that three structures belonging to this period were formally abandoned, with artefact-rich deposits sealing posts in the rectangular structure in Hollow 2 and the interior of Structure 3; one of the gullies associated with Hollow 1 had been deliberately infilled. It has been suggested above that formalized abandonment of buildings during the Roman period is likely to have developed from earlier Iron Age traditions. It has been argued that these practices were much more widespread than has often been thought (Figs 12.4, 12.5 and 12.6).

As argued above, however, not every pit was filled with formality and neither is it suggested

Figure 12.5 Photograph of the Roman period bell found within the midden deposit covering Penhale Round structure 2045/5054.

that the site encapsulates more than 1000 years of unbroken and unchanging tradition or religious belief. Nonetheless, the results are significant as they demonstrate links over time between different types of context and the types of feature which were marked for more formalized deposition.

To conclude, the richness of the results and the span of time covered by the features revealed by the project surpassed what had been anticipated. They again demonstrate the importance of properly funded archaeological mitigation in areas which may appear to be blank on county HER mapping and on aerial photographs, on which archaeological features may show only very rarely. These results therefore highlight the need to undertake full geophysical survey and, as far as possible, full excavation of all promising anomalies. Even seemingly inconsequential pits and ditches need to be excavated and sampled (Chadwick 2015).

Greater consideration also needs to be given to the site formation process and 'odd', 'special' or structured deposits actively evaluated for what they really represent, rather than either labelled as such to avoid thought or missed entirely through lack of it. Perhaps above all, appropriate levels of radiocarbon dating need to be carried out. Pottery or other artefacts, where recovered in redeposited or suspicious contexts, cannot be taken as a proxy dating for the features in which they are found. The 16 radiocarbon determinations undertaken for this project hugely altered our understanding of the site phasing; another 16 would probably have achieved a similar advance in understanding of the chronology.

Figure 12.6 Photograph of the Roman period tin dish which had been placed within a pit at Killigrew Round.

Bibliography

Alcock, L, 1960. Castell Odo: an embanked settlement on Mynydd Ystum, near Aberdaron, Caernarvonshire. *Archaeologia Cambrensis* 109, 78–135.

Aldhouse-Green, M J, 2002: Any old iron! Symbolism and ironworking in Iron Age Europe. In M J Aldhouse-Green and P Webster, eds, *Artefacts and archaeology; aspects of the Celtic and Roman world*. Cardiff: University of Wales Press, 8–19.

Allen, R S, 1901. Two Kelto-Roman finds in Wales. *Archaeologia Cambrensis* 1, sixth series, 20–44.

Appleton-Fox, N, 1992. Excavations at a Romano-British round; Reawla, Gwinear, Cornwall. *Cornish Archaeology* 31, 69–123.

ApSimon, A and Greenfield, E, 1972. The excavation of the Bronze Age and Iron Age settlement at Trevisker Round, St Eval, Cornwall. *Proceedings of the Prehistoric Society* 38, 302–381.

Ashbee, P, 1974. *Ancient Scilly: From the first farmers to the early Christians*. Newton Abbot: David and Charles.

Baires, S E and Baltus M R, 2016. Matter, places, and persons in Cahokian depositional acts. *Journal of Archaeological Method and Theory*. DOI: 10.1007/s10816-016-9304-0

Baldwin, A and Joy, J, eds, 2017. *A Celtic feast: The Iron Age cauldrons from Chiseldon, Wiltshire*. London: British Museum.

Barber, M. 2005. 'There wur a bit of ould brass': Bronze Age metalwork and the Marlborough Downs landscape. In G Brown, D Field and D McOmish, eds, *Avebury landscape: Aspects of the field archaeology of the Marlborough Downs*. Oxford: Oxbow, 137–148.

Barnatt, J, Bevan, B and Edmonds, M, 2017. *An upland biography: Landscape and prehistory on Gardom's Edge, Derbyshire*. Oxford: Windgather Press.

Barrett, J and McOmish, D, 2009. The Early Iron Age in southern Britain: Recent work at All Cannings Cross, Stanton St Bernard and East Chisenbury, Wiltshire. In M J Roulière Lambert, ed, *De l'âge du Bronze a l'âge du Fer en France et en Europe occidentale XeViie siècle avant J.C. - La Moyenne vallée du Rhône aux âges du Fer*. Revue archaéoloqique de L'Est.

Basso, K, 1996. *Wisdom sits in places; landscape and language amongst the western Apache*. Albuquerque: University of New Mexico Press.

Bate, C S, 1864. On the discovery of a Romano-British cemetery near Plymouth. *Report of the Transactions of the Devonshire Association* 1, 123–133.

Beck, R A, 2016. The iron in the posthole: Witchcraft, women's labor, and Spanish folk ritual at the Berry site. *American Anthropologist* 118, 525–540.

Bell, C, 1992. *Ritual: Perspectives and dimensions*. Oxford: Oxford University Press.

Bertsch, K, 1941. *Fruchte und samen. Handbucher der praktischen Vorgeschichtsforschung*. Stuttgart: Ferdinand Enke.

Birbeck, V, 2002. Excavations at Cannards Grave. *Somerset Archaeological and Natural History Society* 144, 41–116.

Bland, R, 2015. Hoarding in Britain from the Bronze Age to the 20th century. In J Naylor and R Bland, eds, *Hoarding and the deposition of metalwork from the Bronze Age to the 20th century: A British perspective*. Oxford: British Archaeological Reports, British Series 615, 1–20.

Borlase, M and Wright, M, 2014. A Late Iron Age and Romano-British settlement at Middle Amble Farm, St Kew. *Cornish Archaeology* 53, 183–208.

Borlase, W, 1769. *Observations on the antiquities historical and monumental, of the county of Cornwall. Consisting of several essays on the first inhabitants, druid-superstition, customs, and remains of the most remote antiquity, in Britain, and the British Isles*. Oxford: W Jackson.

Borlase, W C, 1872. *Naenia Cornubiae: a descriptive essay, illustrative of the sepulchres and funereal customs of the early inhabitants of the county of Cornwall*. London: Longmans, Green, Reader and Dyer.

Bourdieu, P, 1977. *Outline of a theory of practice*. Cambridge: Cambridge University Press.

Bowden, M, Soutar, S, Field, D and Barber, M, 2015. *The Stonehenge landscape: Analysing the Stonehenge World Heritage Site*. London: Historic England.

Bradley, R, 1990. *The passage of arms: An archaeological analysis of prehistoric hoards and votive deposits*. Cambridge University Press: Cambridge.

Bradley, R, 1993. *Altering the earth: The origins of monuments in Britain and Continental Europe*. Edinburgh: Society of Antiquaries of Scotland.

Bradley, R, 2002. *The past in prehistoric societies*. London: Routledge.

Bradley, R, 2005. *Ritual and domestic life in prehistoric Europe*. London: Routledge.

Bradley, R, 2012. *The idea of order: The circular archetype in prehistoric Europe*. Oxford: Oxford University Press.

Bradley, R, 2017. *A geography of offerings: Deposits of valuables in the landscapes of ancient Europe*. Oxford: Oxbow.

Bradley, R, Lewis, J, Mullin, D and Branch, N, 2015. Where water wells up from the earth': excavations at the findspot of the Late Bronze Age hoard from Broadward, Shropshire. *Antiquaries Journal* 95, 21–64.

Bradley, R and Nimura, C, 2016. *The use and reuse of stone circles: Fieldwork at five Scottish monuments and its implications*. Oxford: Oxbow.

Brück, J, 1995. A place for the dead: the role of human remains in Late Bronze Age Britain. *Proceedings of the Prehistoric Society* 61, 245–278.

Brück, J, 1999a. Ritual and rationality: Some problems of interpretation in European archaeology. *European Journal of Archaeology* 2, 313–344.

Brück, J, 1999b. Houses, lifecycles and deposition on Middle Bronze Age settlements in southern England. *Proceedings of the Prehistoric Society* 65, 245–278.

Brück, J, 2001. Body metaphors and technologies of transformation in the English Middle and Late Bronze Age. In J Brück, ed, *Bronze Age landscapes tradition and transformation*. Oxford: Oxbow, 149–160.

Brudenell, M and Cooper, A, 2008. Post-middenism: depositional histories on later Bronze Age settlements at Broom, Bedfordshire. *Oxford Journal of Archaeology* 27, 15–36.

Budd, P and Taylor, T, 1995. The faerie smith meets the bronze industry: magic versus science in the interpretation of prehistoric metal-making. *World Archaeology* 27, 133–143.

Buckley, V, 1990. *Burnt offerings: International contributions to burnt mound archaeology*. Bray: Wordwell.

Bullen, R A, 1912. *Harlyn Bay and the discoveries of its Prehistoric remains*. Harlyn Bay: Colonel Bellers.

Bunn, D, 2011. *Geophysical survey; proposed Newquay Growth Area, Cornwall. Land at Higher Trencreek, Newquay*. Lincoln: Pre-construct Geophysics.

Burl, A, 1976. *The stone circles of the British Isles*. New Haven and London: Yale University Press.

Butcher, S A, 1978. Excavations at Nornour, Isles of Scilly, 1969–73: The pre-Roman settlement. *Cornish Archaeology* 17, 29–112.

Butcher, S A, 2000–1. Roman Nornour, Isles of Scilly: A reconsideration. *Cornish Archaeology* 39–40, 5–44.

Butcher, S A, 2014. The Roman brooches from Nornour, Isles of Scilly. *Cornish Archaeology* 53, 1–81.

Butler, C, 2005. *Prehistoric flintwork*. Stroud: Tempus.

Cappers, R T J, Bekker, R M and Jans, J E A, 2006. *Digital Seed Atlas of the Netherlands*. Groningen: Barkhuis Publishing and Groningen University Library.

Carruthers, W, 1998. Atlantic Road, Newquay, Unpublished report for Cornwall Archaeological Unit.

Carsten, J, 2018. House-lives as ethnography/biography. *Social Anthropology*, 26, 103–116.

Casey, P J and Hoffman, B, 1999. Excavations at the Roman temple in Lydney Park, Gloucestershire in 1980 and 1981. *Antiquaries Journal* 79, 81–143.

Chadwick, A M, 2004. Heavier burdens for willing Shoulders? Writing different histories, humanities and social practices for the Romano-British countryside. In B Croxford, H Eckardt, J Meade and J Weekes, J, eds, *TRAC 2003: Proceedings of the Thirteenth Annual Theoretical Roman Archaeology Conference, Leicester 2003*. Oxford: Oxbow, 90–110.

Chadwick, A M, 2012. Routine magic, mundane ritual: towards a unified notion of depositional practice. *Oxford Journal of Archaeology* 31, 283–316.

Chadwick, A M, 2013. Some fishy things about scales: Macro and micro-approaches to later prehistoric and Romano-British field systems. *Landscapes* 14, 13–32.

Chadwick, A M, 2015. Doorways, ditches and dead dogs – material manifestations of practical magic in Iron Age and Roman Britain. In C Houlbrook and N Armitage, eds, *The materiality of magic: An artifactual investigation into ritual practices and popular beliefs*. Oxford: Oxbow, 37–64.

Chadwick, A M, Martin, L and Richardson, J, 2013. The significance of goats and chickens? Iron Age and Roman faunal assemblages, deposition and memory work at Wattle Syke, West Yorkshire. In A M Chadwick and C Gibson, eds, *Memory, myth, place and long-term landscape inhabitation*. Oxford: Oxbow, 165–188.

Challinor, D, 2012. Charcoal. In A M Jones, S R Taylor and J Sturgess, A Beaker-associated structure and other discoveries along the Sennen to Porthcurno South West Water pipeline. *Cornish Archaeology* 51, 39–41.

Challinor, D, 2015a. The wood charcoal. In A M Jones and S R Taylor, Archaeological investigations of Late Iron Age settlement at Sir James Smith's Community School, Camelford, Cornwall, 2008–9. *Cornish Archaeology* 54, 65–69.

Challinor, D, 2015b. Charcoal. In A M Jones, J Gossip and H Quinnell, *Settlement and metalworking in the Middle Bronze Age and beyond: New evidence from Tremough, Cornwall*. Leiden: Sidestone Press, 137–148.

Clarke, S, 1997. Abandonment, rubbish disposal and "special" deposits at Newstead. In K Meadows, C Lemke and J Heron, eds, *TRAC 96, proceedings of the sixth annual theoretical Roman archaeology conference, Sheffield 1996*. Oxford: Oxbow, 73–81.

Cole, R and Nowakowski, J A, Forthcoming. Killigrew Round excavation 1996. *Cornish Archaeology*.

Connerton, P, 1989. *How societies remember*. Cambridge: Cambridge University Press.

Cool, H E M and Richardson, J E, 2013. Exploring ritual deposits in a well at Rothwell Haigh, Leeds, *Britannia* 44, 191–217.

Cornish, T, 1883. Meetings of the Society. *Transactions of the Penzance Natural History and Antiquarian Society* 1, 429.

Cornish, J B, 1906. Ancient earthworks. In W Page, ed, *The Victoria County History of Cornwall. Volume 1*. London: Archibald and Company, 451–473.

Cotswold Archaeology, A, 2012. Tregunnel Hill, Newquay. *Cornish Archaeology* 51, 225–227.

Cotton, J, nd. Prehistoric and Roman settlement at Tothill Street, Minster in Thanet, Kent, London (Museum of London Archaeology) http://www.kentarchaeology.org.uk/10/042.pdf.

Crane, P and Murphy, K, 2010. The excavation of a coastal promontory fort, at Porth y Rhaw, Solva, Pembrokeshire, 1995–8. *Archaeologia Cambrensis* 159, 53–98.

Crofts, C B, 1954–55. Maen Castle, Sennen: The excavations. *Proceedings of the West Cornwall Field Club* 1, 98–115.

Crosby, V, Baker, P and Hembrey, N, 2013. The Romano-British settlement at Silbury In J Leary, D Field and G

Campbell, eds, *Silbury Hill: The largest prehistoric mound in Europe*. Swindon: English Heritage, 279-284.

Cunliffe, B, 1973. The early pre-Roman Iron Age. In E Crittall, ed, *Victoria County History of Wiltshire. Volume 1, Part 2*. Oxford: Oxford University Press, 408-416.

Cunliffe, B, 1988. *Mount Batten Plymouth, a prehistoric and Roman port*. Oxford: Oxford University Press.

Cunliffe, B, 1993. *Wessex to 1000 AD*. London: Longman.

Cunliffe, B, 2010. *Iron Age communities in Britain - an account of England, Scotland and Wales from the seventh century BC until the Roman Conquest*. London: Routledge (fourth edition).

Cunnington, M, 1923. *The Early Iron Age inhabited site at All Cannings Cross Farm, Wiltshire. A description of the excavations, and objects found, by Mr and Mrs B H Cunnington, 1911-1922*. Devizes: Simpson and Company.

Dark, K R, 1993. Roman-period activity at prehistoric ritual monuments in Britain and the Armorican peninsula. In E Scott, ed, *Theoretical Roman archaeology: First conference proceedings*. Aldershot: Avebury, 133-146.

Darvill, T, 2012. Sounds from the underground: Neolithic ritual pits and pit digging on the Isle Man and beyond. In H Anderson-Whymark and J Thomas, eds, *Regional perspectives on Neolithic pit deposition*. Oxford: Oxbow, 30-42.

Darvill, T and Wainwright, G, 2009. Stonehenge excavations 2008. *Antiquaries Journal* 89, 1-19.

Davis, O, 2017. Iron Age burial in Wales: Patterns, practices and problems. *Oxford Journal of Archaeology* 37, 1-49.

Dietler, M, 1996. Feasts and commensal politics in the political economy: Food, power, and status in prehistoric Europe. In P Wiessner and W Schiefenhovel, eds, *Food and the status quest: An interdisciplinary perspective*. Oxford: Berghahn, 87-126.

Dolan, B, 2016. Making iron in the Irish midlands: The social and symbolic role of Iron Age ironworkers. *Journal of Irish Archaeology* 25, 31-48.

Douglas, M, 1966. *Purity and danger; an analysis of the concepts of pollution and taboo*. London: Routledge.

Dudley, D, 1960-61. Some cist-graves in Poynters Garden, St Mary's, Isles of Scilly. *Proceedings of the West Cornwall Field Club* 5, 221-229.

Dudley, D, 1967. Excavations on Nor'nour in the Isles of Scilly, 1962-6. *Archaeological Journal* 124, 1-64.

Dudley, D and Jope, E M, 1965. An Iron Age cist-burial with two brooches from Trevone, North Cornwall. *Cornish Archaeology* 3, 18-23.

Edlin, H L, 1949. *Woodland crafts in Britain: An account of the traditional uses of trees and timbers in the British countryside*. London: Batsford.

Edmonds, M, 1995. *Stone tools and society; working stone in Neolithic and Bronze Age Britain*. London: Batsford.

Edwards, K and Kirkham, G, 2008. Gear and Caervallack, St Martin-in-Meneage: excavations by Time Team, 2001. *Cornish Archaeology* 47, 49-100.

Eliade, M, 1962 *The forge and the crucible: The origins and structure of alchemy*. Chicago: University of Chicago Press.

Farnell, A, 2015. Multi-period settlement, burial, industry and agriculture: Archaeological excavations 2007-2012 at Twinyeo Quarry, Chudleigh Knighton. *Proceedings of the Devon Archaeological Society* 73, 185-278.

Field, D and McOmish, D, 2017. *The making of prehistoric Wiltshire: Life, ceremony and death from the earliest times to the Roman invasion*. Amberley: Stroud.

Fitzpatrick, A P, 1994. Outside in: the structure of an Early Iron Age house at Dunston Park, Thatcham, Berkshire. In A P Fitzpatrick and E L Morris, eds, *The Iron Age in Iron Age Wessex: Recent work*. Salisbury: Wessex Archaeology, 68-72.

Fitzpatrick, A P, 1997. Everyday life in Iron Age Wessex. In A T Gwilt and C Haselgrove, eds, *Reconstructing Iron Age societies*. Oxford: Oxbow, 73-86.

Fitzpatrick, A P, 2003. Roman amphorae in Iron Age Britain. *Journal of Roman Pottery Studies* 10, 10-25.

Fitzpatrick, A P, Butterworth, C A and Grove, J, 1999. *Prehistoric and Roman sites in east Devon: the A30 Honiton to Exeter improvement DBFO Scheme, 1996-9*. Salisbury: Wessex Archaeology.

Fowler, P, 1962. A native homestead of the Roman period at Porth Godrevy, Gwithian. *Cornish Archaeology* 1, 17-60.

Fowler, P, 1983. *The farming of prehistoric Britain*. Cambridge: Cambridge University Press.

Fox, A, 1952. Hillslope forts and related earthworks in south-west England and South Wales. *Archaeological Journal* 30, 1-22.

Fox, A and Ravenhill, W J D. 1969. Excavation of a rectilinear earthwork at Trevinnick, St Kew, 1968. *Cornish Archaeology* 8, 89-96.

Fulford, M G, Powell, A B, Entwistle R and Raymond, F, 2006. *The Iron Age and Romano-British settlements and landscapes of Salisbury Plain*. Salisbury: Wessex Archaeology.

Gale, R, 2004. Charcoal analysis. In A M Jones and S R Taylor, *What lies beneath... St Newlyn East and Mitchell archaeological investigations 2001*. Truro: Cornwall Archaeological Unit, 81-85.

Gale, R, 2006. The charcoal. In A M Jones and H Quinnell, Cornish Beakers: New discoveries and perspectives. *Cornish Archaeology* 45, 31-70.

Gale, R, 2009-10. Charcoal. In A Lawson-Jones and G Kirkham, Smithing in the round: excavations at Little Quoit Farm, St Columb Major, Cornwall. *Cornish Archaeology* 48-9, 210-216.

Gale, R, 2011. Charcoal. In J A Nowakowski and H Quinnell, *Trevelgue Head, Cornwall: The importance of C K C Andrew's 1939 excavations for prehistoric and Roman Cornwall*. Truro: Cornwall Archaeological Unit, 314-322.

Gale, R, Forthcoming. Charcoal, in A, Reynolds, Atlantic Road, Newquay: Late Iron Age and Romano-British site. *Cornish Archaeology*.

Gale, R and Cutler, D, 2000. *Plants in archaeology: Identification manual of vegetative plant materials used in Europe and the southern Mediterranean to c. 1500*. Otley: Westbury and Royal Botanic Gardens, Kew.

Gardiner, J, 2000. *Resurgam! Archaeology at Stonehouse Mount Batten and Mount Wise Regeneration Areas, Plymouth*. Salisbury: Wessex Archaeology.

Garland, N, 2013. Ritual landscapes of Pre-Roman Britain: The margins of practice on the margins of the empire. In A Bokern, M Bolder-Boos, S Krmnicek, D Maschek and S Page, eds, *TRAC 2012: Proceedings of the Twenty-Second Annual Theoretical Roman Archaeology Conference, Frankfurt 2012*. Oxford: Oxbow, 183–198.

Garrow, D, 2012. Odd deposits and average practice. A critical history of the concept of structured deposition. *Archaeological Dialogues* 19, 85–115.

Geological Survey of Great Britain, 1974. *Newquay Sheet 346*. Drift Edition, 1:50,000 Series.

Gent, H, 1983. Centralised storage in later prehistoric Britain. *Proceedings of the Prehistoric Society* 49, 143–267.

Germany, M, 2014. Continuity and change in the Mid Chelmer Valley – archaeological excavations at Old Hall and Generals Farm, Boreham 2007. *Essex Archaeology and History* 5, 45–86.

Giddens, A, 1984. *The constitution of society: Outline of the theory of structuration*. Cambridge: Polity Press.

Gilbert C S, 1817. *An historical survey of the county of Cornwall*. Plymouth and London: J Congdon.

Giles M, 2007. Making metal and forging relations: Ironworking in the British Iron Age. *Oxford Journal of Archaeology* 26, 395–413.

Goldhahn, J and Oestigaard, T, 2008. Smith and death: Cremations in furnaces in Bronze and Iron Age Scandinavia. In K Childis., J Lund and C Prescott, eds, *Facets of archaeology: Essays in honour of Lotte Hedeager on her 60th birthday*. Oslo: Oslo Academic Press, 215–242.

Golosetti, R, 2017. Cult places at former oppida in South-East Gaul: Questions of memory, tradition and identity. *Oxford Journal of Archaeology* 36, 171–196.

Good, O, 2015. Romano-British settlement and enclosures at Gover Farm, St Agnes, Cornwall. *Cornish Archaeology* 54, 225–232.

Gordon, S, 2015. Domestic magic and the walking dead in medieval England: A diachronic approach. In C Houlbrook and N Armitage, eds, *The materiality of magic: An artifactual investigation into ritual practices and popular beliefs*. Oxford: Oxbow, 65–84.

Gosden, C and Marshall, Y, 1999. The cultural biography of objects. *World Archaeology* 31, 169–178.

Gossip, J, Forthcoming. Life outside the round – Bronze Age and Iron Age settlement at Higher Besore and Truro College, Threemilestone, Truro.

Gossip, J, 2013. The evaluation of a multi-period prehistoric site and fogou at Boden Vean, St Antony-in-Meneage, Cornwall, 2003. *Cornish Archaeology* 52, 1–98.

Gossip, J and Jones, A M, 2007. *Archaeological investigations of a later prehistoric and a Romano-British landscape at Tremough, Penryn, Cornwall*. Oxford: British Archaeological Reports, British Series 443.

Gossip, J and Jones A M, 2008. A Bronze Age roundhouse at Carnon Gate, Feock. *Cornish Archaeology* 47, 101–115.

Gossip, J and Jones A M, 2009–10. Excavations at Tremough, Penryn, 2000-6. *Cornish Archaeology* 48–9, 1–66.

Gossip, J and Jones A M, Forthcoming. Later Neolithic pits and an Iron Age and Romano-British settlement at Penryn College. *Cornish Archaeology*.

Gossip, J, Jones A M and Quinnell, H, 2012. Early Neolithic activity and an Iron Age settlement at Penmayne, Rock, St Minver. *Cornish Archaeology* 51, 165–189.

Graves, R, 1999. *The white goddess: A historical grammar of poetic myth*. London: Faber.

Green, M J, 1986. *The gods of the Celts*. Stroud: Sutton.

Green, T, 2009. Excavation of a hillside enclosure at Holworthy Farm, Parracombe displaying Bronze Age and Iron Age activity. *Proceedings of the Devon Archaeological Society* 67, 39–97.

Greig, J R A, 1991. The British Isles. In W Van Zeist, K Wasylikowa and K Behre, *Progress in old world palaeoethnobotany. A retrospective view on the occasion of 20 years of the International Work Group for Palaeoethnobotany*. Rotterdam: Balkema.

Guthrie, A, 1969. Excavation of a settlement at Goldherring, Sancreed, 1958-1961. *Cornish Archaeology* 8, 5–39.

Gwilt, A T, Lodwick, M, Deacon, J, Wells, N, Madgwick, R and Young, T, 2016. Ephemeral Abundance at Llanmaes: Exploring the residues and resonances of an Earliest Iron Age midden and its associated archaeological context in the Vale of Glamorgan. In J Koch and B Cunliffe, eds, *Celtic from the West 3*. Oxford: Oxbow, 277–303.

Hall, A, 2003. *Recognition and characterisation of turves in archaeological occupation deposits by means of macrofossil plant remains*. Centre for Archaeology Report 16/2003, English Heritage.

Hammon, A, 2011. Iron Age mammal and fish remains. In J A Nowakowski and H Quinnell, *Trevelgue Head, Cornwall: the importance of C K C Andrew's 1939 excavations for prehistoric and Roman Cornwall*. Truro: Cornwall Archaeological Unit, 294–305.

Harris, O, 2009. Making places matter in early Dorset. *Oxford Journal of Archaeology* 28, 111–124.

Hart, J and Sheldon, S, 2017. Cloakham Lawns, Axminster: Archaeological excavation. *Proceedings of the Devon Archaeological Society* 75, 51–96.

Harte, J, 2018. Superstitious observations: fortune-telling in English folk culture. *Time and Mind* 11, 67–88.

Hartgroves, S, Jones, A M and Kirkham, G, 2006. The Eathorne Menhir. *Cornish Archaeology* 45, 97–108.

Haselgrove, C, 2015. Hoarding and other forms of metalwork deposition in Iron Age Britain. In J

Naylor and R Bland, eds, *Hoarding and the deposition of metalwork from the Bronze Age to the 20th century: A British perspective*. Oxford: British Archaeological Reports, British Series 615, 27–40.

Hather, J G, 2000. *The identification of northern European woods; a guide for archaeologists and conservators*. London: Archetype Books.

Heaney, S, 1999. *Beowulf: A new translation*. London: Faber and Faber.

Hencken, H O'N, 1932. *The Archaeology of Cornwall and Scilly*. London: Methuen.

Hencken, H O'N, 1933. An excavation by H M Office of Works at Chysauster, Cornwall, 1931. *Archaeologia* 83, 237–284.

Henderson, J C, 2007. *The Atlantic Iron Age: Settlement and identity in the first millennium BC*. London: Routledge.

Herring, P, 1994. The cliff castles and hillforts of West Penwith in the light of recent work at Maen Castle and Treryn Dinas. *Cornish Archaeology* 33, 40–56.

Hill, J D, 1995. *Ritual and rubbish in the Iron Age of Wessex*. Oxford: British Archaeological Reports, British Series 242.

Hill, J D, 1996. Hillforts and the Iron Age of Wessex. In T Champion and J Collis, eds, *The Iron Age in Britain and Ireland: Recent trends*. Sheffield: University of Sheffield Press, 95–116.

Hill, J D, 2002–3. The mirror. In C Johns, An Iron Age sword and mirror cist burial from Bryher, Isles of Scilly. *Cornish Archaeology* 41–42, 32–36.

Hingley, R, 1990. Iron Age "currency bars": The archaeological and social context. *Archaeological Journal* 147, 91–117.

Hingley, R, 1997. Iron, ironworking and regeneration: a study of the symbolic meaning of metalworking in Iron Age Britain. In A T Gwilt and C Haselgrove, eds, *Reconstructing Iron Age societies*. Oxford: Oxbow, 9–18.

Hingley, R, 2006. The deposition of iron objects in Britain during the later prehistoric and Roman periods: Contextual analysis and the significance of iron. *Britannia*, 213–257.

Hirst, F C, 1937. *Excavations at Porthmeor, Cornwall, 1933, 1934 and 1935*. Truro: Oscar Blackford (Reprinted from Journal of the Royal Institution of Cornwall, XXIV).

Hitchins, M, 1803. Account of Roman urns discovered in Cornwall, and of a cromlech discovered in the parish of Madron in the same county. *Archaeologia* 14, 224–230.

Holbrook, N and Bidwell, P T, 1991. *Roman finds from Exeter*. Exeter: Exeter City Council and University of Exeter Press.

Hughes, J, 2017. Souvenirs of the self: Personal belongings as votive offerings in ancient religion. *Religion in the Roman Empire* 3, 181–201.

Humphreys, O J, 2017. Context, continuity, correspondence, and continental connections: New approaches to the ironwork hoards of Roman Britain. *Archaeological Journal* 174, 363–408.

Hurcombe, L, 2014. *Perishable material culture in prehistory: investigating the missing majority*. London: Routledge.

Hutton, R, 1993. *The pagan religions of the British Isles, their nature and legacy*. London: Routledge.

Hutton, R, 2013. *Pagan Britain*. London: Yale.

Ingold, I, 2016. *Lines: A brief history*. London: Routledge.

Jacomet, S, 2006. *Identification of cereal remains from archaeological sites*. Archaeobotany Lab IPAS, Basel University, www.ipna.unibas.ch/archbot/pdf.

Johns, C, 2002–3. An Iron Age sword and mirror cist burial from Bryher, Isles of Scilly. *Cornish Archaeology* 41–42, 1–79.

Johns, C, 2008. The excavation of a multi-period archaeological landscape at Trenowah, St Austell, Cornwall, 1997. *Cornish Archaeology* 47, 1–48.

Johns, C and Taylor, S R, Forthcoming. Excavation of a Porthcressa-type cist burial at Churchtown Farm, St Martin's, Isles of Scilly, 2013. *Cornish Archaeology*.

Johnson, N, 1981. The location of rural settlement on Pre-medieval Caernarvonshire. *The Bulletin of the Board of Celtic Studies* 24, 381–415.

Johnston, D A, Moore D and Fasham, P, 1998–99. Excavations at Penhale Round, Fraddon Cornwall. *Cornish Archaeology* 37–8, 94–100.

Jones, A M, 1998–9. The excavation of a later Bronze Age structure at Callestick. *Cornish Archaeology* 37–8, 5–55.

Jones, A M, 2000–1. The excavation of a multi-period site at Stencoose, Cornwall. *Cornish Archaeology* 39–40, 45–94.

Jones, A M, 2008. A note on the Harlyn Bay structure. *Cornish Archaeology* 47, 117–121.

Jones, A M, 2010. Misplaced monuments?: A review of ceremony and monumentality in first millennium cal BC Cornwall. *Oxford Journal of Archaeology* 29, 203–228.

Jones, A M, 2013. Memory, myth, place and landscape inhabitation: A perspective from the south-west peninsula. In A M Chadwick and C Gibson, eds, *Memory, myth, place and long-term landscape inhabitation*. Oxford: Oxbow, 55–75.

Jones, A M, 2014. Hay Close, St Newlyn East: Excavations by the Cornwall Archaeological Society, 2007, Cornwall. *Cornish Archaeology* 53, 157–170.

Jones, A M, 2015. Ritual, rubbish or everyday life? Evidence from a Middle Bronze Age settlement in mid Cornwall. *Archaeological Journal* 172, 30–51.

Jones, A M, Forthcoming a. Castle an Dinas, St Columb, Cornwall; investigating the 1962-1964 excavation archive. *Cornish Archaeology*.

Jones, A M, Forthcoming b. Remembering and forgetting: reusing stones and bones, and making and unmaking monuments. In C Gibson, D Brown and J Pyzel, eds, *Gone...but not forgotten. forgotten...but not long gone. Mundane memories, artificial amnesia and transformed traditions*. Oxford: Oxbow.

Jones, A M, Forthcoming c. Mid-fourth millennium cal BC activity at Penans Farm, Grampound, Cornwall. *Cornish Archaeology*.

Jones, A M., Gossip, J and Quinnell, H, 2015. *Settlement and metalworking in the Middle Bronze Age and beyond: New evidence from Tremough, Cornwall*. Leiden: Sidestone Press.

Jones, A M and Quinnell, H, 2006a. Cornish Beakers: new discoveries and perspectives. *Cornish Archaeology* 45, 31–70.

Jones, A M and Quinnell, H, 2006b. Redating the Watch Hill barrow. *Archaeological Journal* 163, 42–66.

Jones, A M and Quinnell, H, 2014. *Lines of investigation along the north Cornish coast*. Oxford: British Archaeological Reports, British Series 594.

Jones, A M and Shepherd, F, 2009–10. Romano-British activity at Gerrans, Cornwall. *Cornish Archaeology* 48–9, 313–315.

Jones, A M and Smith, R P, 2015. A Late Bronze Age pit, burnt bone and stones at Quintrell Downs, Newquay, Cornwall. *Cornish Archaeology* 54, 193–204.

Jones, A M and Taylor, S R, 2004. *What lies beneath ... St Newlyn East and Mitchell archaeological investigations 2001*. Truro: Cornwall Archaeological Unit.

Jones, A M and Taylor, S R, 2009–10. Discoveries along the Treyarnon SWW pipeline. *Cornish Archaeology* 48–9, 243–252.

Jones, A M and Taylor, S R, 2010. *Scarcewater, Pennance, Cornwall, archaeological excavation of a Bronze Age and Roman landscape*. Oxford: British Archaeological Reports, British Series 516.

Jones, A M and Taylor, S R, 2015. Archaeological investigations of Late Iron Age settlement at Sir James Smith's Community School, Camelford, Cornwall, 2008-9. *Cornish Archaeology* 54, 1–87.

Jones, A M, Taylor, S R and Sturgess, J, 2012. A Beaker-associated structure and other discoveries along the Sennen to Porthcurno South West Water pipeline. *Cornish Archaeology* 51, 1–67.

Jones, J, 2014. Charred plant remains from Churchill Farm, Hemyock, Devon. Unpublished report for Exeter Archaeology.

Jope Rogers, J, 1873. Romano-British or late Celtic remains at Trelan Bahow, St Keverne, Cornwall. *Archaeological Journal* 30, 267–272.

Joy, J, 2011. Exploring status and identity in later Iron Age Britain: re-interpreting mirror burials. In T Moore and X L Armada, eds, *Atlantic Europe in the first millennium BC: crossing the divide*. Oxford: Oxford University Press, 468–487.

Joy, J, 2014. 'Fire burn and cauldron bubble': Iron Age and early Roman cauldrons of Britain and Ireland. *Proceedings of the Prehistoric Society* 80, 327–362.

Joy, J, 2015. 'Things in process': Biographies of British Iron Age pits. In D Böschung, P A Kreuz and T Kienlin, eds, *Biography of objects: Aspekte eines kulturhistorischen Konzepts*. Paderborn: Wilhelm Fink, 125–141.

Joyce, S, 2011. *Newquay Strategic Route Newquay, Cornwall: Archaeological evaluation and watching brief*. Cirencester: Cotswold Archaeology.

Karl, R, 2016. Emerging settlement monumentality in North Wales during the Late Bronze and Iron Age: the case of Meillionydd. In J Koch and B Cunliffe, eds, *Celtic from the West 3*. Oxford: Oxbow, 265–293.

Kirkham, G, 2005. Prehistoric linear ditches on the Marlborough Downs. In G Brown, D Field and D McOmish, eds, *Avebury landscape: Aspects of the field archaeology of the Marlborough Downs*. Oxford: Oxbow, 149–155.

Kirkham, G, 2012. "Rip it up and spread it over the field": post-medieval agriculture and the destruction of monuments, a case study from Cornwall. *Landscapes* 13, 2, 1–20.

Kis-Jovak, J, Nooy-Plm, H, Schefold, R and Schultz-Dornburg, U, 1988. *Banua Toraja: Changing patterns in the architecture and symbolism among the Sa'dan Toraja, Sulawesi*. Indonesia. Amsterdam: Royal Tropical Institute.

Kuijpers, M H G, 2013. The sound of fire, taste of copper, feel of bronze, and colours of the cast: Sensory aspects of metalworking technology. In M L S Sørensen and K Rebay-Salisbury, eds, *Embodied knowledge: Historical perspectives on belief and technology*. Oxford: Oxbow, 137–150.

Ladle, L and Woodward, A, 2009. *Excavations at Bestwall Quarry, Wareham, 1992-2005, volume 1: The prehistoric landscape*. Dorchester: Dorset Archaeological and Natural History Society.

LaMotta, V and Schiffer, M, 1999. Formation of house floor assemblages. In P Allison, ed, *The archaeology of household activities*. London: Routledge, 19–29.

Larrington, C, (trans), 1999. *The Poetic Edda*. Oxford: Oxford University Press.

Lawson, A J, 2000. *Potterne, 1982-5: Animal husbandry in late Prehistoric Wiltshire*. Salisbury: Wessex Archaeology.

Lawson-Jones, A, 2011. *Land at Trevithick Manor, Newquay, Cornwall: Archaeological assessment and geophysical survey*. Truro: Cornwall Archaeological Unit.

Lawson-Jones, A, 2013. Discoveries along the North Land's End pipeline. *Cornish Archaeology* 52, 197–222.

Lawson-Jones, A and Kirkham, G, 2009–10. Smithing in the round: excavations at Little Quoit Farm, St Columb Major, Cornwall. *Cornish Archaeology* 48–9, 173–226.

Leary, J, Field, D and Campbell, G, eds, 2013. *Silbury Hill: The largest prehistoric mound in Europe*. Swindon: English Heritage.

Leonard, K, 2015a. Arranged artefacts and materials in Irish Bronze Age ritual deposits: A consideration of prehistoric practice and intention. In C Houlbrook and N Armitage, eds, *The materiality of magic: An artefactual investigation into ritual practices and popular beliefs*. Oxford: Oxbow, 23–36.

Leonard, K, 2015b. *Ritual in Late Bronze Age Ireland*. Oxford: Archaeopress.

Lee, K, 2001. Experimental heat-treatment of flint. *Lithics* 22, 39–44.

Lewis, J, 2007. The creation of round barrows on the Mendip Hills, Somerset. In J Last, ed, *Beyond the Grave: new perspectives on barrows*. Oxford: Oxbow, 72-82.

Lönnrot, E, (Bosley, K, trans), 2008. *The Kalevala*. Oxford: Oxford University Press.

Lynch, F, Aldhouse-Green, S and Davies J L, 2000. *Prehistoric Wales*. Stroud: Alan Sutton.

Lynn, C, 2003. *Navan fort, archaeology and myth*. Bray: Wordwell.

Madgwick, R and Mulville, J, 2015. Feasting on forelimbs: conspicuous consumption and identity in later prehistoric Britain. *Antiquity* 345, 629-44.

Madgwick, R, Grimes, V, Lamb, A and McCormick, F, 2017. Isotope analysis reveals that feasts at Navan Fort, Ulster, drew people and animals from across Ireland. *PAST* 87, 15-16.

Maltby, M, 1994. The animal bones from a Romano-British well at Oakridge II, Basingstoke. *Proceedings of the Hampshire Field Club and Archaeological Society* 49, 47-76.

Manning, P and Quinnell, H, 2009. Excavation and field survey at the Iron Age hillfort of Berry Ball, Crediton Hamlets. *Proceedings of the Devon Archaeological Society* 67, 99-132.

Manning, W H, 1972. Ironwork hoards in Iron Age and Roman Britain. *Britannia* 3, 224-250.

McAvoy, F, 1980. The excavation of a multi-period site at Carngoon Bank, Lizard. *Cornish Archaeology* 19, 31-62.

McOmish, D, Field, D and Brown, G, 2010. The Late Bronze Age and Early Iron Age midden site at East Chisenbury, Wiltshire. *Wiltshire Archaeological and Natural History Magazine* 103, 35-101.

Mercer, R J, 1981. Excavations at Carn Brea, Illogan, Cornwall 1970-73. *Cornish Archaeology* 20, 1- 204.

Merrifield, R, 1987. *The archaeology of ritual and magic*. London: Batsford.

Midgley, M S, 2005. *The monumental cemeteries of prehistoric Europe*. Stroud: Tempus.

Mikkelsen, P H, 1998. The growth of the field-agricultural systems and strategy of cultivation in the Iron Age agriculture. Archaeobotanical investigations of iron-smelting furnaces from the 1st to 8th centuries AD. Unpublished PhD Thesis, Institut for Forhistorik Arkaeologi, Århus Universitet, Denmark.

Miles, H, Davey, U, Harris, D, Hooper, S, Moreton, P, Padel, O and Staines, S, 1977. Excavations at Killibury hillfort, Egloshayle 1975-6. *Cornish Archaeology* 16, 89-121.

Mlekuž, D, 2012. Messy landscapes manifesto. *AARGnews. The Newsletter of the Aerial Archaeology Research Group* 44, 22-24.

Moore, H, 1982. The interpretation of spatial patterning in settlement residues. In I Hodder, ed, *Symbolic and structural archaeology*. Cambridge: Cambridge University Press, 74-79.

Moore, H, 1986. *Space, text and gender: An anthropological study of the Marakwet of Kenya*. Cambridge: Cambridge University Press.

Morris, J, 2007. Associated bone groups; one archaeologist's rubbish is another's ritual deposition. In O Davis, N Sharples and K Waddington, eds, *Changing perspectives on the first millennium BC: Proceedings of the Iron Age research student seminar*. Oxford: Oxbow, 83-98.

Morris, J, 2011. Animal 'ritual' killing: from remains to meanings. In A Pluskowski, ed, *The ritual killing and burial of animals: European perspectives*. Oxford: Oxbow, 8-21.

Mudd, A and Joyce, S, 2014. *The archaeology of the south-west reinforcement gas pipeline, Devon; investigations in 2005-7*. Cirencester: Cotswold Archaeology.

Muller, K E, 1999. *Soul of Africa. Magical rites and traditions*. Cologne: Konemann.

Naylor, J, 2015. The deposition and hoarding of non-precious metals in early medieval England. In J Naylor and R Bland, eds, *Hoarding and the deposition of metalwork from the Bronze Age to the 20th century: A British perspective*. Oxford: British Archaeological Reports, British Series 615, 125-147.

Needham, S, 2005. Transforming Beaker culture in north-west Europe: processes of fusion and fission. *Proceedings of the Prehistoric Society* 71, 171-218.

Newberry, J, 2002. Inland flint in prehistoric Devon: sources, tool-making quality and use. *Proceedings of the Devon Archaeological Society* 60, 1-36.

Nowakowski, J A, 1991. Trethellan Farm, Newquay: the excavation of a lowland Bronze Age settlement and Iron Age cemetery. *Cornish Archaeology* 30, 5-242.

Nowakowski, J A, 2001. Leaving home in the Cornish Bronze Age: insights into the planned abandonment process. In J Brück, ed, *Bronze Age landscapes tradition and transformation*. Oxford: Oxbow, 139-148.

Nowakowski, J A, 2007. Digging deeper into barrow ditches: Investigating the making of Early Bronze Age memories in Cornwall. In J Last, ed, *Beyond the Grave: new perspectives on barrows*. Oxford: Oxbow, 91-112.

Nowakowski, J A, 2011. Appraising the bigger picture – Cornish Iron Age and Romano-British lives and settlements 25 years on. *Cornish Archaeology* 50, 241-261.

Nowakowski, J A, 2016. Remarkable Landscapes of ancient fields – the later prehistoric and Romano-British legacy. In P Herring, N Johnson, A M Jones, J A Nowakowski, A Sharpe and A Young, eds, *Archaeology and Landscape at the Land's End*. Cornwall. Truro: Cornwall Archaeological Unit, 160-191.

Nowakowski, J A, Gwilt, A T, Megaw, V and La Niece, S, 2009. A late Iron Age neck-ring from Pentire, Newquay Cornwall, with a note on the find from Boverton, Vale of Glamorgan. *Antiquaries Journal* 89, 35-52.

Nowakowski, J A and Johns, C, 2015. *Bypassing Indian Queens. Archaeological excavations 1992-1994. Investigating prehistoric and Romano-British settlement and landscapes in Cornwall*. Truro: Cornwall Archaeological Unit.

Nowakowski, J A and Quinnell, H, 2011. *Trevelgue Head, Cornwall: the importance of C K C Andrew's 1939 excavations for prehistoric and Roman Cornwall*. Truro: Cornwall Archaeological Unit.

O'Brien, W, 1999. *Sacred ground: Megalithic tombs in coastal south-west Ireland*. Galway: University of Galway Press.

O'Brien, W, Hohan, N and O'Driscoll, J, 2014–2015. Archaeological investigations at Toor More (Corrandhu) Hillfort, Co. Kilkenny. *Journal of the Royal Society of Antiquaries of Ireland* 144–145, 7–26.

O'Kelly, M J, 1982. *Newgrange: Archaeology, art and legend*. London: Thames and Hudson.

Olson, L, 1981. Crantock, Cornwall, as an early monastic site. In S Pearce, ed, *The early church in western Britain and Ireland: studies presented to C A Ralegh Radford*. Oxford: British Archaeological Reports, British Series 102, 177–185.

Ovid, (Raeburn, D, trans), 2004. *Metamorphosis*. London: Penguin.

Palmer, S C, 2017. Any more old Iron Age? An archaeological resource assessment for the Middle Bronze Age to Iron Age in Warwickshire and Solihull. In D Hurst, ed, *Westward on the high-hilled plains: The later prehistory of the West Midlands*. Oxford: Oxbow, 37–69.

Parker-Pearson, M, 1990. The production and distribution of Bronze Age pottery in south-west Britain. *Cornish Archaeology* 29, 5–32.

Parker Pearson, M, 1996. Food, fertility and front doors. In T Champion and J Collis, eds, *The Iron Age in Britain and Ireland: Recent trends*. Sheffield: University of Sheffield Press, 117–132.

Parker Pearson, M and Richards, C, 1994. Ordering the world: Perceptions of architecture, space and time. In M Parker Pearson and C Richards, eds, *Architecture and order, approaches to social space*. London: Routledge, 1–37.

Peacock, D P S, 1969. A Romano-British salt working site at Trebarveth, St Keverne. *Cornish Archaeology* 8, 47–65

Peacock, D P S and Williams, D F, 1991. *Amphorae and the Roman economy. An introductory guide*. London: Longman.

Pearce, S, 1976. The Middle and Late Bronze Age of the South-West and its relationship to settlement. *Proceedings of the Devon Archaeological Society* 34, 136–145.

Pearce, S, 1978. *Kingdom of Dumnonia: Studies in history and tradition in south western Britain, AD 350–1150*. Padstow: Lodenek Press.

Penhallurick, R D, 1986. *Tin in antiquity: its mining and trade throughout the ancient world with particular reference to Cornwall*. London: The Institute of Metals.

Penhallurick, R D, 1997. The evidence for prehistoric mining in Cornwall. In P Budd and D Gale, eds, *Prehistoric extractive metallurgy in Cornwall*. Truro: Cornwall Archaeological Unit, 23–34.

Penhallurick, R D, 2009. *Ancient and early medieval coins from Cornwall and Scilly*. London: Royal Numismatic Society.

Perkins, D R J, 1990. *Archaeological remains at Cottington Hill, Ebbsfleet, Ramsgate: an evaluation report by the Trust for Thanet Archaeology*, http://archaeologydataservice.ac.uk/archiveDS/ArchiveDownload?t=arch-1352 1/dissemination/pdf/Kent/GL9002.pdf

Peter, T, 1896. The Exploration of Carn Brea. *Journal of the Royal Institution of Cornwall*, XIII, 92–102.

Pitts, M, 2009. Urine to navel fluff: the first complete witch bottle. *British Archaeology* 107, 7.

Quinnell, H, 1986. Cornwall during the Iron Age and Roman period. *Cornish Archaeology* 26, 111–134.

Quinnell, H, 1992a. Stone objects. In N Appleton-Fox, Excavations at a Romano-British round; Reawla, Gwinear, Cornwall. *Cornish Archaeology* 31, 106–112.

Quinnell, H, 1992b. The pottery. In N Appleton-Fox, Excavations at a Romano-British round; Reawla, Gwinear, Cornwall. *Cornish Archaeology* 31, 94–106.

Quinnell, H, 1993. A sense of identity: distinctive Cornish stone artefacts in the Roman and post-Roman periods. In M Carver, ed, *In search of cult; archaeological investigations in honour of Philip Rahtz*. Woodbridge: Boydell Press, 69–78.

Quinnell, H, 2004. *Trethurgy; excavations at Trethurgy Round, St Austell: community and status in Roman and post-Roman Cornwall*. Truro: Cornwall Archaeological Unit.

Quinnell, H, 2011a. The pottery. In J A Nowakowski and H Quinnell, *Trevelgue Head, Cornwall: the importance of C K C Andrew's 1939 excavations for prehistoric and Roman Cornwall*. Truro: Cornwall Archaeological Unit, 144–208.

Quinnell, H, 2011b. A summary of Cornish ceramics in the first millennium BC. *Cornish Archaeology* 50, 213–240.

Quinnell, H, 2011c. Stonework. In J A Nowakowski and H Quinnell, *Trevelgue Head, Cornwall: the importance of C K C Andrew's 1939 excavations for prehistoric and Roman Cornwall*. Truro: Cornwall Archaeological Unit, 257–280.

Quinnell, H, 2014a. The pottery from the North Cornwall pipeline. In A M Jones and H Quinnell, *Lines of investigation along the north Cornish coast*. Oxford: British Archaeological Reports, British Series 594, 51–57.

Quinnell, H, 2014b. Tregunnel Hill pottery assessment. Unpublished report for Cotswold Archaeology Project No 9139.

Quinnell, H, 2014c. A pit with Beaker pottery at St Stephen-in-Brannel: A note. *Cornish Archaeology* 53, 233–238.

Quinnell, H, 2015. The prehistoric ceramics. In A M Jones, J Gossip, J and H Quinnell, *Settlement and metalworking in the Middle Bronze Age and beyond: New evidence from Tremough, Cornwall*. Leiden: Sidestone Press, 53–79.

Quinnell, H and Watts, S, 2004. Rotary querns. In H Quinnell, *Trethurgy; excavations at Trethurgy Round, St Austell: community and status in Roman and post-Roman Cornwall*. Truro: Cornwall Archaeological Unit, 145–152.

Rahtz, P A, 1951. The Roman temple at Pagans Hill, Chew Stoke, Somerset. *Proceedings of the Somerset Archaeological and Natural History Society* 96, 112–142.

Rainbird, P and Pears, B, Forthcoming. The excavation of an Iron Age Site at Nansledan, Newquay. *Cornish Archaeology*.

Rawlings, M and Fitzpatrick, A P, 1996. Prehistoric sites and a Romano-British settlement at Butterfield Down, Amesbury. *Wiltshire Archaeological and Natural History Magazine* 89, 1–43.

RCHM, Wales, 1964. *Caernarvonshire, Volume III: The West*. London: Her Majesties Stationery Office.

Reynolds, A, In preparation. Atlantic Road, Newquay: Late Iron Age and Romano-British Site. *Cornish Archaeology*.

Reynolds, P, 1982. Substructure to superstructure, in P J Drury, ed, *Structural reconstruction: approaches to the interpretation of the excavated remains of buildings*. Oxford: British Archaeological Reports, British Series 110, 173–198.

Richardson, J E, 1997. Economy and ritual: the use of animal bone in the interpretation of the Iron Age to Roman cultural transition. In K Meadows, C Lemke and J Heron, eds, *TRAC 96, proceedings of the sixth annual theoretical Roman archaeology conference, Sheffield 1996*. Oxford: Oxbow, 73–81.

Riley, D, 1980. *Early landscape from the air: Studies of crop marks in South Yorkshire and North Nottinghamshire*. Sheffield: University of Sheffield Press.

Rippon, S, Smart, C and Pears, B, 2015. *The fields of Britannia: Continuity and change in the late Roman and early medieval landscape*. Oxford: Oxford University Press.

Roberts, D, Moorhead, S, Robinson, P, Payne, A, Winton, H, Hembrey, N, Bishop, B, Campbell, G, Dungworth, D, Forward, A, Middleton, A, Russell, M, Timby, J, Worley, F, Carpenter, E, Edwards, Z, Linford, N, Linford, P, Vallender, J, Henry, R, Marshall, P, Reimer, P and Russell, N, 2017. Recent work on Urchfont Hill, Urchfont, Wiltshire. *Wiltshire Archaeological and Natural History Magazine* 110, 134–170.

Robinson, G, 2013. Re-building memory, identity and place: the long-term re-use of prehistoric settlements on the Isles of Scilly. In A M Chadwick and C Gibson, eds, *Memory, myth and long-term landscape inhabitation*. Oxford: Oxbow, 146–164.

Rogers, W, 1923. The shingles and sands of Cornwall. *Nineteenth annual report of the Royal Cornwall Polytechnic Society* 5, 1, 45–50.

Romankiewicz, T, 2018. Room for ideas: Tracing non-domestic roundhouses. *Antiquaries Journal* 98, 1–26.

Ross, A, 1974. *Pagan Celtic Britain*. London: Cardinal.

Russell, N, Wright, K I, Carter, T, Ketchum, S, Ryan, P, Yalman, E N, Regan, R, Stevanović, M and Milić, M, 2014. Bringing down the house: House closing deposits at Çatalhöyük. In I Hodder, ed, *Integrating Çatalhöyük: Themes from the 2000-2008 seasons*. Los Angeles: Cotsen Institute of Archaeology, University of California, 109–121.

Russell, V, 1971. *West Penwith survey*. St Austell: Cornwall Archaeological Society.

Russell, V and Pool, P, 1963. Excavation of a Romano-British hut, Boscreege, Gulval. *Cornish Archaeology* 2, 19–22.

Saunders, A and Harris, D, 1982. Excavation at Castle Gotha, St Austell. *Cornish Archaeology* 21, 109–153.

Sharpe, A, 1992. Treryn Dinas: cliff castles reconsidered. *Cornish Archaeology* 31, 65–68.

Sharples, N, 2010. *Social relations in later prehistory: Wessex in the first millennium BC*. Oxford: Oxford University Press.

Schweingruber, F H, 1990. *Microscopic wood anatomy*. Birminsdorf: Eidgenössische Forschungsanstalt WSL (third edition).

Schwieso, J, 1976. Excavations at Threemilestone Round, Kenwyn, Truro. *Cornish Archaeology* 15, 51–67.

Scudder, B, (trans), 2004. *Egils saga*. London: Penguin.

Seager Smith, R H, 2006. Late Iron Age and Roman pottery. In M G Fulford, A B Powell, R Entwistle and F Raymond, *The Iron Age and Romano-British settlements and landscapes of Salisbury Plain*. Salisbury: Wessex Archaeology, 113–121.

Smith, C, 1979. *Fisherwick: The Reconstruction of an Iron Age Landscape*. Oxford: British Archaeological Reports, British Series 61.

Smith, G, 1984. Penhale coastal promontory fort, Perranzabuloe, 1983, *Cornish Archaeology* 23, 180.

Smith, G, 1988. Excavation of the Iron Age cliff promontory fort and of Mesolithic and Neolithic flint working areas at Penhale Point, Holywell Bay, near Newquay, 1983, *Cornish Archaeology* 27, 171–199.

Smith, G and Harris, D, 1982. The excavation of Mesolithic, Neolithic and Bronze Age settlements at Poldowrian, St Keverne, 1980. *Cornish Archaeology* 21, 223–232.

Smith, R P, 2015. *Newquay Strategic Route Phase 1, Cornwall: Archaeological mitigation archive report*. Truro: Cornwall Archaeological Unit.

Smythe, J, 2006. The role of the house in Early Neolithic Ireland. *Journal of European Archaeology* 9, 229–257.

Soutar, S, 2013. Castle-an-Dinas, St Columb Major: A new survey. *Cornish Archaeology* 52, 1–48.

Sparey Green, C, 1987. *Excavations at Poundbury, Volume 1: The settlements*. Dorchester: Dorset Natural History and Archaeological Society.

Stace, C, 1997. *New flora of the British Isles*. Cambridge: Cambridge University Press (second edition).

Straker, V, 1991. Charred plant macrofossils. In J A Nowakowski, Trethellan Farm, Newquay: the excavation of a lowland Bronze Age settlement and Iron Age cemetery. *Cornish Archaeology* 30, 162–179.

Straker, V, 1995. Plant macrofossils. In J Ratcliffe, Duckpool, Morwenstow: A Romano-British and early medieval industrial site and harbour. *Cornish Archaeology* 34, 155–158.

Straker, V, 1997. The ecofactual assemblage. In R Harry and C D Morris, Excavations on the lower terrace, Site C, Tintagel Island 1990–94. *Antiquaries Journal* 77, 82–101.

Straker, V, Brown, A, Fyfe, R, Jones, J and Wilkinson, K, 2008a. Later Bronze Age and Iron Age environmental background. In C J Webster, ed, *The Archaeology of South West England*. Taunton: Somerset County Council, 103–116.

Straker, V, Brown, A, Fyfe, R and Jones, J, 2008b. Romano-British environmental background. In C J Webster, ed, *The Archaeology of South West England*. Taunton: Somerset County Council, 145–150.

Tabor, R, 2008. Woolston Manor Farm, North Cadbury: An outline report of fieldwork in 2006–7 by the South Cadbury Environs Project. *Proceedings of the Somerset and Natural History Society*, 151, 83–96.

Taylor, H, 1951. The Tynings Farm barrow group: Third report. *Proceedings of the University of Bristol Speleological Society* 6, 111–173.

Taylor, S R, forthcoming. *Down the bright stream: the prehistory of Woodcock Corner and the Tregurra Valley*, Leiden: Sidestone Press.

Ten Harkel, L, Franconi, T and Gosden, C, 2017. Fields, ritual and religion: Holistic approaches to the rural landscape in long-term perspective. *Oxford Journal of Archaeology* 36, 413–443.

Thomas, A C, 1985. *Exploration of a drowned landscape: archaeology and history of the Isles of Scilly*. London: Batsford.

Thomas, G, 2008. The symbolic lives of late Anglo-Saxon settlements: A cellared structure and iron hoard from Bishopstone, East Sussex. *Archaeological Journal* 165, 334–398.

Thomas, J, 2017. Glenfield Park: Living with cauldrons. *British Archaeology* 158, 14–21.

Thomas, J S, 2012. Some deposits are more structured than others. *Archaeological Dialogues* 19, 124–127.

Thomas, K, 1971. *Religion and the decline of magic: Studies in popular beliefs in sixteenth and seventeenth century England*. London: Weidenfeld and Nicolson.

Thomas, N, 2005. *Conderton Camp, Worcestershire; a small Middle Iron Age hillfort on Bredon Hill*. York: Council for British Archaeology.

Threipland, L M, 1956. An excavation at St Mawgan-in-Pyder, North Cornwall. *Archaeological Journal* 113, 33–81.

Tilley, C, 2017. *Landscape in the longue durée: a history and theory of pebbles in a pebbled heathland landscape*. London: University College London Press.

Timberlake, S and Hartgroves, S, forthcoming. New evidence for Bronze Age tin / gold mining in Cornwall: the date of the antler pick from the Carnon Valley Streamworks, Devoran near Truro. *Cornish Archaeology*.

Tingle, M, 1998. *The prehistory of Beer Head: field survey and excavations at an isolated flint source on the south Devon coast*. Oxford: British Archaeological Reports, British Series 270.

Trow, S, James, S and Moore, T, 2009. *Becoming Roman, being Gallic, staying British. Research and excavations at Ditches 'hillfort' and villa 1984-2006*. Oxford: Oxbow.

Tullett, A, 2008. Black earth, bone and bits of old pot: The Pewsey middens. Recent work by the University of Sheffield. In O Davis, N Sharples and K Waddington, eds, *Changing perspectives on the first millennium BC*. Oxford: Oxbow, 11–20.

Waddell, J, 1998. *The prehistoric archaeology of Ireland*. Galway: University of Galway Press.

Wailes, B, 1963. Excavations at Castle-an-Dinas, St Columb Major: Interim Report. *Cornish Archaeology* 2, 51–55.

Wainwright, G, 1967. *Coygan Camp: A prehistoric, Romano-British and Dark Age settlement in Carmarthenshire*. Cardiff: Cambrian Archaeological Association.

Waterson, R, 1997. *The living house: An anthropology of architecture in South-East Asia*. London: Thames and Hudson.

Watts, S, 2014. *The structured deposition of querns; the contexts of use and deposition of querns in the south-west of England from the Neolithic to the Iron Age*. Southampton: The Highfield Press.

Watts, S, 2017. The quernstones of Glastonbury and Mere. In R Shaffrey, ed, *Written in Stone: Papers on the function, form, and provenancing of prehistoric stone objects in memory of Fiona Roe*. Southampton: The Highfield Press, 166–194.

Webley, L, 2007. Using and abandoning roundhouses: a reinterpretation of the evidence from Late Bronze Age-Early Iron Age southern England. *Oxford Journal of Archaeology* 26, 127–144.

Webster, J, 1997. Text expectations: the archaeology of 'Celtic' ritual wells and shafts. In A T Gwilt and C Haselgrove, eds, *Reconstructing Iron Age societies*. Oxford: Oxbow, 134–144.

Weiner, A B, 1987. *The Trobrianders of Papua New Guinea*. Belmont: Wadsworth / Thomson.

Wessex Archaeology 2017. *East Chisenbury midden excavation, Salisbury Plain, Wiltshire: Archaeological evaluation report (Report Ref: 70241.01)*. Wessex Archaeology: Salisbury.

Wheatley, D, 2015. Myth, memento, and memory: Avebury, Wiltshire, England. In M Díaz-Guardamino, L García Sanjuán and D Wheatley, eds, *The lives of prehistoric monuments in Iron Age, Roman, and medieval Europe*. Oxford: Oxford University Press, 99–118.

Wheeler, R E M, 1943 *Maiden Castle, Dorset*. Oxford: Oxford University Press.

Wheeler, R E M and Wheeler, T V, 1932. *Report on the excavation of the prehistoric, Roman, and post-Roman site in Lydney Park, Gloucestershire*. London: Oxford University Press.

Whimster, R, 1977. Harlyn Bay reconsidered: the excavations of 1900-1905 in the light of recent work. *Cornish Archaeology* 16, 60–88.

Whimster, R, 1981. *Burial practices in Iron Age Britain; a discussion and gazetteer of the evidence c. 700 BC-AD 43*. Oxford: British Archaeological Reports, British Series 90.

Wiessner, P, 1996. Introduction: Food, status, culture and nature. In P Wiessner and W Schiefenhovel, eds, *Food and the status quest: An interdisciplinary perspective*. Oxford: Berghahn, 1–18.

Wilkes, E M, Griffith, F M, Quinnell, H, Allason-Jones, L and Randall, C, 2012. Cadbury Castle, Devon, reconsidered. *Archaeological Journal* 169, 237–280.

Williams, G, 1988. *The standing stones of Wales and South-West England*. Oxford: British Archaeological Reports, British Series 197.

Williams, H, 1998. The ancient monument in Romano-British ritual practices. In C Forcey, J Hawthorne and R Witcher, eds, *TRAC 97 Proceedings of the Seventh Annual Theoretical Roman Archaeology Conference*. Oxford: Oxbow, 71–87.

Williams, H, 2004. Ephemeral monuments and social memory in early Roman Britain. In B Croxford, H Eckardt, J Meade, J and J Weekes, eds, *TRAC 2003: Proceedings of the Thirteenth Annual Theoretical Roman Archaeology Conference, Leicester 2003*. Oxford: Oxbow: 51–61.

Williams, M, 2003. Growing metaphors. The agricultural cycle as metaphor in the later prehistoric period of Britain and north-west Europe. *Journal of Social Archaeology* 3, 223–255.

Williamson, T, 1987. Early co-axial field systems on the East Anglian boulder clays. *Proceedings of the Prehistoric Society* 53, 419–431.

Williamson, T, 1998. The 'Scole-Dickleburgh field system' revisited. *Landscape History* 20, 19–27.

Wilson, D and Blunt, C, 1961. The Trewhiddle Hoard. *Archaeologia* 98, 75–122.

Wood, I I, 2015. *Gunwalloe through the ages: Middle Bronze Age to the 12th century AD, Lizard Peninsula, Cornwall*. Exeter: National Trust.

Woodward, A, 1992. *Shrines and sacrifice*. London: Batsford.

Woodward, A and Cane, C, 1991. The Bronze Age pottery. In J A Nowakowski, Trethellan Farm, Newquay: The excavation of a lowland Bronze Age settlement and Iron Age cemetery. *Cornish Archaeology* 30, 103–131.

Woodward, A and Leach, P, 1993. *The Uley shrines: Excavation of a ritual complex on West Hill, Uley, Gloucestershire 1977-9*. London: English Heritage.

Young, A, 2012. Prehistoric and Romano-British enclosures around the Camel estuary, Cornwall. *Cornish Archaeology* 51, 69–124.